HER QUEST FOR SELF: A JOURNEY

HER QUEST FOR SELF: A JOURNEY

Revisiting Select Novels of
Two American Women Writers

GAYREEN LYNGDOH

PARTRIDGE

A Penguin Random House Company

To order additional copies of this book, contact
Partridge India
000 800 10062 62
orders.india@partridgepublishing.com

www.partridgepublishing.com/india

CONTENTS

To

The amazingly strong and extremely loving women in my family whose lives and stories have shaped my own: my late Meirad Methili, my beloved Mei, Ep my incorrigible aunt, my beautiful sisters, Kong Sonia and Christina.

To my late father, Bah John Robert Fancon. This Book, as was the study that inspired it, is a culmination of his dream. I know that he would have been extremely proud of his daughter.

For Tej, my wonderfully supportive and encouraging husband, my love and heartfelt gratitude. You must know that I couldn't have done it without you.

To the One who is the ultimate inspiration and author of this work, whose faithful love and blessings sustained and guided me throughout this journey – My Almighty God and Saviour. I cannot even begin to comprehend what you have done in my life, and what you continue to do . . . and the story goes on . . .

Acknowledgement

I believe that the writing process is always collaborative and intertextual. Every text is, consciously or unconsciously, informed by layers of ideas and insights embedded in other texts. This is particularly true of a scholarly work such as this one. I would, therefore, like to thank and acknowledge on record, my indebtedness to the many scholars and writers whose work and research has contributed in far-reaching ways, to the build-up of knowledge and thinking process in my own research, eventually culminating in this book. Though I will never have the opportunity to thank them individually, yet their names are gratefully acknowledged in the Bibliographic section of the book.

I would like to express my deepest gratitude to Professor Esther Syiem, my doctoral supervisor. Her constant 'nudges' towards completing (and publishing) my work, her mentorship and her expert and insightful critique over the years, has done much to broaden my thinking and help me grow in my scholastic efforts.

I am deeply appreciative of the Publishing team at Partridge, particularly Ms Gemma Ramos my Publishing Service Associate, for their professional expertise and technical inputs in bringing out this book.

I would like to say a big 'Thank You' to Wilbur Manners, a doctor by profession and an artist by vocation, whose artistic brilliance and sensitivity is clearly etched out in the cover design and illustration. His sketch evokes the theme and the essence of the text beautifully.

Thank you Doreen, my amateur-photographer friend, for the lovely 'author's shot'. I pray that you capture many more (and much more), beautiful things through your lens.

I am grateful to God for this work, and for the many people who have, in one way or the other, helped in making this book a reality: my beloved family and all my friends. A big 'Thank You' to you all and God Bless!

ABBREVIATIONS

Wind: *East Wind: West Wind*

Earth: *The Good Earth*

Mother: *The Mother*

Pavilion: *Pavilion of Women*

Kinfolk: *Kinfolk*

Joy: *The Joy Luck Club*

Kitchen: *The Kitchen God's Wife*

Hundred: *The Hundred Secret Senses*

Bonesetter: *The Bonesetter's Daughter*

Fate: *The Opposite of Fate*

Introduction

For a long time, woman has existed as a gap, as an absence in
literature . . . This is not only true of the fiction created by men,
but also by women, who have mostly confined themselves to
writing love stories or dealing with the experiences of women in
a superficial manner . . . [which] represses the truth about the
majority of their sisters and their lives.

(Sarla Palkar, 'Breaking the Silence:
That Long Silence', 163)

There's no room for her if she's not a he.

(Helene Cixous, 'The Laugh of the Medusa', 888)

Woman as a central space in literature has long been ignored. Objectified,
rather than depicted as a subject of interest and significance in her own
right, it was commonly assumed that hers is 'a life whose story cannot be
told as there is no story' (Eichner 620). Even when stories about women
are told, these come filtered through the phallocentric world view which
either 'obscures' the real picture, or 'reproduces the classic representations
of women as sensitive – intuitive – dreamy, etc' (Cixous 878). This book is
partly an attempt to show that the female reality and experience are as valid
and legitimate a story as that of any other human being's.

Pearl S. Buck and Amy Tan may both be described as writers who have,
in their own ways, written about 'the experiences of women' (Palkar 163).
Through their work, they challenged the patriarchal assumptions about
women, by attempting to fashion a distinctive feminine voice that allows for

the articulation of women's experiences in their own voices, and /or through the female perspective. This book takes a relook at the women characters in select novels of Pearl S. Buck and Amy Tan, examining and analysing their experiences and subjectivities as they journey in quest of the self. The novels included in this volume are those relating specifically to China and the Chinese experience, with the main subject being the Chinese women, both local and *emigre*.

Pearl S. Buck, an American writer, was born in 1892 to Absalom and Caroline Sydenstricker who were American Presbyterian missionaries in China in the late nineteenth and early twentieth century. Although she was born in America (Hillsboro, West Virginia) and did her higher education there (Randolph-Macon Woman's College, 1914; Cornell, 1926), Buck spent her entire childhood and adolescent years in China, and later lived and taught in China irregularly between 1910 and 1934, when she permanently relocated to the United States. Having been reared and having lived in China, it is therefore inevitable that China and the Chinese people, as well as her own experiences there, would leave a strong mark on her, both as a person and as a writer. As a child, she learned Chinese as her first language and grew up on Chinese folk stories, especially the Buddhist and Taoist legends told to her by her Chinese nurse. These stories are, according to her, the first literary influence in her life. She also received a formal Chinese education in Chinese reading and writing, as well as in Confucian ethics and Chinese history. As a writer, therefore, Buck is greatly moulded by the Chinese literary culture, particularly, the Chinese novel, a fact she proudly asserted in her Nobel lecture in 1938. Her work also displays a multicultural literary amalgam such as the 'traditional Chinese novel, the King James Bible, classic American and English fiction . . . as well as the models in other literary genres'(Rabb 7). Critics have also noted the influence of European Naturalism, particularly that of Emile Zola, in her writings. This attests to the wide range of literary traditions that is embedded in the work of Pearl Buck and lends richness to it. She has written almost eighty books in various genres, with thirteen of the novels dealing with China and Chinese characters.

In 1938, she was awarded the Nobel Prize for Literature, becoming the first American woman to achieve that honour. She died in 1973, in Vermont, United States of America, at the age of 80.

Amy Tan, an American of Chinese ancestry, was born in 1952 in Oakland, California. Though born to Chinese immigrant parents, John and Daisy Tan, Amy Tan grew up with largely American sensibilities and mindset. The rejection of her Chinese culture during childhood and adolescence, spurred by the desire to assimilate into the mainstream, is often a cause of discord between her and her parents (mainly her mother), as well as within herself, leading to a crisis of identity. It is only later, as an adult, that Tan begins to understand and appreciate the value and importance of acknowledging her roots and embracing the dual aspects of her identity as a Chinese-American. It is this experience from her own life that colours all her writing. And yet, though spanning both the Chinese and American experience, a by-product of her bicultural reality, her novels are largely dominated by China and its social, political, historical, and cultural milieu. Chinese folklore and myths abound in her works. This is because Tan's childhood is filled with her parents' stories, particularly, her mother's tales and memories about China, about her life there, and about relatives and friends who have died, or were left behind. Tan's three half-sisters from her mother's first marriage to Wang Zo, a wife-and-child batterer, were among those who were left behind in China, an event that deeply affected Daisy, and in one way or the other, keeps surfacing in Tan's work. Thus, early in life, Tan imbibed the art of storytelling from her parents, especially the Chinese 'talk-story' narratives employed by her mother.

The 'talk-story' is a common and popular form of traditional Chinese storytelling, including within its ambit, fables and folklore, wisdom and didactic tales, gossips and family anecdotes, exchanged mainly between women as they sit and work together in informal settings. Often, this becomes the only means available for these women entrapped within a patriarchal world, to express themselves and bond with each other. As Elizabeth McHenry notes, for women living in cultures where their experience and existence are continually conditioned and limited by race, class, and gender, storytelling is, and continues to be, 'vital to their cohesion and literal survival' (14). It is this rich literary heritage of 'talk-stories', mined from her ancestral culture, which Tan later incorporates into her work as a major part and technique of her fiction.

The common theme that binds these two writers together in the present context is their portrayal of female Chinese subjects as the main focus of their novels. As noted, the two writers' works belong to two different periods. Buck's works are written during the earlier half of the twentieth century, while Amy Tan's work spans the last decade of the twentieth, and the beginning of the twenty-first, century. In bringing these two writers together, the attempt is to interrogate whether there is a transition and evolution in the image of the Chinese woman as depicted in their novels.

As already mentioned, the female subject is a largely peripheral figure in Western literature. The Chinese woman is doubly so. She is 'doubly colonised by both imperial and patriarchal ideologies' (Ashcroft *et al.* 250). Representation of Chinese characters in American literature has generally been stereotypical and highly derogatory. In her thesis, 'The Chinese as Portrayed in the Writings of Several Prominent American Authors' (1989), Li Bo examines the work of five American authors who have depicted Chinese characters in their writings: Bret Harte, Mark Twain, Frank Norris, John Steinbeck, and Pearl Buck. What she concluded in her thesis is that apart from Pearl Buck, and to a certain extent John Steinbeck, almost all of the mentioned writers portray the Chinese, either stereotypically or derogatorily. For instance, in the play *Ah Sin*, a collaborated work by Harte and Twain which was first performed in 1877, the character, Ah Sin, is perceived as 'a poor dumb animal, with his tail on top of his head instead of where it ought to be' (53). According to Li Bo, the Chinese is always referred to by the nomenclature, 'the Chinaman' by most Americans, as a way of decimating his individuality and identity. What is more remarkable, however, is the noticeable invisibility of Chinese female characters in the works of the writers mentioned, except for that of Pearl Buck. The Chinese woman is almost completely nonexistent in the fiction of the other writers.

What is interesting to note, furthermore, is that even in works by Chinese-American male authors such as Frank Chin, the Chinese woman, even if she features in the story, is depicted very marginally, and as being 'totally devoid of subjectivity', a point brought out by Sau-Ling C. Wong in her essay on Amy Tan. According to Wong, in Chin's play, *Year of the Dragon* (1981), which is about a disintegrating Chinatown family in the 1960s, Chin portrays the female characters either as 'scatterbrained American-born' mothers, or as the silent China Mama transplanted from China to America. Known as the *gum sahn paw* (gold mountain wife), China Mama is brought to America just to assuage a dying husband's familial guilt, and dumped unceremoniously into the Eng family's living room. Unable to communicate, she is rendered 'mute, except for sporadic attempts to communicate with the children in gibberish-like Cantonese' (55). Wong further contends that in Chin's play, the old immigrant woman from China is just a convenient symbol, not a human being with decades' worth of experiences and grievances to recount. According to her, Tan's work, along with that of other Chinese-American female writers like Maxine Hong Kingston, represents 'China Mama's revenge', because their women characters 'get not only their own voices back but equal time with their American offspring' (55). By foregrounding Chinese female characters in their novels, both local and immigrant, giving them a central space, both Buck and Tan attempt to give voice and presence to the long-silenced and invisible Chinese woman. This is the central theme in both the authors, even though their ways of doing this may vary, and follow different trajectories and paths.

The Chinese presence in America started with the gold rush in 1848, which witnessed the first wave of Chinese emigration to America. Chinese men came mainly as labourers and worked in the California and San Francisco gold mining camps as miners, laundrymen, and household servants (Chinn 61–63). The building of the Central Pacific Railroad in the 1860s further escalated the flow of Chinese emigrants who provided ready and cheap labour for the railroad companies. The pattern of emigration continued up to 1949 when the Communist Party came to power in China and closed the doors for further emigration. It was towards this latter part of the Chinese emigration wave that most of Amy Tan's fictional characters, including her own mother, came to the United States.

Pearl Buck's novels about China were written mainly during the earlier half of the twentieth century, at a time when anti-Asian sentiments, and particularly, sinophobia, still held sway in America. Gregory B. Lee offers some revealing examples of how the Chinese, particularly those in America, were constructed as the 'other'. He quotes the following article from the *New York Times* of 3 September 1865 to emphasise his point:

> We are utterly opposed to any extensive emigration of Chinamen or other Asiatics to any part of the United States . . . With Oriental thoughts will necessarily come Oriental social habits . . . [and if] there were to be a flood-tide of Chinese population – a population befouled with all the social vices . . . with heathenish souls and heathenish propensities, whose character, and habits, and modes of thought are firmly fixed by the consolidating influence of ages upon ages . . . we should be prepared to bid farewell to republicanism and democracy. (1)

And as mentioned, this racial polemics was further augmented by popular literary works such as Bret Harte's *The Heathen Chinee* (1870), one among many such works of its kind, which projects the Chinese as sinister and inscrutable creatures from another world.

Living and writing in such a climate, Buck's primary purpose in writing her Chinese novels is to challenge and critique the existent exoticisation of, and ignorance about, China. In 'Spectacle of the Other', Stuart Hall documents the various ways in which the racial 'other' has been constructed in Western popular culture and imagination, which he terms as the 'politics of representation'. What is seen in Buck's work is an attempt to 'contest "negative" images' of China and the Chinese people, and reorient these images towards 'a more positive direction' (Hall 225–6). Her work is therefore directed primarily to Western readership. Consequently, this has necessitated a style of writing and a language mode that is familiar and acceptable to Western readers. Thus, even though her novels depict China and Chinese life, there is no allusion or reference even to a single Chinese word or phrase. As Phyllis Bentley points out, her work is completely 'English – very plain English' (793). Similarly, it is only in her first novel, *East Wind: West Wind* that Buck employs the Chinese talk-story mode as a narrative technique. To reiterate, her attempt is to render her work as approachable as possible to Western readers rather than alienating it from them. In her endeavour to present the Chinese as completely credible and ordinary as any other human beings, Buck is fairly successful. Carl Van

Doren, for instance, states that, '*The Good Earth* for the first time made the Chinese seem as familiar as neighbours' (353).

Amy Tan, on the other hand, wrote her novels during the later part of the twentieth and early twenty-first century, when multicultural and multiethnic narratives were gaining currency in the American sociohistorical landscape. Her work is, therefore, a bold assertion and celebration of Chinese and the Chinese-American identity. Like Buck, she too writes within the American context. Her work, however, may be read as a means of writing back, of reconstructing a Chinese-American literary tradition and breaking away from 'the discursive imprisonment of American Orientalist discourse (D.L. Li 324). This is clearly expressed in her essay, 'Required Reading and Other Dangerous Subjects' where she confidently states that

> I am an American writer. I am Chinese by racial heritage. I am Chinese-American by family and social upbringing. But I believe that what I write is American fiction by virtue of the fact that I live in this country and my emotional sensibilities, assumptions, and obsessions are largely American. My characters may be largely Chinese-American, but I think Chinese-Americans are part of America. (*Fate* 310)

Tan's act of writing back is observed, particularly, in her appropriation and use of language, the deployment of Chinese narrative strategies such as the talk-story, the recovery of Chinese-specific myths and folklore, and the multiplicity of previously silent narrative voices in her fiction, as a means of subverting the traditional, Western, monolithic narrative. In his speech titled 'The African Writer and the English Language' (1975), Chinua Achebe states:

> Is it right that a man should abandon his mother tongue for someone else's? It looks like a dreadful betrayal and produces a guilty feeling. But for me there is no other choice. I have been given the language and I intend to use it. (qtd. in Thiong'O 285)

Like Achebe, Tan chooses to write her Chinese and Chinese-American narratives in English because 'there is no other choice'. Brought up with

English as her first language, Tan's Chinese is limited to a smattering of colloquial Mandarin and Shanghaiese words and phrases uttered by her mother every now and then. Again, like Achebe who wrote of 'a new English' that is 'altered to suit new African surroundings' (qtd. in Thiong'O 286), Tan, too, creates 'a new English', or 'Englishes', in her fiction, one that she grew up with, a patois of Chinese and broken English that is commonly used by first-generation Chinese immigrants like her mother. In her appropriation of the English language and remoulding it to reflect the linguistic reality of her Chinese-American characters, Tan is, as mentioned, writing back, using language as a tool. Thus, in her collection of essays, *The Opposite of Fate* (2003), she writes:

> I began to write stories using all the Englishes I grew up with: the English I spoke to my mother, which for lack of a better term might be described as 'simple'; the English she used with me, which for lack of a better term might be described as 'broken'; my translation of her Chinese, which could certainly be described as 'watered down'; and what I imagined to be her translation of her Chinese if she could speak in perfect English, her internal language, and for that I preserve the essence, but neither an English nor a Chinese structure. (278–79)

Pearl Buck's depiction of China may, therefore, be described as that of a writer looking in from the outside, her 'outsider' status being a necessary outcome of her American race and birth. This fact is recognised by Buck even though she claims deep emotional and spiritual kinship with China. The fact was vividly impressed upon her during the Boxer Uprising of 1900 in China, which witnessed strong anti-West sentiments. She writes after the incident:

> My worlds no longer interwove. They were sharply clear, one from the other. I was American, not Chinese, and although China was as dear to me as my native land, I knew it was not my land. Mine was the country across the sea, the land of my forefathers, alien to China and indifferent to the Chinese people. (Buck 1954, 55)

Tan's work, on the other hand, may be said to be that of a writer looking from the inside. Her Chinese ancestry marks her as an 'insider' and gives her a certain claim of ownership to the culture that she depicts, even though the China that she attempts to recapture in her work is largely a 'familially mediated' entity (Grice 45), culled from the memories and impressions of her mother, rather than personally experienced. However, though the two writers may approach the subject from two completely different perspectives, what emerges from their fiction is a realistic rendition of China as they experienced it, or envision it, individually.

Because the novels discussed relate specifically to China and Chinese characters, both local and immigrant, therefore, what is also taken into account here is the Chinese cultural context that shapes, and has shaped, these characters' lives and conceptions of self. Pertinent questions emerge from this: Does China and its cultural ideology play a role in shaping the consciousness of these women, affecting their lived experiences, and the way they perceive themselves? What kind of culture/society is one confronted with in these novels? In this chapter, therefore, the broad contours of China's history is traced out, both socioculturally, as well as politically, in order to show how these have impacted women's lived realities and defined their self-image. In all the novels analysed, special attention is drawn to the role and position that women occupy within traditional Chinese society.

The traditional image of the Chinese woman has, largely been, one of ambivalence. In their study, *Women in Chinese Society* (1975), women scholars in Asian studies, Margery Wolf and Roxane Witke, note that the Chinese conception of women is a highly discrepant one. Women are seen as 'weak, timid, and sexually exploitable, as well as dangerous, powerful and sexually insatiable' (2). Echoing this observation, Veronica Wang states that in 'the traditional Chinese society, women were expected to behave silently with submission, but act heroically with strength. They were both sub-women and super-women' (24). This dual perspective of the Chinese woman is one that finds expression in Buck's fiction. In her years in China, Buck is constantly confronted with the sense of duality that seems to surround the Chinese woman. She found them trapped in an immutable 'sexual caste system' (Conn 26), that render them weak and thwart their potentialities, many times. At the same time, she also observed how powerful Chinese women often were: 'among farmers and gentry alike, homes were typically ruled by the senior women in a kind of domestic matriarchy' (Conn 26). Thus, in Buck's novels, one encounters women such as Madame Wu in *Pavilion of Women*, who seems to wield extraordinary power and influence in the family, the epitome of Wang's 'super-women'. At the other end of the spectrum, however, one also finds women like O-lan in *The Good Earth*, voiceless and invisible, relegated by society to the 'sub-women' status. It is this social reality that is reflected in Buck's novels, and to a large extent, in Tan's fiction.

However, the nature of a woman's power in Chinese society is, again, a claim that needs to be inquired into. What is observed is that though some women may seem to be powerful and are indeed powerful figures, that power is solely determined by Confucian patriarchy. Confucianism, or the doctrines of the Chinese philosopher/teacher Confucius, is perhaps one of the dominant social ideologies and most influential schools of thought in China and in the Orient, beginning approximately from 200 BCE to almost 1949, when the Communists came to power in China. One of the defining characteristics of Confucianism is its deeply seeded prejudice against women. A particular passage in *Lun Yu*, a collection of Confucius' teachings and dialogues compiled by his disciples is a telling instance: 'It is not pleasing to have to do with women or people of base condition. If you show them too much affection, they become too excited, and if you keep them at a distance, they are full of resentment' (Chap. 17, qtd. in Gao 31). Thus, a woman is equated to a person of 'base condition', or an inferior being who must be controlled and reined-in by superior male power. During the Han Dynasty (206 BCE–219 CE), 'feminine ethics' were rigidly codified into the 'Three Obediences and Four Virtues' or the *San Cong Si De.* (qtd. in Lin 140). According to the code of 'thrice-obeying', or *san-tsung*, (Wolf and Witke 13), women were expected to obey the father before marriage, the husband after marriage, and the first son should she be a widow. Her whole existence revolved around the male figures in her life whom she is expected to submit to and obey.

Thus, a woman in the traditional Chinese social structure is allowed power only as she fits in with the patterns laid down by the patriarchal norms. Women are powerful only because they have the potential to produce male descendants to perpetuate the family name and to perform the ceremony of ancestor worship, which is the cornerstone of a clan/lineage-centric culture like China. In Buck's *Pavilion of Women*, Madame Wu's power and authority clearly stems from the fact that she has borne four sons. However, as Xiongya Gao observes, a woman's 'power lies solely behind the doors; she has no legal and property rights' (33). Furthermore, if a woman fails to produce a son for the family, according to Confucian standards, she is considered to have committed 'the worst moral crime' (33). Thus, a woman's power and identity in old China comes and is sustained only through her identification with, and subscription to, the male-controlled institutions of marriage, and specifically, motherhood. It is primarily through these two institutions that Chinese women define themselves. Therefore, in the novels considered here, the marriage-and-motherhood theme, whether as a means of personal fulfilment, or as a hindrance to women's growth, or as a tool of male oppression, occupies a major space, because it is so much a part of these women's worldview. Thus their quest for selfhood is viewed against the backdrop of this reality.

In her book, *Of Woman Born* (1976), Adrienne Rich states thus:

> At certain points in history, and in certain cultures, the idea of woman-as-mother has worked to endow all women with respect, even with awe, and to give women some say in the life of a people or a clan . . . But . . . motherhood as institution has ghettoized and degraded female potentialities. (1)

Rich goes on to say that 'under patriarchy, female possibility has been literally massacred on the site of motherhood' (1). In China, both marriage and motherhood have been used by the male-dominated culture as tools for subjugating women and keeping them 'in their place'. If a woman submits to these institutions, she is 'rewarded' with a certain semblance of power and acceptance. Should she fail in these, she is, as Rich says, 'ghettoized' and discarded. Consequently, therefore, women's activities are circumscribed wholly within the domestic sphere and have no place outside of it. Yang Chen, a famous Confucianist, theorised thus:

If women are given work that requires contact with the outside, they will sow disorder and confusion throughout the Empire. Shame and injury will come to the Imperial Court, and the Sun and the Moon [Emperor and Empress] will wither away . . . Women must not be allowed to participate in the affairs of government. (qtd. in Van Gulik 121)

This worldview is also reflected in its folklore and folksongs, its legends and myths. The legend of Mu-Lan is one representative example. One of the most famous female mythical figures in Chinese lore is Hua-Mu-Lan, the woman warrior, also known as Fa-Mu-Lan. There are different versions of the tale recounting the adventures of the heroine Mu-Lan, who disguises herself as a male warrior in order to fight in battle in her father's place. Notwithstanding the slight variations, all these versions end on the same note: with the heroine returning home and assuming her traditional female duties of wife, daughter-in-law, and mother. Two pertinent points are observed in this story: first, Mu-Lan must conceal her identity as a woman and masquerade as a man in order to be allowed to venture out into, and participate in, the public space which is traditionally considered a man's world; second, in spite of her abilities as a warrior who successfully led and won the battle, Mu-Lan, true to the Chinese ideal of womanhood, returns to her rightful place, the domestic domain, and dutifully reassumes her female roles. In Maxine Hong Kingston's version of the story which is narrated in her groundbreaking work, *The Woman Warrior* (1975), the tale ends with Mu-Lan remarking thus:

Wearing my black embroidered wedding coat, I knelt at my parents-in-law's feet, as I would have done as a bride. 'Now my public duties are finished,' I said. 'I will stay with you, doing farmwork and housework, and giving you more sons'. (1989 ed, 45)

Thus, though in very exceptional situations women may be allowed to step out of the bounds of the 'female space' and that, too, for the sake of family filiality (in Mu-Lan's case, for the sake of her father, another male, authoritative figure) and not for their own sakes, what is clearly understood is that there is an eventual return to 'womanly duties' and roles.

A song found in the *Book of Poems*, composed approximately around 200 BCE, exemplifies the cult of male veneration further: 'When a baby boy was born, he was laid on the bed, and given jade to play with, and when a baby girl was born, she was laid on the floor and given a tile to play with' (qtd. in Lin, 137).

In her collection of lectures and essays, *Managing Monsters: Six Myths of Our Time* (1994), Marina Warner, noted mythographer and writer, argues that myths and archetypes are not neutral or innocent symbols. They come laden with highly political and social meanings and invisible enforcements, which shape not only individuals' but also societies' and people's lives and thinking (xiii–xiv). Furthermore, feminist criticism, as early as the 1970s, has consistently argued that traditional myths and fairy tales have been employed by patriarchy to endorse archetypal gender roles that marginalise women, and depict them negatively/passively. As Mary Daly note, 'patriarchy perpetuates its deception through myth' (44). This has, therefore, led to the revisiting and re-visioning of traditional myths and lore by women writers who, as Nicola Pitchford notes, are 'engaged in the double project of challenging traditional mythic images of women', and at the same time, 'revamping them, uncovering the female strength latent in these figures' (131). This is an important part of Amy Tan's fiction. In her novels, one observes Tan not only critiquing the male-defined Chinese myths and '(hi)stories' that have been passed down for generations, but also engaged in the task of reworking these narratives to present the woman's '(her)story' from her viewpoint, a story that has largely been passed over, or silenced by patriarchal discourse. Thus, popular myths and folktales like 'The Moon Lady' in *The Joy Luck Club*, and the 'Kitchen God's Wife' in a novel of the same name, are explored and given a different slant and interpretation in her novels, one that gives scope for the woman's side of the story to be heard.

The traditional Chinese social structure is, therefore, one that is predominantly male centred, with women existing only as a decentred object somewhere on the fringes of that male universe. And, as noted, this gender inequity and bias are vividly reflected in its literature and folk narratives, which has, in turn, shaped the popular imagination and social practices for centuries, altogether.

Two of the predominant social practices regarding women, which were prevalent, and almost institutionalised, in Confucian China were female foot binding and concubinage. Both these terms are examined here because they are seen to be instrumental in shaping and affecting, the lived experiences of the women characters in the novels discussed.

Foot binding is perhaps the ultimate expression of a Chinese woman's oppression, both physically and psychologically. Believed to have started sometime in the beginning of the tenth century, between the end of the Tang dynasty (906 CE) and the beginning of the Sung Dynasty (960 CE) (Gao 36), the custom began as a fashion in the imperial court, but soon spread to the common people. In her essay, 'Female Bodily Aesthetics, Politics, and Feminine Ideals of Beauty in China' (2000), Eva Kit Wah Man notes that the 'sexual adoration of miniature female feet represents a Confucian patriarchal aesthetic perversion . . . The practice enhanced the sexual appeal of women . . . but it also controlled the mobility and behaviour of Confucian women and tied them to their homes' (181). The binding process which is usually performed by the mother begins in early childhood and lasts for ten to fifteen years, resulting in unimaginable pain and permanent crippling. The outcome is a bound foot reduced to three inches in length from heel to toe, with the toes bent under the sole. For this reason, it is also euphemistically termed as the 'three-inch golden lilies'/*san-tsun-gin-lian* (J. Chang 24). The small bound feet became such an ideal of feminine beauty standards that it increases daughters' worth in marriage. In her book *About Chinese Women* (1974), Julia Kristeva remarks:

> It is not at all shocking that women of many classes rush to submit themselves to the torture: after so many years of suffering, it presents a unique opportunity to gain the respect and recognition of the in-laws, who will praise the beautiful tiny feet even beyond her dowry, as an undeniable proof of her capacity to suffer and obey. (82)

Thus, a woman's bound feet are celebrated not so much because of any aesthetic appeal, but rather, because it symbolises 'her capacity to suffer and obey'. A woman's natural and unbound feet were looked upon as an object of gross ugliness and unfemininity not only by men, but by women themselves. The custom is, therefore, one that has come to shape not only the psyche of a society, but more importantly, a woman's perception of herself. This point is clearly brought out in Buck's *The Good Earth*. O-lan, the female protagonist, perceives herself as ugly and unwanted not only because of her dark swarthy appearance, but also because of her large, unbound feet which marginalises her even in her own eyes and leads to her low self-esteem. The idea of beauty as a social and historical construct, and as a crucial determiner of a person's self-image, is also an argument brought forth by Christine Battersby in *Phenomenal Woman: Feminist Metaphysics and the Patterns of Identity*.

Concubinage is another key element that defines Chinese feudal culture. It is a practice where men take on additional wives known as 'small wives' into their homes, apart from the first wife. Again, it is a custom that endow men with all the rights and privileges of choice, while women have almost no say in the matter. Usually, men could take a concubine when their first wives fail to bear them a male child. However, as Gao points out,

> The husband did not have to have a reason for taking concubines. He could, through no 'fault' whatsoever on the wife's part, but simply for his own sexual pleasure, have found a woman outside, . . . and take her home for a concubine. . . . Usually, the one that first bore a male child for the family would be the proudest. Once a wife lost her husband's favor, her life would be spent in loneliness, misery, and constant jealousy, . . . fighting with other wives for the favour of both the husband and the parents-in-law. As a way out of her emotional desperation, she may choose to commit suicide. (40)

Concubinage and its accompanying ramifications feature as an important element in the novels discussed. In both Buck's and Tan's work, it is portrayed as an instrument of male oppression and women's humiliation and pain, one that has an adverse impact on their lives and psyche. This is particularly depicted in Buck's *East Wind: West Wind, Pavilion of Women*, and *The Good Earth*, as well as in Tan's *The Joy Luck Club* and, to some extent, in *The Kitchen God's Wife*.

This is the social reality that informs the background of most of the women characters met with in these novels. An-Mei Hsu, an immigrant Chinese woman in Tan's *The Joy Luck Club*, remarks on the constrictive burden of being a woman in such a society: 'I was raised the Chinese way, . . . taught to desire nothing, to swallow other's people misery, to eat my own bitterness. . .I taught my daughter the opposite, still she came out the same way! . . .she was born a girl' (215).

In a society where girls are considered to be only 'small happiness', whereas, a boy, 'big happiness' (Conn 26), being born a female is tantamount to a curse. Often, even the women themselves conform, consciously and unconsciously, to gynophobic views of women, having internalised patriarchal values and been conditioned by them for centuries. In Buck's *The Good Earth*, when O-lan gives birth to a girl, she announces the news to her husband thus: 'It is only a slave this time – not worth mentioning' (65). This is a powerful and tragic indication of women's psychological enslavement in feudal China. In her book, *The Resisting Reader: Feminist Approaches to American Fiction* (1978), Judith Fetterley urges on the necessity of 'exorcising the male mind that has been implanted in [women]' (xxii). Thus, for the Chinese women characters in these novels, the journey to the self is one that entails the 'exorcising' of deeply embedded negative modes of thinking that is inimical not only to one's self as a woman but also to the whole experience of being female. It is only as they learn to come out of the 'cramped confines of patriarchal space' (Showalter 201) and recognise their own worth as women that these protagonists arrived at some level of self-realisation and personal growth and succeed in reinventing their lives.

Apart from the sociocultural factors of traditional China, its political configurations also play a role in determining the experiences and the direction that these women's lives take. The New Culture Movement, for instance, that came in the wake of the May 4th Movement 1919, is a significant one. Influenced by the movement's democratic ideas of freedom and equality, and the struggle to break away from feudalist social evils, women, hitherto suppressed and silent, begin to awaken to their rights and to articulate their discontent with the prevailing social system. He Jing notes that '[c]ompared to western feminist movement, . . .China did not have women's movement in the real sense. The awakening of women's awareness was a by product of the May 4th Movement for cultural rejuvenation' (He 2011, 96). It is this period of Chinese political history that is reflected in Buck's *Pavilion of Women*. Characters such as Madame Wu and Rulan are seen as being more open and expressive of their own needs and desires to unshackle themselves from male-imposed 'female' duties and to carve out their own destinies in life.

Most of Tan's immigrant heroines are also born, or grew up during this period and are impacted by it, in one way or the other. With relatively more education and more freedom than their female counterparts before them, this emboldens them to finally break away from their restrictive social environment and migrate to America. The Sino-Japanese War (1930s–40s) and the civil wars that wracked China's political history before the Communists came to power in 1949 are, again, major events that affect not only the national history but also personal histories and individual psyches. It is within this backdrop of war that most of the novels discussed are situated. This is reflected poignantly in all of Tan's novels, particularly, *The Kitchen God's Wife*, and in Jing-Mei Woo's account of her mother in *The Joy Luck Club* (19–26). It was during the Sino-Japanese War that Suyuan, Jing-Mei's mother, was forced to abandon her twin children, an event that haunted her throughout her life. Thus, these novels attest to the fact that politics does play a role, to some extent, in shaping and reconfiguring the lived realities and experiences of people, affecting them not only materially but also psychically. As Walter Shear remarks of Tan's characters, their stories convey 'the terror of a vulnerable human consciousness torn and rent' in a country's and culture's 'contortions' (193).

However, it is not just China and its sociopolitical context that determine the lived realities and experiences of these women. In all of Amy Tan's novels and in Pearl Buck's *Kinfolk*, America features as an integral presence defining the lives and self-conception of these women characters. What is also examined here, therefore, is the dual aspect of America as depicted in these novels. Most of these characters came to America during the earlier half of the twentieth century, prompted by various reasons. For the Liang family in *Kinfolk*, the relocation is necessitated by the political climate in pre-Communists China which was marked by civil wars and in-fightings. For Tan's characters, America provides a means of escape from the 'unspeakable tragedies' (*Joy* 20), and oppressiveness of their lives in China. At the same time, all of these characters are lured by the promise of the 'American Dream' – the belief that people of talent in this land of opportunity and plenty could reasonably aspire to material success if they adhered to a fairly well-defined set of behavioural rules. This is clearly brought out in Tan's *The Joy Luck Club*. Jing-Mei Woo, one of the characters in the novel, remarks of her mother:

> My mother believed you could be anything you wanted to be in America. You could open a restaurant. You could work for the government and get good retirement. . . . You could become rich. You could become instantly famous. . . . [It] was where all my mother's hopes lay. She had come here in 1949 after losing everything in China. . . . [in America] there were so many ways for things to get better. (132)

The American Dream with its promise of unlimited opportunities and hopes of success is, thus, one of the factors that draw these characters to America. In one sense, these characters are living out the American Dream. Most of them are depicted as being materially successful in one way or the other, if not in their own selves, at least in and through their children. At the same time, however, the American experience is also one of marginalisation, especially for the first-generation Chinese-American characters. They find themselves marginalised on the basis of their racial/cultural difference and perceived inferiority from the mainstream. Their 'fractured' English (Tan, *Fate* 274) further alienates them not only from the larger society but also from their own children who have imbibed American values and mindsets and are ignorant and dismissive of their mothers' tongue and culture. Consequently, this results in a deep sense of displacement, alienation, and estrangement within themselves, as well as between them and their American-born offspring.

What is observed about these characters, however, is the fact that they eventually manage to use language (the factor that had disadvantaged them in the first place), as a means of rewriting their own lives and destinies. It is interesting to note that many of these women's careers in America are connected with words and language, in one way or the other: Winnie Louie's florist business is made even more successful by the banners accompanying the flowers, replete with writings of 'her own inspiration, her thoughts about life and death, luck and hope' (*Kitchen* 18–19); Similarly, Luling Liu, in *The Bonesetter's Daughter*, supplements her income as a teacher's aide with side businesses, one of which is 'bilingual calligraphy, Chinese and English' (57).

America, thus, provides a platform for these women to use language by readapting it to their own needs and special purposes, eventually, crafting out a language of their own, one which enables them to speak/write themselves into being. As Tan writes in *The Opposite of Fate*, of the many advantages of being an American, one is the freedom of expression, 'to write whatever I want. I claim that freedom' (316). Paralleling her own position with that of her half-sisters living in China, Tan mourned their 'creative incarceration', especially during the Cultural Revolution. She remarks: 'They, too, once had imagination but it was pretty much stifled. . . . They were taught so long what to think, it was as if they lost the use of that muscle. The imagination rusted' (qtd. in Snodgrass 15–6). Thus, in the novels discussed, America represents both a site of conflict and tension, as well as a space of freedom and opportunities. It is within this ambivalent space that the characters negotiate their quest for redefinition and discover their identity.

The title of this book, *Her Quest for Self: A Journey*, draws attention to the fact that the women characters' quest for selfhood is not a singular event, but rather, a continuous process which must be negotiated and travelled through, much like a journey. In *More than Cool Reason: A Field Guide to Poetic Metaphor* (1989), George Lakoff and Mark Johnsen note that the journey metaphor is a pervasive one both in describing people's daily lives, as well as in literature:

> Our understanding of life as a journey uses our knowledge about journeys. All journeys involve travellers, paths travelled, places where we start, and places where we have been. Some journeys are purposeful and have destinations that we set out for, while

others may involve wandering without any destination in mind.
(60–61)

The journeying portrayed in the works of both Buck and Tan is not a
desultory, aimless one, but rather, an exploratory and a goal-directed journey
with the destination being the discovery, actualisation, and affirmation of
the characters' selfhood.

Though the characters portrayed in Pearl Buck's and Amy Tan's novels
are impelled on a journey to discover the self, the journey undertaken carries
them through separate routes and varying paths. For Buck's characters,
the journey is one that takes them inward, into self-introspection. But the
journey is also one that carries them beyond, and outside of, themselves,
into a recognition of, and acceptance of, the 'other'. It is only in relation
to this 'other' that Buck's characters succeed in rediscovering themselves.

The term 'other', in the context of this book, is one that carries a triple
connotation: it is employed in the Sartrerian sense to refer to a person(s)
other than one's self, 'a thinking substance of the same essence as I am', but
nonetheless, different from me (Sartre 303). In this definition, therefore,
the other is understood as someone who shares my basic attribute of being
human, but at the same time, one who is also different from me, the
difference being marked in terms of gender and race, among many other
factors. In *East Wind: West Wind*, Kweilan's journey to selfhood is one
that is facilitated through her relationship with her husband, the gendered
other, and also with her American sister-in-law who represents the racial
other. Simultaneously, the term 'other' is also and more frequently used in
the post-colonial and feminist sense to denote the colonised/marginalised
'other', who by virtue of their difference from the dominant group have been
disempowered and robbed of a voice in the social, religious, and political
world. Feminist thinker and writer Simone de Beauvoir calls the 'other'
the minority, the least favoured one, and often, a woman when compared
to a man (qtd. in McCann 33). Thus, the term 'other' refers to (i) others
(other human beings apart from oneself), (ii) the gendered and racial other
(marked by difference from oneself, in terms of gender, race, etc) with
whom the characters interrelate, (iii) the women characters themselves, the

marginalised others, who have been 'doubly colonised' (Ashcroft *et al*, 250), by virtue of their sex and race.

The journey motif for Amy Tan's immigrant characters encapsulates both the literal one – the trans-pacific crossings between China and America – as well as the figurative journey into the past. The physical voyage is an essential theme in Tan's fiction because of the dual-cultural/national affiliations of the characters. In *Coping with Threatened Identities* (1986), G. Breakwell argues that places/physical locations are important sources of identity elements and self-formation because places have symbols that have meaning and significance for us. They are linked to both personal as well as social memories, which in turn build up the individual's larger concept of self. Thus, the physical journeys are important because they serve to connect and reconnect the characters with spatial domains that have shaped, and will continue to reshape, the characters' lives and realities. Incidentally, the significance of the physical journey as a means of reclaiming one's identity is also explored by Buck in her novel *Kinfolk*.

Simultaneously, for the characters of Tan, the journey also involves revisiting the past via the realm of storytelling and 'rememory'. Storytelling, both oral and scripted, is integral to Tan's work and she weaves it into the fabric of her fiction to reconnect the characters with the past. 'Rememory' is a term coined by Toni Morrison in her novel *Beloved*. In Morrison's novel, Sethe, the female protagonist who is a former slave tries to describe the process of 'rememory' to her daughter Denver by using the following imagery:

> Where I was before I came here, that place is real. It's never going away. Even if the whole farm – every tree and grass blade of it dies. The picture is still there and what's more, if you go there . . . and stand in the place where it was, it will happen again. (36)

These lines emphasise the potency and ability of the past to retain its hold upon people's lives and impact them emotionally, especially if that past is a particularly painful and traumatic one, as it is for Sethe. The only way for her to come out of the stranglehold of the past and find healing and closure is through the process of 'rememory'. 'Rememory', therefore, involves the deliberate act of reliving and evoking past images by articulating them and learning to deal with the pain that remembering necessarily entails. Amy, one of the characters in *Beloved*, tells Sethe, '[a]nything dead coming back to life hurts' (42). The act of 'rememory' is therefore both an ordeal (because of the pain that is evoked) as well as an act of reconciliation with the past; it is a process that necessitates the reopening of old wounds, but at the same time, one that eventually brings healing and closure.

In Amy Tan's novels, the process of 'rememory' is an especially crucial one for the characters. Most of these women come laden with traumatic emotional baggage from the past that imprisons them psychically and stunts their personal growth. This has served to alienate them from their loved ones, and even from themselves, resulting in disjointed lives and fragmented personalities. A crucial means by which these women find inner healing and learn to reassume control over their own lives and selves is through 'rememoring', the telling and retelling of the past, through their stories. Storytelling, therefore, both the written and the oral 'talk-stories' function as a strategic tool by which these women reassert agency and autonomy in their lives and situations. It serves as a conduit for these women to 'talk out' their pain, and in the process, disencumbers them from the iron grip of bitter memories that keep them from moving forward. Thus, the journey to the past, through storytelling and 'rememory', is extremely significant for Tan's women characters. It brings internal healing and helps them to move forward into the future, armed with wisdom and life's lessons learnt from the past. In her essay, 'My Grandmother's Choice', Tan compares the past to 'a tomb of memories':

> We open it and release what has been buried for too long – the terrible despair, the destructive rage. We hurt, we grieve, we cry. And then we see what remains: the hopes, broken to bits but still there. (*Fate* 104)

The journey motif in both Pearl Buck's and Amy Tan's novels, therefore, functions both at the physical and geographical plane, as well as in the metaphorical and symbolic sense.

The quest for self is a central motif and functions as the supporting framework in analysing the novels. In *Literary Constructs of the Self: Socio-Cultural Contexts* (2010), the text begins thus: 'To know one's self has been a persistent and perennial human endeavour and has been the foremost concern of disciplines like Philosophy, Psychology, Literature, and Religion.' It implies the 'realization of the multilayered and multishaded complex reality of the inner core of being, called the self' (Gupta *et al.*, 1). If the search for self, therefore, is seen as the ultimate human goal, the question that necessarily arises is, 'What is the self?' or 'What defines it?' In Jean Paul Sartre's, *Being and Nothingness* (1956), the self is defined as 'the *essence* of man' (72), or that which constitutes the inner core of one's being. The self is, thus, understood as that which is the ultimate defining characteristic of what it means to be human.

In this book, however, the focus is not on the philosophical or abstract understanding of self, but rather, on the self as an experiential reality, one that evolves from 'the interrelatedness between the individual and the immediate surrounding social and cultural milieu' (Gupta *et al.*, 4). The quest for selfhood that is negotiated by the women characters here is not a hermetic search or one that is experienced in isolation, but rather, one that develops, and is actualised, through a network of relationships and interactions with the greater world outside oneself. This world-outside-oneself encompasses the human relationships in their lives, the social and cultural environment in which they lived, and even the political realities that shape and inform the lives of the characters, as well as the way they view and understand themselves. As such, the self that is realised by these women is not a fixed or unchanging entity, but a fluid one. It is a self that constantly grows and evolves along with the shift and change in the personal, sociocultural, and political context(s) which defines their lived realities.

The twin concepts of 'self' and 'identity' have been used interchangeably even though scholarship makes a distinction between the two. K. Deaux, for instance, in his article 'Personalizing Identity and Socializing Self', describes the 'self' as a more abstract, and encompassing concept, whereas 'identity' is linked to specific aspects of self-definition. However, the two concepts are used synonymously here, based on the underlying assumption that selfhood can never be fully realised without also comprehending and knowing one's own identity / 'Who am I?' The two concepts are thus, seen as mutually related, deriving their meanings from each other: If the 'self' is the essence or the inner core of a person's being, 'identity' is 'the essential core of who we are as individuals, the conscious experience of the self inside' (Kaufman 68). It is in discovering their identity, or in knowing 'who they are', that the characters move closer towards a reclamation and reaffirmation of the self.

Section 1 of this book, titled, 'Bridging the Gap: Rereading Pearl S. Buck,' explores the delineation of the Chinese women characters in the select fiction of Pearl S. Buck, in the context of their quest for self-discovery and personal meaning and fulfilment. The attempt is to define and identify the various 'gaps' that characterise these women's lives and to show how they negotiate their journey to the self, by attempting to bridge these gaps/divides/absences that mark their lives. What is examined is, whether these women succeed in bridging these gaps? What are the factors that facilitate/impede their attempt to do so? These are the questions that are dealt with in this section.

Section 2, 'Bridging Divides; Crossing Two Worlds: The Role of Storytelling in Amy Tan's Fiction', is an attempt to understand the multilayered divides that characterise the characters' lives and impede their journey to selfhood. The 'divides' that are outlined here pertains particularly to the mother-daughter divide which constitutes one of the themes in all the novels discussed. The various chapters also attempt to probe into the intercultural differences between the Chinese culture and the American one which the characters constantly confront, as a necessary outcome of their bicultural placement. The centrality and role of storytelling, particularly the Chinese oral 'talk-stories', as a means of bridging these divides and as a way of understanding and reclaiming the self is explored in detail. Finally, what is underlined in this section is how in the bridging of their relationships – interpersonally, interculturally, and intrapersonally – the characters manage to reinvent their lives and discover their own identities in the process.

Finally, the concluding chapter, 'Two Perspectives: Two Voices', compares the work of both, Pearl S. Buck and Amy Tan, tracing out the similarities as well as the distinguishing features that mark their works, and sums up the theme of the book.

SECTION ONE

BRIDGING THE GAP

Rereading Pearl S. Buck

PROLOGUE

> If Willa Cather was the writer who created the first strong
> American Woman in literature, Pearl Buck was the writer who
> created the first strong ordinary Chinese Woman in literature.
>
> (Kang Liao, *Pearl S. Buck:*
> *A Cultural Bridge across the Pacific* 4).

This section attempts to define and identify the various 'gaps' that characterise the lives and experiences of Pearl Buck's women characters; to show how they negotiate their journey to the self by attempting to bridge the gaps/divides/absences that mark their lives. The analysis of Buck's novels in the proceeding chapters probes into the nature of the gaps and lacunae that these women characters encounter and negotiate with in order to come to terms with their lives and achieve some form of personal meaning and self-actualisation.

Chapter 1 focuses on *East Wind: West Wind* (1930), chapter 2 on *The Good Earth* (1931), chapter 3, *The Mother* (1934), chapter 4, *Pavilion of Women* (1946), and chapter 5, *Kinfolk* (1949). These particular novels have been chosen because they represent a wider and more varied picture of Chinese life and Chinese women, as drawn from the different sections of Chinese society: *East Wind: West Wind* and *Pavilion of Women* depict the lives of Chinese women from the aristocratic circles, while *The Good Earth* and *The Mother* portrays rural women drawn from peasantry. *Kinfolk*, again, represents yet another aspect of Chinese life in its depiction of educated Chinese immigrant characters who live their lives on two sides of the globe – China and America. The different backgrounds of these characters facilitate in providing a wider platform for a more rounded and comprehensive exploration and understanding of the Chinese woman.

The gaps or chasms encountered in the novels are multifarious and often overlap one another: *East Wind: West Wind* depicts the ensuing conflict but also the eventual growth in the protagonist, when she is forced into a situation where she has to negotiate the intergenerational and intercultural gaps that the novel presents; in *Kinfolk*, the gap is geographical but also psychological. This novel is set within the bicultural context of China and America, and as such, it explores the diasporic experience and the conflict of identity that follows from such a transaction. The novel also highlights the gap between the China created out of the parents' memory and the actual China encountered by the children when they eventually went there. In *Pavilion of Women*, Buck dramatises the dichotomy between the domestic/female space and the public/male domain, and the character's attempt to bridge this socially constructed gap. In *The Mother*, which is perhaps Buck's most explicit portrayal of female sexuality, what is underlined is the intrapsychical gap (embodied by the deep sense of guilt) that the protagonist goes through when she attempts to explore her own sexuality as a woman. This, as a study of the novel reveals, is a result of the negative conditioning of women by a society which views woman only as a mother figure and/or a wife, as a sexual object but not a sexual being; the intrapsychical gap is again explored, though through a different angle, in *The Good Earth*. What is portrayed in this novel through the character of O-lan is the tragic sense of fragmentation, inner rift, and psychological stunting that result when a woman is silenced and seen as the 'other'.

What is examined in this section is, whether these women succeed in bridging these gaps. What are the factors that facilitate/impede their attempt to do so? As mentioned above, the women characters are drawn from varied segments of the Chinese society. As such, these characters are uniquely individualised and diverse from one another. They differ in their backgrounds, their circumstances and experiences, their outlook, and also in their sense of self-awareness and ability to self-reflect. While Madame Wu consciously asserts her right to self-determination and individual freedom, the other characters, with the exception of the Liang women, and the mother to some extent, seems to be unaware, and almost apathetic, to their needs and desires as women. It is only when propelled by situations into a space where they are forced to interrogate their lives and inner beings that a sense of self is awakened in them. This is not because of any deficiency on the part of these women, but rather, the conditioning impact of a society that treats women as objects and possessions, robbing them of their voice and individuality, and alienating them from their very personhood.

What is attempted in this section, therefore, is to trace the circumstances leading to the reawakening and re-emergence of self in these women, and the different paths that their journey takes as they reclaim their dormant selves. The nature of these women's journey is so different and unique one from the other, that each merits a special study, even as the larger and shared context of patriarchy shapes their common background.

CHAPTER ONE

SPANNING THE INFINITY
East Wind: West Wind

I am like a frail bridge, spanning the infinity.
(*East Wind: West Wind*, 167)

In his tribute to Pearl S. Buck, the late president Nixon of the United States of America describes her as 'a human bridge between the civilisations of East and West' (qtd. in Stirling 330). It is significant therefore, that Pearl Buck made her debut as a writer with *East Wind: West Wind*, a novel which underlines this theme. This novel describes China at a time when the West had begun to make inroads into a country steeped in tradition. The novel is aptly titled for it portrays two worlds – China and the West, the 'East Wind' and the 'West Wind'. The book also serves as a backdrop to another of Buck's recurrent theme, which is, the conflict between youth and age, tradition and modernity.

The twin themes highlighted in the novel are thus the conflict between two broad cultures, namely, the East and the West, and the intergenerational rift between the old China and the new, emerging China. As Isidore Schneider points out, 'the clash between modern and traditional China' (1930, 24), informs the thrust of the novel.

The plot is structured into two parts and centres on the experiences of a young Chinese woman, Kweilan, who becomes the human interface whereby the themes of the novel are explored. Written in the first-person narrative, Kweilan tells her story – the story of the turmoil that is suddenly brought to bear upon her and her family, by the intrusion of Western values and thinking into their hitherto structured lives. This turmoil results from Kweilan's marriage to a modern Chinese man who has been exposed to new ways of thinking and living. The subsequent marriage of her brother to an American woman complicates Kweilan's situation further. Thus, the novel dramatises the conflict that is generated in the life of the family, in the wake of the above two events. The narrative focuses particularly on Kweilan's reaction to the situation and her individual journey towards self-discovery and personal growth, triggered by this conflict in her life.

Belonging to a rich, old, and respected aristocratic Chinese family, Kweilan was brought up 'in all the honoured traditions' (*Wind* 3–4) of the ancient Chinese. Betrothed to her husband before she was born, her whole education right through childhood was directed to one sole purpose alone – her marriage, and how to conduct herself with propriety in it. On the eve of her marriage, her mother addresses her with these words: 'You have been reared for this end. . . Through these seventeen years of your life I have had this hour of your marriage in mind' (*Wind* 9). Kweilan is therefore brought up to believe in the Chinese ideal that marriage, and subsequently motherhood, is the ultimate, and indeed, the sole purpose and destiny of a woman. Living within the cloistered environment of courtyard walls, Kweilan was never led to challenge or question this assumption. She says, 'I went, as I was taught, in the approved ways of my ancestors, nothing from the outside ever touched me. *I desired nothing*' (emphasis added, *Wind* 4). Remarking on this, Xiongya Gao notes:

> If the molding of women into a source of pleasure for their husbands was unfair and tragic, the impact this tradition had on women's way of thinking was even more disturbing. They generally did not realize that they were victims of such prejudice and mistreatment. (48)

The seclusion and under-exposure of Chinese women to the outside world, particularly those from the aristocratic circles, and the lack of educational opportunities and interactions such as is given to their male counterpart, account to a large extent, for their subservience and general perception of themselves as lesser beings. Thus, while Kweilan's brother enjoys the privilege of education, studying in the national university, and eventually, America, Kweilan is denied the same, simply because she was born a girl. What Virginia Woolf writes in her novel *A Room of One's Own*, of her fictional character, Judith, Shakespeare's sister, may well be said to describe Kweilan, and other women like her who are denied access to opportunities simply on the basis of their gender: 'She was as adventurous, as imaginative, as agog to see the world as he was. But she was not sent to school' (47). Kweilan's only education consists in learning to be a model/ wife/mother/daughter-in-law. In her groundbreaking book, *The Second Sex*, de Beauvoir further exposes the myth of gender inequality that is prevalent in patriarchal societies:

> The universe does not wear a similar aspect for the adolescent boy . . . and for the adolescent girl . . . The one constantly questions the world; he can, at any moment, rise up against whatever is . . . The Other simply submits; the world is defined without reference to her (15).

Interestingly, the subtitle in part 1 of the novel significantly reads: 'A Chinese Woman Speaks'. This is extremely important. First, it centres a Chinese woman as the subject, rather than the object other. Second, it gives woman a voice that had hitherto been denied to her in Chinese feudal society. An age-old Confucian maxim reads:

> The girl's eyes should never be used for reading, only for sewing. The girl's ears should never be used for listening to ideas, only to orders. The girl's lips should be small, rarely used, except to express appreciation or ask for approval. (qtd. in Tan's *The Kitchen God's Wife* 121)

With her debut novel, therefore, Buck clearly announces her intention of foregrounding, and giving voice to, the Chinese women in her fiction who, according to her, 'possess the finest qualities that can be possessed' (Gao 46).

In this novel, the story unfolds through the first-person narration of Kweilan. She is the central consciousness, the 'I', that informs the narrative. It is on her sensibility and on her perception of her environment that the whole novel is rooted. The insertion of a narrating 'I' in this narrative, is of extreme significance. According to American-Chinese author Jade Snow Wong, in traditional Chinese writing, 'the submergence of the individual is literally practiced . . . the word "I" almost never appears' (vii). It may appear, therefore, that Buck's inscription of a narrating 'I' in a work which is totally Chinese in context betrays a lack of knowledge about its basic rules and traditions. However, as a fluent speaker, reader, and writer of the language, Buck is perfectly aware of the nuances and trends in Chinese literary tradition, a tradition in which she was born and reared, and one that she consistently tries to emulate in her own work about China and Chinese characters. The break with Chinese tradition (in this novel), in the employment of a narrating 'I', and that too, in a woman's voice, must therefore be read as Buck's deliberate attempt to give voice to the suppressed Chinese woman. In this sense, therefore, this novel may also be read as an early feminist text.

French psychologist Jacques Lacan asserts that when a child begins to recognise himself/herself in a mirror, it is then that 'the "I" is precipitated' (2). Lacan's assumption suggests that the 'I' or the self is realised through the journey of self-recognition and exploration. One of the means undertaken by Kweilan to explore her lived reality and to make sense of her own experience is through the mode of storytelling. She says, '[m]y life is confused with strange events' (*Wind* 40). The novel commences with Kweilan trying to weave together the 'strange events' that make up the fabric of her story.

The use of storytelling in this context is significant. Storytelling is, often, the only means available for women in segregated societies to express themselves and to bond with each other. As H.W. Wong points out, 'for women living in male-dominated societies where they were silenced and excluded from public forms of involvement . . . storytelling provides a realm of voice and of building communities with other women' (4). Storytelling, therefore, becomes a platform for Kweilan to articulate the self and give voice to her own experiences when no other medium sufficed, or is available. The act of telling her story, articulating her experiences and perspectives to her listening friend, becomes a tool in facilitating Kweilan's move towards self-awareness and propels her on her search for meaning and validation. In the process, she becomes an active agent of her own self-development and gradually comes closer to a better understanding of herself.

It is interesting to note that 'the Chinese phrase for story-telling is "talking-story"' (Juhasz 175) and is extremely relevant in the context of this novel. It postulates a conversation, a negotiation, with a listener/participant who is as actively engaged in the telling of the story as the teller herself. In this novel, the story unfolds through the interaction between the 'I' (Kweilan, the narrator-protagonist), and the 'you', affectionately called 'my sister' (*Wind* 5), who listens and supposedly interjects with her own questions, remarks, and observations. Thus, storytelling, particularly the 'talking-story', lends itself as a significant means of connection between the teller and the listener. The interaction between Kweilan and the listener, the self and the other, becomes one of the means that help Kweilan to come closer to a better understanding of her own impulses and situation. This reiterates the point that the quest for self-knowledge and realisation is one that is transacted not in isolation, but in conjunction with others. As Sartre reiterates in his book *Being and Nothingness*, 'to establish itself as a knowing self-consciousness it [the self] must be aware of other knowing consciousnesses from which it is also distinct, and these other consciousnesses are the "Others"' (qtd. in Rath 90).

It is important to note that in this novel, the listening other is also the racial other because the listener of Kweilan's story is a Western woman. By depicting the close relationship between her Chinese heroine and the Western woman, Buck attempts, through her art, to span the intercultural divide that she sees existing between East and West, at the time. Her main belief, as Liu Haiping points out, is that 'all under heaven are one' (56). Thus, for both Buck and Kweilan, the stories that they tell function as a tool to bridge the intercultural divide between East and West, represented here by Kweilan and her Western friend, respectively.

Kweilan's journey towards selfhood is, therefore, one that is mapped out through a network of relationships and transactions in her life, both interculturally and interpersonally. One of the most significant relationships in Kweilan's life that, in a sense, triggers the crisis that initiates her on the path of self-interrogation and self-exploration is her relationship with her husband. Educated in America, he has learnt 'to love new things and new ways' (*Wind* 4). He finds her feminine demureness dull, and her submissiveness, irritating. She was horrified to discover that her small bound feet, pride of every high-born Chinese woman, are viewed by him as unhealthy and terribly regressive. To win his affection, therefore, Kweilan finds that she must learn to accommodate herself to new ways and ideas. Seeing her openness towards change, her husband helps her in this 'new path' *(Wind* 37). This 'new path' compels her to interrogate and rethink many of her previously held assumptions and worldview, leading eventually to the reframing of new sensibilities.

It is interesting to note that in most women's narrative, written from the feminist perspective, marriage is often portrayed as debilitating and restricting, a state of 'growing down' rather than 'growing up', as Annis Pratt puts it (14). And although certain feminist themes are clearly evident in most of Buck's novels discussed here, in this particular novel, Buck evinces a marked departure from the general feminist stance regarding marriage. In *East Wind: West Wind*, marriage does not reduce or decimate Kweilan's identity and personality in any way. In fact, it becomes an enriching experience for her and it is within the sphere of this relationship that her ideas and sensibilities about herself and about the world are reshaped and redefined: 'It is my husband who has changed me,' she says, 'so that I dare, in spite of my fear, to speak for love even against my ancestors' (*Wind* 183).

One of the tangible evidences marking Kweilan's transformation is the unbinding of her feet which she had steadfastly refused to do earlier. In her book *Unbound Feet*, Judy Yung notes that foot binding, practiced extensively from the twelfth to the early twentieth century in China, is perhaps, the ultimate expression of a Chinese woman's oppression. It has come to symbolise the Chinese woman's restricted life, both physically and socially. One of the most difficult decisions that Kweilan makes after her marriage is the unbinding of her feet. The decision is difficult because it entails not merely the physical act but, more importantly, implies a decisive break with a familiar pattern of life that has grown comfortable in its very familiarity. The unbinding of feet, therefore, becomes a metaphor for Kweilan's attempt to unbind herself from the patriarchal bind of the

Chinese ancestral culture. It connotes not merely a physical change but the internal changes taking place in Kweilan's inner being. Through this act, she metaphorically frees herself from the fetters of feudal imposition and mindset which has enslaved Chinese women for centuries. The process of change, however, as Kweilan realises, is one that is not easily negotiated. It is painful and difficult. Nonetheless, it is a road that must be travelled if she is to grow and survive in a world where, as Gloria Naylor puts it, all of us are 'in some measure victims of something' (576). Although for Kweilan, 'the unbinding process was almost as painful as the binding had been', yet as a consequence of the unbinding, she begins to experience 'a new freedom' (*Wind* 84–5). She could walk more freely and manage her steps without much difficulty. However, the freedom experienced by Kweilan in this context is more than physical, for it entails, the freedom of the inner spaces of her being, which is a crucial prerequisite for personal fulfilment and self-growth.

Interestingly, Buck scholars, such as Caoly Doan, critique the way the change is brought about in Kweilan. He argues that her resolution to change is motivated by external forces rather than by any inclination on her own part:

> Kweilan may well represent the soul of ancient China: though she becomes a convert to modern life, the conversion is forced upon her by marriage rather than by a genuine conviction. (47)

Doan's argument is valid to a certain extent, in that Kweilan's acquiescence to the changes in her life is indeed prompted by the desire of pleasing and obeying her husband. But to understand why this is so, one must take into account the times and cultural context in which the story is situated. In old China, there is no safety and security for a woman on her own. A woman's well-being, both physically and socially, is firmly tied to home and family. Women, especially the aristocratic ones like Kweilan, have been so insulated that apart from the home environment, they 'would not know . . . how to survive in the outside world even if they wanted to. . .' (Gao 46). Living within such a context, Kweilan is astute and practical enough to realise that her happiness and well-being lies in pleasing her husband.

Therefore, her apparent conformity to his wishes may, in fact, be read as a tool of personal empowerment. It empowers her to establish herself in her husband's life and find happiness within the allocated space of home and family that makes up her reality.

Modern readership may critique this as a powerful example of the circumscriptions that women inadvertently impose upon themselves. It is from such 'cramped confines of patriarchal space' that Showalter urges women to break away (201). At the same time, however, it is important to remember that this was the prevalent social reality in China at that particular time. Women like Kweilan had no other recourse than to wrest out the best options available to them within the limited space that informs their social reality. As she schools herself to embrace, and adapt to, the changes in her life, Kweilan finds herself attaining to a certain measure of self-contentment and rewriting a new story in her life. 'I ceased to be lonely,' she remarks, '[w]here he was became my home, and I thought no more of my mother's house' (*Wind* 93).

As Kweilan interacts with her husband and with the outside world, she learns to question and re-examine many of the beliefs and the value system that she had always accepted and taken for granted: 'Could it be that he was right, after all?' (*Wind* 77), she asks herself. In her essay, 'When We Dead Awaken: Writing as Re-vision', Adrienne Rich writes about the importance of 're-visioning' as a crucial means of female self-discovery and finding one's identity. She defines 're-vision' as 'the act of looking back, of seeing with fresh eyes, of entering an old text from a new critical direction.' The re-visioning process is extremely important for women, according to Rich, because 'until we can understand the assumptions in which we are drenched, we cannot know ourselves' (18–19).

An important motif that stands out in this novel is Buck's pervasive use of the home space as the arena in which the drama of Kweilan's personal growth and self-definition is played out. The home functions both as a physical entity and as a lived experience in this novel. Paraphrasing Gayatri Spivak, Dorinne Kondo defines home as 'a safe place, where there is no need to explain oneself to outsiders; it stands for community' (97). In *East Wind: West Wind*, however, the home assumes an ambivalent role. This argument finds a parallel in M. Jackson's work, *At Home in the World*, which asserts that the home 'may evoke security in one context and seem confining in another' (122). Kweilan's story is played out within the domestic domain of three homes – her ancestral home, her in-law's home, and finally, her own home.

The first seventeen years of life spent under the ancestral roof birthed and nurtured Kweilan's assumptions and perceptions about life, about the world, and her role in it. Here she is taught that the ultimate destiny of a woman is marriage and that her worth comes only from pleasing her husband and his family, through the begetting of sons to perpetuate the ancestral name. It is also here that Kweilan is taught to believe the patriarchal myth that different sets of rules and norms exist for men and women. Talking of her childhood with her brother, Kweilan recalls thus: 'When we played together I dared not cross him, partly because he was a boy, and it would not have been seemly that I, a girl, should set my will against his' (*Wind* 127). So deeply ingrained is this presumption that she sees nothing unjust or discriminatory when, at an early age, she had to stop her book-studies because she 'could not spare the time from the many things necessary to fit me for marriage to pursue further the Classics' (*Wind* 18). Her brother, on the other hand, goes to a foreign school in Peking and on to the university, before he eventually goes to America to study further.

If the ancestral house is the fomenting ground for Kweilan's self-devaluation and abnegation, her brief sojourn in her in-laws' home further reinforces this notion. Having been scrupulously instructed in all the duties of a daughter-in-law, Kweilan now sets herself to the task of obeying her mother-in-law unquestioningly. 'I may refuse her nothing,' she says, 'and her reproaches, however unjust, I must bear in silence. I am prepared to subject myself to her in all things' (*Wind* 42). In old Chinese society, 'once married, a woman, in a way, became homeless' (Gao 39). She can no longer claim her parents' home as hers, just as she cannot experience a true sense of home in her in-laws' house either, because of the traditional joint family system which is usually ruled by the matriarch of the family. Thus, stripped of a sense of home, the woman's psyche becomes a splintered one. She is caught adrift in a world that does not want her to belong. This feeling of dislocation, this sense of belonging nowhere, is also echoed by Kweilan immediately after her marriage:

> I ran to the door, thinking in my wildness that I might escape
> and return to my mother's home. But my hand upon the heavy
> iron bar recalled me . . . my mother would be there waiting to
> send me back to my duty . . . I no longer belonged to her family.
> (*Wind* 38–39)

It is out of these trapped confines that Kweilan must venture forth if she is to acquire a sense of freedom and self-expression so fundamental to self-reclamation.

It is interesting to note that in this novel, the decision to break away from a suffocating and sterile environment is initiated not by the heroine but by her husband who belongs to the new school of educated Chinese. He tells his wife, 'I wish to regard you in all things as my equal. . . You are not my possession . . . you may be my friend if you will' (*Wind* 36). He, along with Kweilan's brother, represents the voice of modern China in conflict with the old-world traditions and values. Refusing to allow himself and his wife to be shackled by outdated customs and regressive practices, he moves out of the ancestral courts. For the traditional Chinese brought up to believe in filial piety as the norm, rather than the exception, this act embodies the ultimate expression of *bu xiao*, or 'failure of filial piety' (Gao 33). Kweilan's husband chooses for their abode, a Western-style house. The relocation to a space that Kweilan eventually comes to regard as her own is extremely strategic. It opens up a wider and freer space for her to express herself uninhibitedly, without being constrained by the self-effacing rules and diktats of her previous homes. In this new, open space, Kweilan finds the freedom to be herself, renegotiating life daily without fear of being caught in the wrong foot, and exploring relationships and friendships that would not have been possible in her earlier milieux.

The painstaking attention to the physical details of the new house is symbolically significant. The windows are made of 'large panes of clear glass', giving access to 'merciless light'. Kweilan tells her friend, 'This light searches,' as she contrasts it with a traditional Chinese house where 'the light is dimmed by lattice and carving' (*Wind* 46–47). The new house, thus, represents a space for introspection and soul-searching for Kweilan. Removed from the constricting atmosphere of her earlier environment and exposed to new ideas and beliefs, Kweilan learns to look at things in a new light. As she interacts with a world far broader than the one she has known, she finds her old prejudices and ignorance being stripped away, gradually. For instance, when she observes the openness and frankness in the way her brother and his American wife relate to each other, the once reticent and highly conservative Kweilan can now say:

> Watching them I marvelled that only warmth came into my heart for them. Had I ever seen them thus before my marriage I should have sickened at such emotion between man and wife . . . and thought it fit only for concubines and slave-girls. And now, you see how I am changed. (*Wind* 254–55)

This shift in her thought processes, this 'changed consciousness' (Collins 111–12), is a defining moment in Kweilan's journey for it ushers her on the path towards maturity. She remarks, 'Once I was willing to change, a complete new life poured in upon me' (*Wind* 88).

An interesting feature about *East Wind: West Wind* is that it may also be read as a female Bildungsroman, although it may not adhere to each and every feature typical of the genre. Like a traditional Bildungsroman which traces the hero's path towards self-discovery and self-realisation, a female Bildungsroman is one which depicts the female protagonist on her journey to selfhood. According to Annie Estyuroy, this genre is marked by certain features: It focuses on the character's 're-examination of the past' as an important means by which the character 'arrive[s] at an understanding of her female self', a self which emerges from its interaction with the world (Estyuroy 3–4). Other writers have built further on the defining elements that make up this literary genre: Xie contends that most female Bildungsroman 'begin where the traditional Bildungsroman ends, with marriage and family' (21); According to Ardanzazu, 'these texts consists of a long series of circular reflections on the past, connected to the present by the character's circular and always repetitive reflections' (329–330). Unlike the traditional Bildungsroman that presents a full account of the protagonist's life, this genre spotlights only certain defining 'moments or specific experiences' (Estyuroy 6) that act as building blocks in the character's development.

A reading of *East Wind: West Wind* shows that it lends itself perfectly to the pattern of these definitions. Marriage, and to some extent, motherhood, provides the 'specific experiences' that lead to the personal growth of Kweilan. Marriage – her own and that of her brother's – serves to push the hitherto unquestioning and conservative Kweilan into a space of conflict where tradition battles hard against a new wave of thinking. Kweilan's revolt against tradition such as in the unbinding of her feet and the equally sacrilegious act of leaving the in-laws' home (both consequences of her marriage), enacts, in a smaller scale, China's subsequent revolt against Confucian feudalism that had held sway for centuries, such as the New Culture Movement (1919), and the even more radical, Cultural Revolution (1960s–70s). Thus, Kweilan's personal narrative both mirrors and anticipates the larger cultural narrative of her people, particularly the younger generations of Chinese, as they too journey, also through conflict, from the past and into a new way of living and thinking.

If Kweilan's marriage forces her into a new space which challenges her assumptions, her brother's marriage to a Westerner poses an even greater challenge. Brought up in a cocooned and self-contained environment, one largely limited in its contact with the outside world, Kweilan is thrust into an unanticipated encounter with the other – a person and a situation totally alien and incomprehensible to her. 'What will it be like when my brother comes, bringing her?' Kweilan asks herself, 'I fear such strangeness' (*Wind* 168). Her first impulse on meeting Mary, her American sister-in-law, is one of confusion, resentment, and apprehension. Her assessment of her is tinged with prejudice and condescension as she measures her by her own social and cultural standards:

> When we sit down to rice all together, she cannot eat with the chopsticks . . . her hands are unskilled in delicate things. . . We like to hear a woman's voice light and soft like a small stream of water trickling between two rocks . . . But her voice is deep and full. (*Wind* 175)

But gradually, as she begins to relate and interact with Mary, her perceptions are altered and widened. She learns to accept, and even appreciate, the difference that she sees existing between them: 'Living with her day after day, I have grown to like her, and as I watch her, there are times when I even see something of beauty in her strange looks and ways' (*Wind* 198).

Motherhood is another event that shapes the protagonist's growth and self-awareness. Recognised as a crucial element of the female Bildungsroman (Ardanzazu 333), the experience of motherhood fosters in Kweilan a deeper understanding of, and sensitivity to, the older generation, particularly her own mother. At a time when old values and ways were crumbling and disintegrating in the wake of the new culture that threatens to obliterate the stable flow of their lives, the period was particularly trying for the old in China. Women especially, having lived such sheltered and insulated lives, 'had the most difficulty in coping. . . . If one failed to survive the whirlwind, she would be discarded by it, thus becoming a victim of the change (Gao 46).

Kweilan's mother is one such victim. She stubbornly clings to the old tenets, refusing to the end of her life, to surrender to the new ways, even while admitting wryly that 'the times are changed' (*Wind* 71). Viewing her son's love marriage against his parents' consent as a violation of the age-old Confucian ethics of filial obedience, she refuses to recognise his marriage till her death, disowning him and breaking her own heart in the process. As a mother herself, Kweilan empathises with the sense of pain and betrayal felt by her mother. Simultaneously, however, she can no longer find it in her heart to reproach her brother's love marriage, having come to realise the importance of love in her own life and marriage. She says, 'When I remembered my husband, my heart turned to my brother, and when I held my son in my arms, my heart cleaved to my mother' (*Wind* 213). This dual perspective reveals her maturing sensibility, one that is gradually learning to see life in its entirety. She describes herself thus:

> I am like a frail bridge, spanning the infinity between past and present. I clasp my mother's hand; I cannot let it go, for without me she is alone. But my husband's hand holds mine; his hand holds mine fast. I can never let love go! (*Wind* 167)

Thus, the two marriages in the text, as well as motherhood, positions Kweilan in the unique role of a mediator, one who tries to bridge the gap between youth and age, old and new, East and West. In the attempt, she finds her own character taking on a new stature and dimension.

The importance of reviewing 'the past' as a means of understanding the present is also stressed by Ardanzazu as an integral element of the female Bildungsroman (329–30). As Kweilan strives to make sense of the present, she resorts to the only standards she has known: the experiences and knowledge gleaned from the past. The narrative, therefore, alternates between the two time frames of past and present. As she struggles to fit into the present with all its unfamiliarity and tension, she reflects back on the past to find answers to the new situation that she finds herself in. But as she measures the past in light of current realities, she is forced to conclude that the legacies she has inherited are terribly insufficient, limited, and even erroneous at times: 'I had been taught all wrong, I began to realize' (*Wind* 77).

This realisation of the inadequacy of past knowledge and experiences to address her present needs serves as a crutch, enabling her to step out of the shadows of the past. It also enables her to reshape herself and reinvent her life. This new path, completely at variance with the one she has known, is what finally leads Kweilan to chart out a new identity and discover personal truths for herself.

What is further observed in this novel is that the protagonist's quest for self-discovery is also facilitated by her relationship with a community of women. Noted women writer, Rita Felski, notes that the '[e]ncounters with other women' is a crucial part of 'the discovery process . . . the group of women providing the organic and harmonious community which opposes the rationalized world of male society' (135). The anonymous confidante in Kweilan's story is one of the 'organic and harmonious' links in this chain of network. Simply referred to as 'sister', her unobtrusive presence is integral to the heroine's self-articulation. She is privy to the inner landscapes of Kweilan's heart, drawing her out through her queries and responses implicitly embedded in the narrative. This interface between listener and narrator is repeatedly observed in the text.

Mary, Kweilan's American sister-in-law, is another female figure instrumental in the protagonist's growing maturity and understanding. Educated and broad in her outlook, she serves as a foil to Kweilan. From this woman whose presence she had initially viewed as intrusive, Kweilan learns to look beyond surface realities. As Mary tells of her life back in America and what she had left behind, Kweilan is humbled by the strength of this woman whose love had prompted her to give up 'a world for the other's sake' (*Wind* 271). Her relationship with Mary also teaches her that difference does not imply wrong or evil. It is a viable and enriching reality in a world of pluralities and variety. At the birth of Mary's son, Kweilan exultingly exclaims: 'He has tied together the two hearts of his parents into one . . . with all their difference in birth and rearing – differences existing centuries ago! What union' (*Wind* 277). This is a telling statement, revealing a woman whose vision of life is greatly expanded, finding harmony and beauty in the differences that she had once abhorred and recoiled from.

Though a minor character, Mrs Liu plays a major role in the re-visioning of the protagonist's thought pattern. A Chinese graduate from Vassar, she has learnt to amalgamate the best of both East and West. She may also be said to represent the voice of modern China, eschewing old customs and practices that she deems oppressive. It is through her interactions with Mrs Liu that Kweilan partly arrives at the decision to unbind her feet. However, unlike Kweilan's husband who advocates a complete break from all 'old, useless things!' (*Wind* 277), Mrs Liu recognises the importance of retaining certain aspects of the culture that are good and worthwhile. She advises Kweilan: 'Learn the good that you can of the foreign people and reject the unsuitable' (*Wind* 109). Her practical wisdom and common sense provides Kweilan with a moral compass to navigate the new course that she must journey through. Her support and advice are invaluable to Kweilan, helping to boost her wavering confidence and morale in times of intense stress and pressure.

In his article, 'Forming an Authentic Self in an Inauthentic World', Kenneth Boa differentiates between two types of 'role models' which he terms as 'valid' and 'invalid'. According to him, 'valid and palpable role models . . . are visible compasses that help us discern the authentic in a world of image, posing and externalism' (13). Kweilan's husband, as well as the three women discussed above – the confidante, Mary, and Mrs Liu – may be said to be positive and valid role models for Kweilan. Her interaction with them leads her to a clearer perspective and understanding of self and of others.

There are, however, other women in Kweilan's life – her mother, and La-may, her father's concubine – whose influences may be said to be largely, inimical to the heroine's conception of the female self. A typical first lady in an aristocratic household, managing her family with firmness and efficiency, Kweilan's mother is twice a victim. First, she is a victim of the changing times. The values and beliefs of feudal China are so entrenched in her psyche that she can no longer accommodate herself to new ways and dies a bitter and broken woman. Resisting change to the end, she is crushed under its weight and becomes a victim to it. But she is also a victim of the old system. The first of four wives, she experienced first-hand the repercussions of a system that treats a woman as a mere sex object living for the pleasure of her husband. Her eyes are like 'sad jewels . . . dying from over-much knowledge of sorrow' (*Wind* 13), the self-same sorrow that marks 'the anguish of a hundred generations of women who loved their lords and lost their favour' (*Wind* 162). This has spawned in her a contempt and distrust of the emotion of love. She tells her daughter bitterly, 'There is no such thing as this [love] between man and woman. . . It is only desire – the man's desire for the woman, the woman's desire for a son. When that desire is satisfied, there is nothing left' (*Wind* 166). She is a tragic figure, 'a character who lives a life of sorrow and dies with the death of the old system. The tragedy is that she insists until death on keeping the very system that has crushed her own happiness. . . However, like most women of and before her times, she does not realize that she has been mistreated and oppressed' (Gao 57).

Seeing her mother relentlessly bent on a self-destructive path, disappointed with both husband and son, Kweilan is determined to choose a path vastly different from hers. She opts for change rather than resisting it, seeing it as a strategy for survival and a hope for happiness and a better future. Ironically enough, Kweilan's mother who had so bitterly opposed change in her own life, admits that 'the times are changed' (*Wind* 71). She therefore, encourages her daughter to keep up with the permutations of time in order to 'please her husband' (*Wind* 71), even to the extent of allowing her to unbind her feet. Her function, therefore, is that of a catalyst, instrumental in the metamorphosis of her daughter while she herself remains unmoved by it.

La-may, the beautiful dancing girl from Soochow, third concubine of Kweilan's father, had fascinated Kweilan as a child and held her husband captive to her charms. But, like Kweilan's mother before her, she soon lost her husband's favour after the birth of a child. After a failed suicide attempt, she becomes a woman twisted by hate and anger, a victim of a system that reduces a woman to a mere play-thing, a beautiful object with no intrinsic worth. La-may had lived her life under the illusion that physical beauty connotes power, giving her control over men, a belief that even Kweilan shared initially:

> Ah, and so it was with me as well! . . . I dressed my hair with the jade and onyx ornaments, and I hung jade in my ears . . . I had learned from La-may . . . the guile of colorless cheeks and a lower lip touched with vermilion, and the witchery of scented, rosy palms. (*Wind* 73–74)

However, this myth was shattered by the reality of La-may's experience. As her own relationship with her husband grows, Kweilan discovers that love is formed and sustained not on the basis of the external but rather on intrinsic worth and integrity. Thus, the life lessons that Kweilan learns from both her mother and La-may are largely negative ones. From them she learns what *not* to build her life on, rather than what to emulate and follow.

While Kweilan's journey to self-realisation may, to some extent, evoke certain elements of the female Bildungsroman, there are, however, as mentioned earlier, points of deflection from the genre. In her definition, Rita Felski emphasises upon the importance of a community of women to aid the protagonist's growth, while indicting the 'rationalized world of male society' (135). This novel, however, indicates that the 'world of male society', represented here by Kweilan's husband, is as instrumental to the heroine's self-knowledge and self-discovery. He is, in a sense, the first key that unlocks the door to a world of myriad experiences and encounters that would alter and shape the heroine's mental vista. In her journey to selfhood, he is the supporting figure, encouraging the thorny process of growth and self-learning every step of the way. Towards the end of the narrative, Kweilan acknowledges thus: 'And now you see how I am changed, and how my lord has taught me! I knew nothing indeed until he came' (*Wind* 255).

The affirmation, rather than the indictment of the male-female alliance, is what is upheld in this novel. It primarily serves to highlight Pearl Buck's firm belief in the mutuality and reciprocity of life and of relationships. The world that we live in, as she repeatedly affirms in her work, is a world of both men and women:

> Ultimately, that vision of reconciled men and women, of integrated lives involved in work and family – regardless of whether Buck herself achieved it – is still what matters most, and in that vision, Buck still has something to teach. (d'Entremont 53)

Second, it conforms to the over-arching theme of the novel that welds together diametrically opposite elements: the East wind and the West wind; the self and the other; man and woman. The novel begins on a highly polarised note – the clash between tradition and modernity, the East wind versus the West wind invading each other's space, and the conflict that ensues. But, as these opposites interlock each other, a new space is created, and a new identity emerges. The novel ends symbolically with the birth of a child, the son of Mary and Kweilan's brother, a new entity who fuses into his being the dualities of his parents: as Kweilan exclaims, 'into this tiny knot' are 'tied two worlds' (*Wind* 275).

The engagement between East and West, the bridging of gaps of man's own making, Buck seems to suggest through this novel, is where hope for the future lies. In her autobiography, *My Several Worlds*, she declares her abiding belief in the following principles:

> In the brotherhood of peoples, in the equality of the races, in the necessity for human understanding, in the common sense of peace – all these principles in which I have been reared, in which I do believe and must believe fearlessly until I die. (376)

The discovery that Kweilan makes about herself at the close of the novel is that she sees herself as a mediator, a bridge trying to span the dividing lines between youth and age, tradition and modernity, East and West: 'I am like a frail bridge, spanning the infinity. . .' she announces of herself (*Wind* 167). Although she may see herself only as 'a frail bridge', yet Kweilan does succeed, to a certain extent, in bridging the intergenerational and intercultural gaps that the novel presents. In the process of bridging this gap, she finds her sense of self vastly enriched and redefined.

CHAPTER TWO

APPROPRIATING SPACES

Pavilion of Women

Today, after years of giving body and mind to others, she felt that
she needed to drink deeply at old springs

(Pavilion of Women, 48).

In *Pavilion of Women*, Buck dramatises a woman's quest for self-
realisation and personal freedom. Madame Wu, the protagonist, is perhaps
one of Buck's most individualised and protean women characters. Living
in a cultural context where women are not expected to voice their thoughts
and desires, let alone act on them, she exhibits a sense of self-awareness
and self-assertiveness that is highly unusual for a woman of her generation.
The novel has also been described as 'a searching adult study of women'
(McGrory 6). Married into the highly respected House of Wu, Madame Wu
presides as the matriarch over a large, extended family whose destiny she
tries to shape and control. Being the only wife of her husband in a culture
where concubinage is societally sanctioned, her position is highly enviable
in the eyes of female friends and contemporaries. Interestingly, in a society
where marriage is still regarded as the ultimate goal of a woman, Madame
Wu shocks her entire household and social circle when on her fortieth
birthday she announces her decision to arrange a concubine for her husband
so that she may 'retire' (*Pavilion* 51), from her conjugal and maternal duties.

Written in 1946, *Pavilion of Women* is, in many ways, a feminist narrative, of the emerging Chinese woman who is beginning to assert herself and make her voice heard. Simultaneously, like *East Wind: West Wind*, the novel is also a portraiture of a China in transition and the impact that this has on women's way of thinking. While the story revolves predominantly around the figure of Madame Wu, Buck also uses other minor female figures such as Rulan, Madame Wu's daughter-in-law, to show that the new Chinese woman is beginning to question the woman's sequestered position in society. Rulan tells Ch'iuming, the young woman brought into the family as a concubine for Mr Wu, 'Oh, I wish you and I could get out of this house. . . . Here we are all locked behind these high walls. The family preys upon itself' (*Pavilion* 382). Rulan eventually leaves the family court and carves a new life for herself in the ancestral village, teaching the children there. In a culture where silence is the watchword for women, Rulan's frustrated articulation is indicative of the new consciousness among Chinese women. Thus, while *Pavilion of Women* may be said to be the story of an individual woman whose voice dominates the narrative, it also resonates with the voices of other women like Rulan. The individual history of Madame Wu is interwoven with the collective cultural history of other women like her. This is a feature that is often seen in the works of most feminist writers, particularly Gloria Anzaldua and Audre Lorde. Anzaldua coined the term 'autohistoria' to describe her writing because it fuses together both the 'personal and collective' experience, the self and others (578). What is noticed in *Pavilion of Women* is that in the telling of Madame Wu's story, Buck allows other women's stories to emerge as well. What she succeeds in doing through her fiction, therefore, is to capture the sociopolitical mood of women's history in China at that time, making her work a collective document rather than a personal story.

In 1963, Betty Friedan published *The Feminine Mystique*, a feminist text questioning the traditional idea that women are naturally fulfilled by devoting their lives to simply being housewives and mothers. Friedan asserts that 'we can no longer ignore that voice within women that says "I want something more than my husband and my children and my home"' (32). Antedating Friedan's work by almost two decades, *Pavilion of Women* had already articulated women's need for 'something more' than what society traditionally assigns to them.

The traditional, gender-based, public/private dichotomy of social roles has always been used by patriarchy to undermine and limit women's potential. The public sphere, where men participated, was the sphere where culture, intellectual stimulation, and political activities exist. Women, on the other hand, were expected to remain in the private sphere in which household duties were held above all else (Rotman 669). This is even more pronounced and rigidly adhered to, in the traditional Chinese society. As the story of the legendary Chinese warrior woman, Fa Mu-Lan (already discussed earlier), demonstrates, one must be male to venture out into the public domain. What Helene Cixous remarks of the plight of women in general may well be said to describe the situation of the Chinese woman aptly, 'there's no room for her [in the public arena], if she's not a he' (888). The concept of domesticity, because it relegated women solely to the home, denies their intellectual and professional capabilities (Papke, 12). In Madame Wu, Buck delineates a woman who is not only aware of this socially constructed gap, but one who also challenges and attempts to cross the divide. She tells her daughter-in-law Rulan, after announcing her decision to retire from her role as a wife, 'I will spend the rest of my life assembling my own mind and my own soul' (*Pavilion* 61–2). The statement is a significant one reflecting the character's awareness of herself and of her personal needs and longings. It also announces her intention and determination to enter the 'male space' of learning and knowledge and make it her own, in the process, reinventing her life.

Madame Wu's entry into the male space is both literal as well as metaphorical. It is literal because her first act on coming out of her husband's court is to appropriate the library that belonged to her dead father-in-law. A woman of uncommon intelligence and deep thinking from an early age, Madame Wu's yearning for learning and knowledge was not greatly encouraged. Though with more freedom than most women of her time, the context in which she lives is governed by the worldview that 'as far as knowledge goes, a woman need not be extraordinarily intelligent. As for her speech, it need not be terribly clever . . . and for her talents they need only be average' (qtd. in Kristeva 86). Echoing a Confucian maxim, Old

Gentleman, Madame Wu's father-in-law, underlines her role in the family thus, even though he acknowledges her intellect:

> Yet I know that in my house you do not need so much intelligence – Yes, a little is good so that you can keep accounts and watch servants and control your inferiors. But you have reasoning and wonder. What will you do with them? (*Pavilion* 80)

Knowledge, for a woman, is viewed merely as a tool to aid in good household management, rather than as a means to self-cultivation and personal fulfilment. Having given herself to the household for twenty-two years, Madame Wu now decides to cast aside the role that had stunted her potential, and to embark on a new journey, one that she feels will lead to self-actualisation and inner freedom. The gesture of appropriating the library is, therefore, highly symbolic, spelling out the transition of her life from a phase consumed wholly by the domestic and the familial, to a new phase, which is the cultivation of the self. 'It gave her pleasure to think of the library full of books now hers . . . after years of giving body and mind to others, she felt that she needed to drink deeply at old springs' (*Pavilion* 48).

It has been argued that 'the formation of the self is imperceptibly moulded by geographical and temporal specificities' (Gupta 5). This has made the consideration of physical space a critical determiner in the growth of self. In *A Room of One's Own* (1929), Virginia Woolf remarks on the necessity of a physical space and material logisticities as aids to women's intellectual growth and self-expression. According to her, 'intellectual freedom depends', to a certain extent, 'upon material things' (108), such as 'money and a room of her own' (4). In *Pavilion of Women,* the library as a spatial specificity assumes great significance in the self-development of the character. It initiates the protagonist into the realm of books and reading which unlocks a sense of freedom, broadening her perspective and satisfying her mentally.

For Madame Wu, however, reading serves not only as an intellectual stimulus, but is also a means of connecting her with a greater world outside herself. Though physically, she is limited to the four walls of her court; metaphysically, however, she is able to journey the universe through the act of reading, a transcending experience that enlarges her perspective. As she reads, she feels 'as though she were out of her body and travelling in space', seeing 'the whole earth lying before her, the seven seas and the countries and the peoples of whom she had heard only in books' (*Pavilion* 113, 205). Buck's use of this trope is extremely significant in this context, highlighting the nature of a voyage that is metaphysical in nature. In an interview with Mike Wallace, Buck opines that most women make their own homes their graves because 'they stop reading, or reading books that would enlarge their minds', a belief supported by other women writers. Historian Mary Kelley notes that through reading, women could find 'alternative models of womanhood . . . that enabled [them] to resist constraints and to pursue more independent courses of self-definition' (404, 406). Thus, reading serves as an important building block in the character's journey to self-liberation and self-definition. As she reclaims the right to read/study, she is, in a sense, appropriating a space traditionally denied to women, transforming it into a personal space of freedom, wisdom, and inner growth.

Metaphorically, Madame Wu's entry into the male space is symbolised by the act of deciding upon, and choosing, a concubine for her husband. The act symbolically signals her appropriation of a space, a prerogative largely claimed by men. The action, however, is problematic: One may critique that in attempting to assert her autonomy and power via this feudal mode of practice, Madame Wu inadvertently becomes complicit in an act which has contributed to the subjugation of her own gender through the centuries. On the other hand, however, it is imperative to remember the context in which the character lives. In articulating her needs and desires openly, Madame Wu may well be regarded as a precursor of the emerging, liberated women of revolutionary China. Yet, she herself is still the product of an age and a culture where concubinage is very much a part of the system. Brought up in such a milieu, therefore, she sees nothing inherently wrong or unnatural in it. Second, in Madame Wu's view, it is the only recourse available to her if she is to free herself from her marital responsibility and pursue her personal goals and aspirations. Thus, the fact that she unwittingly aligns herself with an act that clearly demeans women did not even occur to her initially. It is only through her discussions with Andre that she gradually becomes aware of the implications of her action. He tells her, 'You have bought a young woman as you would buy a pound of pork. But a woman, any woman, is more than that, and of all women you should know it' (*Pavilion* 264). It is to Madame Wu's credit, however, that when she is made aware of flaws in her judgement and decision, she is quick to rectify her mistakes and make necessary changes. It is this openness towards change, this 'changed self' (*Pavilion* 282), that is, in many ways, instrumental in the eventual growth and self-realisation of Madame Wu.

Madame Wu's attempt to bridge the cleavage between the public/ private spheres also stems from her personal experience of the limitations, frustrations, and insufficiency of life when it is confined solely to the domestic space. It is the same realisation felt by Buck when she asserts that 'even children are not enough. . . There is the individual life' (*Of Men and Women*, 58). It is this quest for 'the individual life', for a personal self and identity beyond the family, that characterises Madame Wu's journey. A reading of Buck's work, both fiction and nonfiction, reveals this as one of her prime concerns. In *The Exile* (1936), a biography of her mother Caroline Sydenstricker, Buck depicts her mother as a woman continuously sacrificing herself for the sake of home and family. Torn between a desire to live life on her own terms and her sense of duty to her family, there rages 'a continual war in her' (69). John d'Entremont writes that this 'exacted a perpetual psychic price, because Caroline Sydenstricker was a conflicted, unhappy, deeply talented, and intelligent woman'. He further notes that,

> Very early in life, Pearl Sydenstricker had learned bitter, searing lessons about . . . the perpetual battle that women fought between duty to others, especially family, and fulfilment of self. . . Her mother, and by extension women generally, were stunted by being all duty and self-abnegation. (47–48)

Perhaps, it is this personal experience so close to home that consciously or subconsciously spurs Buck into depicting her characters as making life choices vastly different from that of her own mother. Hilary Spurling states that 'it is in the daughter's fiction that the mother's voice echoes most insistently between the lines, at times muted, plaintive, and resigned, at others, angry and vengeful' (9). Like Caroline, Madame Wu had sacrificed her own ambitions at the altar of her family, but unlike her, however, she makes a conscious decision to break away from that mould and reinvent her life: 'for the first time in their [family] knowledge of her she had done something for herself alone' (*Pavilion* 62).

The theme of women caught between self and family/society also provides a subtext to *The Mother* and may also be traced in another of Buck's work, *This Proud Heart* (1938), which revolves around a woman sculptor named Susan Gaylord. Finding her relationship with her two husbands (one dies, the other, she separates from) as impediments to her art which is an extension of herself, she finally chooses self over family.

It is important to note, however, that in her later years, Buck seems to reconsider her stand on the issue. In the prefatory note of the 1971 reissue of her essay 'Of Men and Women' (1941), she warns that in the frenzied rush towards self-fulfilment, women must not forget their responsibility to the family either, especially children. Madame Wu, as the narrative reveals, does manage to strike a balance between self and family, eventually. Initially, she too had sought to withdraw completely to herself, naively thinking that she would find freedom in detachment from others. The complete disruption in the family, however, brought about by her action, leads her to rethink her decision (*Pavilion* 289). She comes to realise that if freedom is to be real, it must be rooted in the tangible realities of everyday life, a point that is also made by Sartre when he states that 'to will oneself free is to choose to be in the world confronting others' (674). Once again, therefore, she re-enters the familial space, though not the conjugal one, governing and giving guidance to the family as they 'looked to her for advice and shelter and care' (*Pavilion* 377), without, however, relinquishing the new space of self-cultivation and personal freedom that she has created for herself.

In the prologue, it has been stated that the characters' journey to selfhood is one that is multilayered: for Madame Wu, the journey takes her inward as she probes into the inner recesses of her being to understand herself; at the same time, it takes her outward, beyond herself, and into a negotiation with the other – gendered and racial – who is as instrumental in facilitating her growth and self-actualisation as she herself is. Emmanuel Levinas argues that self-awareness and self-definition cannot occur without the intervening presence of the Other:

I am defined as a subjectivity, as a singular person, as an 'I', precisely because I am exposed to the Other. It is my inescapable and incontrovertible answerability to the Other that make me an individual 'I'. (qtd. in Kearney 62)

East Wind: West Wind portrays Kweilan's husband, as well as a network of women, shaping to some extent, the character's growth and selfhood. *Pavilion of Women*, on the other hand, reveals a network of men – the gendered other – who play a role in Madame Wu's journey to self-discovery. While almost all the womenfolk in the novel feeds on her strength and direction, she herself is influenced and guided by her interactions with this male network, namely, Old Gentleman and Brother Andre, who impact her life deeply.

Given the context in which he lives, Old Gentleman, Madame Wu's father-in-law, exhibits many of the prejudices and biasness of his age and culture, in relation to women. His is a mindset shaped and framed by the patriarchal narratives that inform his day and society. 'As life has proved', he told his daughter-in-law, 'it is true that a woman's body is more important than her mind' (*Pavilion* 79). His conservative views, notwithstanding, Old Gentleman is one of the formative agents in Madame Wu's early years as a bride. Admitting her into his library often, an un-orthodox act in Chinese culture, the old man encouraged his daughter-in-law's probing and questioning mind, recognising her intelligence. Her interaction with him provides her with the intellectual and mental stimulus which her mind seeks. His wisdom, she realises, is one that comes from having lived life. It is to the wisdom gleaned from him that she resorts to in order to comprehend and negotiate the twists and turns of her journey. Twenty years after his death, she realises that 'Old Gentleman had taught her much' (*Pavilion* 277) and that he is 'still the wisest soul' (*Pavilion* 84).

Brother Andre, the foreign Christian priest, is another figure instrumental in Madame Wu's journey to self-discovery. His relationship with Madame Wu is one of polarities: he is the male other to her female self; he represents the West, while she, the East. Andre was primarily engaged in the Wu household as a tutor for the third son, but his wisdom and knowledge soon find an eager learner in the mother herself. Though Madame Wu is already an educated woman, her encounter with Andre further expands her horizon. Through him, she becomes acquainted with new ideas and knowledge, thus satisfying her intellectual need. He 'came to be for her a well, wide and deep, a well of learning and knowledge' (*Pavilion* 229). More significantly, however, her encounter with Andre leads to her emotional awakening. Not only does he help to transform the way she thinks, but also the way she feels. He becomes the facilitating agency who awakens her to the emotional side of her being. Before meeting Andre, Madame Wu's life was characterised by emotional detachment and aloofness. As she candidly admits, in one of her self-searching moments, '[p]erhaps that is my trouble, that I have never been able to love anyone' (*Pavilion* 266):

> All her life she had struggled against her dislike of human beings. None had been wholly to her taste . . . her mother she had disliked because of her ignorance and superstitions. . . And though Mr Wu had been a handsome young man when she married him there were secrets of his person which she disliked. . . Old Gentleman had been dear to her, but she was so delicately made that she could not forget what she disliked while she found what she liked. (*Pavilion* 297–298)

Citing psychologist Abraham Maslow, in their study on psychological well-being, Ryff and Singer asserts that 'feelings of empathy and affection for all human beings and the capacity for great love, deep friendship, and close identification with others' is crucial to self-actualisation (21). It is as she also learns to embrace the emotional side of herself that Madame Wu begins to realise a self, more expansive and integrated. The affinity that she shares with Andre succeeds in awakening love in her heart, love for Andre, but also love for other people. As she gazes upon his dead body, she suddenly recognises the truth that she loves him, and 'the instant she accepted . . . [that] she felt her whole being change' (*Pavilion* 277). This flash of recognition is like an epiphany that leads to a sea-change in her being, one that finally liberates her: 'The four walls stood, but she felt free and whole' (*Pavilion* 278).

Ironically, Madame Wu's realisation of her love for Andre comes only after his death, which occurs in the middle of the story. This may be read as Buck's way of asserting that *Pavilion of Women* is not a conventional love story, but rather, the story of a woman who was awakened to love, leading subsequently to a changed self. The major half of the novel, therefore, deals with the change in Madame Wu and how she renegotiates her environment and learns to relate with others as a result of this transformed self. She takes Andre's orphans into her home, and when they cluster around her, she welcomes their touch, although 'she had often shrunk from the touch of her own children when they were small, and had sometimes disliked even their hands upon her' (*Pavilion* 366). She tells herself, 'I shall no longer live out of duty but out of love.' This is Madame Wu's 'discovery of herself through love' (*Pavilion* 285). What Buck seems to be asserting through this novel is that, at the end of the day, it is this basic and simple human emotion of love that serves as a crutch in the journey of life, one that gives beauty, dignity, worth, and purpose to one's life.

It is important to note that unlike Kweilan in *East Wind: West Wind*, Madame Wu's self-awakening through love is one that comes not through the bonds of marriage but outside of it. On the contrary, in this novel, marriage is depicted as an unequal partnership between a highly intelligent and capable woman and a man who is her mental and spiritual inferior in many ways. This may be seen as Buck's way of reversing and overturning the highly prejudiced myth of the superiority of men and inferiority of women. As Madame Wu relates with her husband, she discovers 'the boundaries of his mind and soul . . . small', eventually compelling her to step out, 'beyond his boundaries' (*Pavilion* 100–01). By breaking physical ties with him through her provision of a concubine, she sets an irrevocable seal upon an already-existent gulf between them. Thus, while in other contexts, she reaches out to the other, in this most basic of relationships, the gap remains un-bridged, and must remain so, if the character is to realise her full potential.

Madame Wu's journey is a paradoxical one, resisting any simplistic understanding of it. Her journey is more of a winding path rather than a straight road. Its complexities and contradictions, notwithstanding, it does, however, help the character to arrive at some measure of self-fulfilment and self-realisation. At the end of the narrative, as she looks back on her life, Madame Wu declares, 'My life is complete. I do not need to add another to it' (*Pavilion*, 416). This sense of completeness, this integrated self that comes from having the will and the courage to chart her own course, even though it goes against the grain of society's expectation of women, is what Madame Wu ultimately comes to discover in her journey.

Chapter Three

THIS SILENCE THAT STIFLES

The Good Earth

> She said no word, but he heard her panting as an animal pants
> which has run a long way . . . quick and loud, like whispered
> oceans, but she made no sound aloud
>
> (*The Good Earth*, 36–37).

In O-lan, the female protagonist of *The Good Earth*, one encounters a woman who is the exact opposite of Madame Wu, the indomitable heroine of *Pavilion of Women*. While Madame Wu freely articulates her own needs and desires, O-lan 'accepts her status and fate without complaint, submerging whatever personal desires she might have in her tasks as wife, daughter-in-law, and mother' (Introd. *The Good Earth* xx–xxi). Brought up as a slave in the rich, decadent House of Hwang and later married off to the peasant Wang Lung, O-lan's life is characterised by an endless cycle of toil, rejection, and subjugation, but above all, silence.

Silence, as a patriarchal strategy to subjugate and keep women under the yoke, has been recognised by women writers and feminists over the years. Feminist critics Sandra Gilbert and Susan Gubar note that '[In history] women have been told that their art . . . is an art of silence' (43). Echoing this claim, Chicana author Sandra Cisneros writes of 'the world of thousands of silent women' (76), whose stories must be recorded so that they can finally be heard. ell ooks contends that, 'Silence is often seen as the sexist "right speech of womanhood" – the sign of woman's submission to patriarchal authority' (1989, 6).

Of all of Buck's Chinese heroines, O-lan stands out as the most inarticulate and verbally inexpressive. When Wang Lung, her husband, saw her for the first time, he noticed that hers is 'a face that seemed habitually silent and unspeaking, as though it could not speak if it would' (19). The adjectives repeatedly used to describe her emphasise this particular aspect of her character: 'her wide face expressionless' (20), 'her eyes dumb' (21), she is 'like a faithful, speechless serving maid' (29). At the same time, the portrayal of O-lan serves to highlight Buck's own awareness of, and concern at, the plight of women who have been crushed into silence and inarticulation by various forces through the centuries. Talking of Chinese women in particular, Buck records in one of her articles:

> From the very fact of her sex at birth, she has had to submit herself, to endure what she did not like, to do without, in many cases, special notice or even affection. Work has been her daily bread and silence her virtue. ('Chinese Women' 905)

Buck also uses O-lan's silence as a comment on the socioeconomic dynamics that are in play in the given context. The silent O-lan is representative of the many others who, like her, belong to the lowest rung of the socioeconomic ladder. The oppressed and disempowered poor are rendered mute by the exploitation of the rich, and the unremitting hardships of their lot. The issue is of such grave concern to Buck that she devotes a whole chapter in the novel to spell out the gruelling cycle of life as it is lived by the poor. In the opulent city where they flee to escape starvation, Wang Lung and his family encounter countless others like themselves, who have to struggle hard for their survival:

> Greybeards pulled rickshaws, . . .wheelbarrows of coal and wood to bakeries and palaces, strained their backs until the muscles stood forth like ropes . . . ate frugally of their scanty food, slept their brief nights out, *and were silent*. Their faces were like the face of O-lan, *inarticulate, dumb*. None knew what was in their

minds. If they spoke at all it was of food or of pence (emphasis added, 115).

The relationship between silence and poverty depicted through O-lan and the silent poor is clearly underlined by Buck in the above passage.

In another of her novel, *Peony* (1948), which is about a servant girl after whom the novel is titled, Buck reveals the kind of behaviour that is expected of female slaves and bondservants in old Chinese society. In the presence of the family, she is to remain 'properly silent' (1) and 'quietly watchful' (2), always ready to obey and serve, to move around the house noiselessly, and to remain in the background until needed or called. Thus, she is depicted more as an absence than a presence. As Gao notes, 'the Chinese tradition did not allow . . . [servants] to be equals with other members of the family . . . they were to obey their masters and were not allowed to talk back' (81).

The habit of servitude and silence imbibed from her years as a slave is so deeply embedded in O-lan's psyche that she carries it even into her marriage. It is important to note that though, in one sense, marriage frees O-lan from slavery to the Hwangs, in another sense, it entails a different kind of servitude to another master, Wang Lung. Though she functions as a wife to Wang Lung and is mother to his children, he often describes her and his relationship with her in the master/servant analogy. Thus, to him, she is 'like a faithful, speechless serving maid, who is only a serving maid and nothing more' (*Earth* 29). Reflecting on her later, he admits that 'she had been a faithful servant' (*Earth* 252) to him. The use of such terminology in the novel is not accidental. It underscores Buck's consciousness of the reality of women's role in Chinese society:

> The sexual object and possession of the man, the childbearing tool to carry on her husband's family name, and the servant to the whole family . . . the first one to get up in the morning to prepare breakfast and to wait on the husband and parents-in-law . . . [and] the last one to go to bed at night after seeing to it that everything was settled. (Gao 34, 39)

This is clearly sketched out in detail in the novel. In such a context, marriage becomes a patriarchal enclosure resulting in 'suffocation, dwarfing and mental illness', a point argued by Annis Pratt (41). Significantly, O-lan suffers from a tumour in her womb that eventually kills her. According to Leard, 'a circumscribed person, whether a man or a woman, whose identity is predominantly defined in someone else's terms, is bound to be lacking in emotional and physical health' (71).

O-lan is further marginalised by her physical appearance. Throughout the novel, her lack of feminine beauty is reiterated again and again by those who make up the small circle of her world and who reject her for it. This social alienation engenders a deep sense of personal worthlessness and self-deprecation, pushing her further into silence. When giving her to Wang Lung, the Old Mistress in the House of Hwang introduces O-lan thus:

> She is not beautiful but that you do not need. Only men of leisure have the need for beautiful women to divert them. Neither is she clever. . . She has not beauty enough to tempt my sons and grandsons even if she had not been in the kitchen. (*Earth* 18)

Later, the reader learns that because of her ugliness, O-lan's service was relegated to the kitchen so that she does not have to appear before the family unnecessarily. Her feverish murmurings of her traumatic childhood as she lays on her sickbed reveals how her appearance was used against her, pushing her to the periphery of her social world, and marking her an outsider: 'I will bring the meats to the door only – and well I know I am ugly and cannot appear before the great lord . . . well I know I am ugly and cannot be loved' (*Earth* 260). What these lines reveal is the damaging extent to which O-lan herself has internalised society's biasness. Having learnt from bitter experience that physical appearance, can, and does, determine a woman's social acceptance or rejection, O-lan makes every effort to see that her daughter conform to the beauty standards of the day. She does this by binding the feet of her youngest daughter, ignoring her cries of pain, to ensure miniature feet, the watermark of a woman's beauty in Confucian China.

A relevant point to note is that in O-lan, Buck intentionally delineates a character who contradicts the stereotypical assumption of heroines as icons of feminine beauty and grace. O-lan is, as Kang Liao notes, 'the first good and ugly Chinese woman character ever created in a novel' (5). The juxtaposition of 'goodness' and 'ugliness' in the person of O-lan also challenges the stock notion that ugly women are morally repulsive and that 'revolting physical appearance is the direct result of grave moral turpitude or some other evil influence' (Wright 25). Thus, through the depiction of O-lan, Buck critiques the social mindset where a person's worth and/ or worthlessness is judged on the basis of physical attributes. Feminist writer Kathleen Lennon underlines this reality when she writes that 'those differently shaped bodies to the dominant ideal, are treated socially as outsiders, "the abject" and subject to social punishments' (5:1). A person like O-lan who does not fit the mould of the prescribed beauty ideal is ostracised and marginalised, leading to psychological oppression which may be termed as an intrapersonal rift.

Perhaps, one of the most painful consequences of O-lan's failure to meet the socially prescribed criteria of beauty is that of being discarded by her husband:

> In times of difficulties, he is happy to have a wife like O-lan who works even harder than a man does. . . But when . . . the family becomes prosperous, and Wang Lung has the leisure to look at his wife as a man looks at a woman, he finds her ugliness intolerable. (Li Bo 97)

Using her lack of feminine appeal as an excuse, Wang Lung contrives to bring home Lotus, a beautiful prostitute, as his concubine, who serves as a foil to O-lan. From the same social stock as O-lan, Lotus manipulates herself into the heart and home of Wang Lung through her beauty: 'She swayed upon her little feet and to Wang Lung there was nothing so wonderful for beauty in the world as her pointed little feet and her curling helpless hand' (*Earth* 201). Christine Battersby argues that biology is a mode of discourse that cannot be separated from other symbolic codes and practices of the social networks of power (20–21). This is amply brought out in *The Good Earth* where physical appearance is linked with a certain amount of power, or powerlessness in O-lan's context, and determines a person's lived experience to a certain extent.

Furthermore, the emphasis on O-lan's physical unattractiveness is also used to explore how the materiality of the body affects a person's sense of self. Many women writers, like Toril Moi, agree that 'the material features of our bodies play a role in our subjective sense of self' (qtd. in Lennon 6:1). O-lan's self-devaluation and self-attenuation springs, in part, from her perception of her supposed physical flaws, spawned and conditioned by prevalent social attitudes. The incident of the pearls serves to highlight this argument. From the handful of jewels that she discovered in the mass looting in the southern city, O-lan kept back two beautiful pearls. The pearls, however, are never worn 'because she feels she is too ugly' (Li Bo 99) for such adornments, a feeling reinforced by her husband. Taking the pearls from her one day, he justifies himself by saying, 'Why should that one wear pearls with her skin as black as earth? Pearls are for fair women!' (*Earth* 188). To the end of her life, therefore, O-lan is haunted by her lack of physical charm and her life-long struggle to come to terms with it. On her dying bed, the last words she utter shows how deeply the stigma has been branded into her consciousness: 'Well, and if I am ugly, still I have borne a son' (268).

What the preceding discussion shows is that O-lan's silence is not the result of an isolated or individual cause but a corollary of the interlocking of powerful and prevalent systems of oppression. The intersecting of three forces – patriarchal ideology, her socioeconomic status, and the beauty bias that marginalises her – works to undermine O-lan physically and psychologically. Feminist critics have pointed out that cultural patterns of oppression, termed by Patricia Collins as 'the matrix of domination' (248), are not only interrelated but are also meshed together to serve as oppressive measures towards women. In their document, The Combahee River Collective, a group of black women feminists also note that the major systems of oppression are interlocking. The synthesis of these oppressions creates the conditions of our lives (264–74). Thus, O-lan's silence results from a combination of societal factors, termed by Mara Faulkner as 'the silencers that stifle creativity', erasing a person's worth through rejection, dismissal, or devaluation (Faulkner xvi).

Like most traditional Chinese women, O-lan's identity is inextricably bound to marriage and motherhood. 'A woman's life in old China' is lived out in 'three stages: as a girl, as a wife, and as a mother' (Gao 35). To add to this category amounts to a transgression of the Confucian norm, which is what Madame Wu succeeds in doing in *Pavilion of Women*. Unlike Madame Wu, however, O-lan's road to selfhood takes her via a different route altogether. While Madame Wu's quest for self-realisation and freedom takes her 'beyond' marriage and motherhood, O-lan's journey is traversed 'within' the bounds of these enclaves that mark out her lived reality. She repeatedly reveals the centrality of marriage and motherhood in her life and worldview. She tells her fellow slave Cuckoo, 'You may have lived in the courts of the Old Lord, and you were accounted beautiful, but I have been a man's wife and I have borne him sons, and you are still a slave' (261). Thus, it is within the framework of marriage and family that she defines her identity. She does not aspire or even think of going beyond these small walls of her existence. While this is indicative of the kind of circumscribed existence that women must fight against, it reflects the reality of the lives of many women in O-lan's position. Through the novel, Buck succeeds in depicting how a woman like O-lan still succeeds in attaining some measure of meaning and self-fulfilment.

From the feminist perspective, O-lan's subservient mentality and her limited vision of life may seem to be self-defeating. What must be kept in mind, however, is that O-lan is located at a particular time in Chinese history when Confucian ideas were acceptable and the political and social upheavals of the twentieth century were still distant rumblings for the common people. Like Kweilan's mother in *East Wind: West Wind*, O-lan is a typical product of her age and culture, conditioned by the cultural patterns of attitudes and behaviour in feudal China. Thus, it is not O-lan's personal belief or value system that is in play here, but rather, the dynamics of two thousand years of feudalist belief and Confucian codes that have been formed in China's long history.

In this novel, the institutions of marriage and motherhood play an ambivalent role. On one hand, it is portrayed as oppressive and debilitating to women, yet, for O-lan and her contemporaries, it represents the very essence of womanhood. Her greatest strength as a character, therefore, lies in her ability to turn a stifling and suffocating space into a personal space of meaning, where she moves from a victim to a survivor. 'Her value lies in her ability to survive all sorts of hardships and adversities' (Liao 69). As Charles Hayford notes, O-lan is a woman 'betrayed', consistently and systematically, 'but not broken' (25). Therein lies her strength and lasting appeal.

O-lan's subservience may also be traced to her lack of exposure to the outside world. Unlike Madame Wu and Kweilan who are exposed to education and to the outside world, O-lan is socially isolated and illiterate. Her life revolves around two alternating spaces, the kitchen and the land, symbols of drudgery and hard toil, where she lives out her life. Her only foray away from home is the gruelling journey to the south, made out of compulsion and desperation to escape starvation. Even then, their brief stay in the city is swallowed up by the daily grind of staying alive. As Doyle says, 'O-lan wants and expects so little from life' (36). This, however, does not imply that she is devoid of any personal aspirations and desires. Like any other woman, she, too, 'has her joys and sorrows and experiences a full range of natural human emotions' (Li Bo 99). Her desires and aspirations, however, are in keeping with her situation and station in life. Practical and realistic to the core, she asks only for what is within her reach. Her gratification comes from realising simple personal goals and ambitions rather than the lofty endeavours that Madame Wu seeks. Her greatest desire after marriage, for instance, is merely to visit the House of Hwang with her son in her arms and present him with pride and dignity to those who had once looked down upon her:

> When I return to that house it will be with my son in my arms. I shall have a red coat on him and red-flowered trousers. . . And I will wear new shoes and a new coat of black sateen and I will go into the kitchen where I spent my days and I will go into the great hall where the Old One sits with her opium, and I will show myself and my son to all of them. (33)

Thus, while she may not be able to effect any life-changing breakthroughs like Buck's other protagonists, in her own way, O-lan does manage to achieve a sense of autonomy by pursuing the goal(s) that she sees as giving meaning and purpose to her life.

Another significant factor adding to O-lan's unquestioning acceptance of the constraints in her life is the absence of valid and palpable human companionship and interaction to function as support mechanisms in her journey. Such human support is indispensable, functioning as 'visible compasses that help us discern the authentic in a world of image-posing and externalism' (Boa 13). Paraphrasing D. H. Lawrence, Panthea R. Broughton states that '[w]e attain our very individuality itself in living contact, the give-and-take of human relations . . . without such relationships we are nonentities' (36). For O-lan, however, there is no real sense of human bonding with any of the characters in the narrative. She is portrayed as a lone figure travelling on a lonely path. Characterised by a 'sense of isolation, of emotional aloneness' (Wolf 124), nobody is privy to the inner sanctum of her heart and mind. Her inner self is a closely guarded and private space. Only in her feverish delirium are her husband and the reader given a glimpse of her inner thoughts and feelings:

> Often she forgot where she was as he sat there in stillness and silence, and sometimes she murmured of her childhood, and for the first time Wang Lung saw into her heart, although even now only through such brief words. (260)

Meaningful and positive engagement with others such as is accessible to the other women characters in Buck's other novels is noticeably absent in O-lan. The novel does not in any way suggest that O-lan is unable to relate or interact with others. Rather, the onus falls on those who shun and dehumanises her, trapped by various prejudices of their own and society's making, and are unwilling to relate meaningfully with her. As asserted in the prologue, the journey to the self also necessitates reaching out to the other. In O-lan's context, however, the possibility does not arise because she is the marginalised other in the equation. Almost all the characters in the novel relate to her largely, in condescending and patronising terms, treating her as an inferior, never as an equal.

Even her marriage to Wang Lung fails to provide her with the strong support base that Kweilan, for instance, finds in her husband in *East Wind: West Wind*:

> Wang Lung saw her only as he saw the table or his chair or a tree in the court, never even so keenly as he might see one of the oxen

drooping its head or a pig that would not eat. And she did her
work alone and spoke no more than she could escape speaking.
(*Earth* 242)

As Charles Hayford points out, O-lan is 'betrayed . . . as much by
her husband's weak character as by social attitudes' (25). The tragic irony
is that it is only towards the end of her life that O-lan finally gains the
acknowledgement and tenderness that had been denied to her throughout
her marriage. As she lies sick and dying, 'for the first time Wang Lung
and his children knew what she had been in the house, and how she made
comfort for them all and they had not known it' (257). It is only after her
death that Wang Lung acknowledges thus: 'There in that land of mine is
buried the first good half of my life and more. It is as though half of me were
buried there, and now it is a different life in my house' (272). It is interesting
to note that it took the permanent gulf/absence that death entails for Wang
Lung to realise this. Paradoxically, death liberates O-lan from her silence
and gives her a voice and presence beyond the grave, through her husband
and children. She 'triumphs in the end', 'over her rivals, though her ugliness
goes clean to the bone' (Liao 69; Cargill 149). She is, as Constance A. Cutler
says, 'courageous and faithful and throughout the novel' maintained 'a
beautiful dignity which gives her a special identity of her own' (2322).

Ultimately, for O-lan, her sense of fulfilment, personal meaning,
dignity, and vindication comes from her awareness that she is a part of the
living continuum of humanity. Even though she dies soon after the marriage
of her eldest son, she is happy in the thought that her 'grandson is stirred
into life and a great grandson for the old one' (263). She sees herself as a
small but indispensable link in the chain of life. And as she recognises and
grasps this truth, she discovers her individual identity.

Chapter Four

BEHOLD! I STAND

The Mother

The willows were full of tender leaves shining green, and the white blossoms of the pear trees were full blown this day and drifting in the winds, and here and there a pomegranate tree flamed scarlet in its early leaves. . . .she did not know which was sweeter, the deep warm silence when the wind died and the smell of the earth came up from the ploughed fields, or the windy fragrance of the gusts. . . . But walking thus in the silences and in the sudden winds, she felt her body strong and full and young, and a great new longing seized her.

(The Mother 108)

In *The Mother*, Buck chronicles the life of an anonymous peasant woman who is simply referred throughout the novel as 'the mother'; a chronicle of loss and heartbreaks, yet, also, a story of survival and strength. Because of the anonymity of the protagonist, critics tend to read in her, 'a universal portrait of the eternal mother' caught in the cyclical flow of time and the tragedies and hardships of existence (Doyle 70). David Garnett concurs with this view when he says that she is 'any Mother from among all of China's teeming millions' with 'no personal characteristics . . . not even a name . . . just an abstract figure of maternity' (120).

The character's anonymity, however, is not a sufficient rationale to brand the mother simply as a type, or an abstract representative of all mothers. In fact, in old China, a woman's namelessness is not an anomaly, especially for those coming from the uneducated and rural class. In her autobiography, *Wild Swans: Three Daughters of China* (1991), Jung Chang records of her great grandmother: 'Because her family was not an intellectual one and did not hold any official post, and because she was a girl, she was not given a name at all' (22). Therefore, in rendering her character anonymous, Buck may be simply adhering to an accepted standard in Chinese social practice, perfectly congruent with the rural-Chinese context of the novel.

Simultaneously, and more significantly, the character's anonymity draw the reader's attention to the peripheral, subsidiary, and insignificant status that women occupy within the androcentric culture in which the novel unfolds, one which views a woman's personal identity as inconsequential.

Most critics and reviewers such as David Garnett, Mark Van Doren, Isidore Schneider, and Paul Doyle tend to draw attention only to the motherhood theme in the novel. Doyle, for instance, describes the protagonist as a perfect example of the 'eternal *mater dolorosa*' or 'the mother of sorrows' (73). Admittedly, while the motherhood theme is explicitly presented, the novel may also be read as a critique of women's confinement within the society's prescribed roles. The traditional Chinese view of women is a very limited and a limiting one. A woman's identity comes only from two broad categories: she is either the wife/concubine/sexual object of the man, or/ and the mother of his children. In this novel, both the main protagonist, 'the mother', and her female friend who is referred throughout only as 'the Cousin's wife,' are identified not by their personal names but by their roles as wives and mothers. Their social identity, therefore, comes only through their personal relations with men.

At the beginning of the novel, the mother is depicted as a typical Chinese woman, one who conforms unquestioningly to the norms and expectations of her culture. She is

> Such a one as could live well content with the man and children
> and think of nothing else at all. To her – to know the fullness
> of the man's frequent passion, to conceive by him and know life

growing within her own body, to feel this new flesh take shape
and grow, to give birth and feel a child's lips drink at her breast –
these were enough. To rise at dawn and feed her house and tend
the beasts, to sow the land and reap its fruit, to draw water at the
well for drink . . . these were enough. (*Mother* 29)

Her whole being is so wrapped up with her husband, her children, and
her home, that the self is completely subsumed in the process. Interestingly,
seventy-nine years after Buck's novel, noted Indian film director Kiran Rao
asserts in one of her interviews that for women, still,

The most challenging role is in finding that little space that you
call the 'self'. It's not really a role, it is You, and that's the one
most difficult to attend to. . . Often, this self gets least priority
in our lives because our children are important, our husbands are
important, our work is important . . . but that little you needs to
be nourished and nurtured. Otherwise, no role will satisfy us.
(*Sunday Times of India*, August 18, 2013)

The crises in the novel is triggered when the mother is suddenly
abandoned by her husband and left with the sole responsibility of caring
for three young children as well as her old mother-in-law. Working herself
to the bone to keep the family going, she is beset with more misfortunes.
Enticed into a sexual relationship with the landlord's agent, the mother
becomes pregnant and is forced to abort the child when the man deserts
her, leading to deteriorating health, trauma, and a major guilt syndrome
that haunts her. Later her only daughter becomes blind and is married off
to a poor family in another village where she dies sometime later, as a result
of mistreatment. Then the youngest son who has become a communist is
executed by the government. At this juncture, the mother is just about ready
to give up on life when she hears that she now has a grandson. This event,
which closes the novel, rekindles the fire of life in her.

The husband's abandonment is a significant episode in this novel. It
marks a turning point in the character's journey and propels her into a
space of crises and conflict that stretches her to the limits. Simultaneously,
however, it is within this conflict zone that the mother begins to awaken

to her female self. Psychoanalyst and woman writer Marianne Hirsch suggests that female awakening, unlike in her male counterpart, 'is often an awakening to limitations, to a world inimical to female growth and development' (qtd. in Goldensohn 339). It is when this familial/domestic world on which she has based her whole life and happiness collapses, that the mother is made aware of the limitations and fragility of that world. The husband's abandonment, therefore, shakes her out of her self-complacency and impels her on a new journey, one that entails mistakes and wrong choices along the way, but that reconnects her to the hidden potential within herself, opening up a space of opportunity for her to explore her inner resources.

Apart from the physical hardships and emotional pain, the first thing that the mother is forced to negotiate with, after her husband's abandonment, is to attempt to protect herself and her family from the social stigma attendant upon an abandoned woman. In patriarchal China, 'a woman abandoned was the most ashamed, the most humiliated, and the most degraded. She would have no dignity, honor, or respect left as a result and be thrown to the very bottom of society' (Gao 116). To protect her dignity and reputation, the mother contrives an elaborate ruse to explain her husband's absence. She goes to the city and has a letter forged in her husband's name saying that he has a decent job in town and cannot come home, putting inside the envelope, some money purportedly sent by him. This goes on year after year, effectively silencing the rumour of abandonment and preserving her honour, and that of her family. Her affair with the agent necessitates another lie when she discovers she is pregnant. She forges a letter saying that the husband has died in a fire, thinking, in her naiveté, that the agent will marry her. Her hopes were dashed when the agent spurns her, callously disregarding her predicament.

Critics have read the mother's apparently devious plots as indicative of a somewhat 'deceptive and manipulative' nature (Gao 116). However, given the social context in which she lives, the mother's actions are to be read rather, as a survival technique, an out-working of the human instinct for survival and self-preservation. French writer Michel de Certeau argues that people who are pushed into a space of powerlessness often employ what he calls 'tactics' and 'clever tricks', which are the manoeuvres of the weak to assert some measure of control into the given situation (xix). These tactics are often the only 'avenues of power accessible to the ostensibly powerless' (Mount 66). Thus, the mother's elaborate ruses may be read as 'tactics' and 'manoeuvres' to circumvent the situation that she is dealt with. It is, in fact, a means of asserting agency and wresting power from a potentially powerless situation.

It is ironical to note, however, that in a patriarchal system, women who exercise power or try to assume control over their lives are seen as 'deviants, manipulators, or at best, exceptions' (Rosaldo and Lamphere 9). When a man exercises power, society lauds him for his leadership skills, whereas a woman who attempts to do the same is regarded as deviant and manipulative. This is a clear example of the double standards that prevail in a phallocentric set-up. It also becomes a powerful patriarchal strategy to undermine women's assertiveness and resourcefulness.

Another important feature observed about the mother, apart from her resourcefulness, is her openness to explore her own sexuality as a woman. Two contradictory strains are noticed in this character. Like most of her female contemporaries, she is governed and conditioned by the mindset of her culture. Simultaneously, however, she also demonstrates a strong sense of individuality and independence that is highly unusual for a woman of her times and status. Her affair with the agent is a powerful example. Though restricted and confined by the norms of her society, she shows herself acutely conscious of her female needs and desires and tries to achieve them. Her sexuality is thus depicted very explicitly in the novel.

In her encounter with the agent, she is shown as being reluctant, and yet cooperative, ashamed and yet excited, 'and the truth was there was something in her, too, that pulled at her to let him be' (*Mother* 126). Though the act results in a feeling of guilt, an impact of society's conditioning, at the same time, it may be seen as a tentative gesture towards assuming agency and control over her own life and body. By ascribing sexuality to her character, 'the mother', Buck critiques society's, particularly Chinese society's, identification of the female as being solely maternal.

The denial of a woman's sexuality, and the excessive veneration of her maternalism, is a point that has been contested by feminist writers right from Adrienne Rich (1976, 1) to Luce Irigaray (1985, 16). In Buck's protagonist, one finds a woman who tries to be true to herself both as a sexual and as a maternal being.

However, although the mother is seen as attempting to articulate her own sexuality, the act also engenders a deep sense of guilt in her. Thereafter, she reads every mishap and misfortune in her life as a punishment for her 'sin', the 'sin' being her affair, as well as the subsequent abortion of the child conceived. She tells her friend, the cousin's wife, 'since sorrows follow me and everything goes wrong with me, I fear sometimes it is that old sin of mine that the gods know about' (*Mother* 260). Thus, in her mind, she holds herself accountable for her daughter's blindness and death, for the death of her youngest son, and even in her daughter-in-law's failure to conceive. She believes 'somehow dimly that her own sins might be the cause' for all the misfortunes in her life and family (*Mother* 261).

What is dramatised in this novel, therefore, is the deep sense of conflict and intrapsychical rift that is engendered in women when there is a clash between their personal needs and aspirations, and what has been ingrained into them by society.

Traditional Chinese society reveals a glaring ambivalence and ambiguity in its perception and expectation of women. As Gao notes, '[t]he man was free to visit flower-houses and to take concubines, but the woman was not supposed to seek other men even if she is widowed or abandoned' (113). This flawed and gender-skewed view is so deeply entrenched that 'even women themselves viewed any encounter with other men than their husbands, alive or dead, as the ultimate sin . . . beyond any means of redemption' (Gao 113). As socioanthropologists Rosaldo and Lamphere note, 'in learning to be women in our society, we have accepted, and even internalised, what is all too often a derogatory and constraining image of ourselves' (1).

It is interesting to note that unlike most of the other women characters depicted in the novels discussed here, whose path to selfhood is facilitated by a network of human relationships in their lives, for the mother, the journey is travelled a little differently. Though she also draws from the circle of human relationships that encompass her world, particularly, her own family and her female friends, there are also other supporting factors that serve as a crutch in her journey.

The first support mechanism may be traced to the internal make-up of the character herself. In spite of the odds that the mother is continually up against, she displays a strong sense of the *joie de vivre* and a remarkable zest for life. She relishes life in all its myriad realities, right from the mundane, to the most sublime of experiences. Buck goes to painstaking details to highlight this particular aspect of her character:

> She relished all her life: giving birth, the labour on the land, eating and drinking and sleeping, sweeping and setting in rude order her house and hearing the women in the hamlet praise her for her skill in work and sewing; even quarrelling with the man was good and set some edge upon their passion for each other. So therefore she rose to everyday with zest. (*Mother* 29)

In his book, *The Practice of Everyday Life*, de Certeau, quoting Witold Gombrowicz, remarks on the sense of well-being and fulfilment that comes from being rooted in the everyday; to find joy in life's 'very small, almost invisible pleasures', for it is in 'these little details' that 'one grows' (xxiv). This ability to tap into the everyday affairs of life and discover joy, and beauty, and meaning, where others would not, is one of the key factors that sustain the mother. Her husband, on the other hand, is depicted as the opposite of everything that she is:

> In this little hamlet so had he himself been born, and . . . he had never once seen anything new in any day he lived. When he rose in the morning there was this circle of low round hills set against this self-same sky, . . .and when night was come there were these hills set against this sky and he went into the house where he had been born . . . to sleep, to rise again to the same next day. (*Mother* 39–40)

Weak and without any inner resources to sustain him, it takes nothing more than a mere quarrel with his wife to up and leave his family. In the Chinese equation of *Yin* and *Yang*, the *yin*, literally meaning 'overcast' or 'shade', is often used to refer to the female, symbolised by the moon, and standing for all things dark, secret, hidden, cold, weak, and passive;

on the other hand, the *yang*, literally meaning 'the sun' and figuratively referring to the male, stands for all things bright, open, overt, warm, strong, and active (qtd. in Gao, 30). In this novel, however, by depicting the man as morally weaker than the woman, Buck succeeds in subverting the Chinese patriarchal narrative by overturning the gender equation which is discriminating to women. Simultaneously, it brings to the fore the character of the Chinese woman so admired by Buck and yet so overlooked by her own society. She writes:

> The quality of character of the Chinese woman is certainly equal to the finest anywhere, and this quality is to be found in the poorest and most unlettered as well as in those more fortunate . . . [she] exhibits more integrity, more steadfastness, more endurance in the crisis and affairs of life than does the Chinese men. ('Chinese Women' 905)

This belief is consistently affirmed in the character of the mother. Her ability to embrace life whole, with all its up-turns and down-turns, proves to be one of the mainstays in her journey, giving her the strength to go forward.

Second, in her journey, the character is sustained and facilitated by the relationships in her life – one which is double-strand: (i) her organic relationship to the natural world and (ii) her relationship to the human community that makes up her world. This two-fold relationship is extremely important to the character's growth and sustenance. It defines the journey of the mother and leads her closer towards self-actualisation.

While interpersonal relationships have been acknowledged as being vital to an individual's well-being, the ecofeminist discourse stretches the parameters further, by contending that the human-nature relationship is as crucial as the interpersonal one, in framing and defining the self. Nancy Howell, a proponent of this school of thought, writes:

> We can understand and learn about ourselves and who we are through our relationships with other people, . . .[as well as] with the natural world and those things it entails . . . through our interactions and relationships with those entities, both living and non-living. (232)

In *The Mother*, Buck depicts a heroine who relates not only with the human community but also with the more-than-human world that makes up her environs. Unlike her husband who 'hated' the land (*Mother* 51) and eventually alienates himself from it, the mother's rootedness to the land and the natural world is clearly and repeatedly spelled out by Buck. Working on the land fills her with a deep sense of fulfilment and satisfaction, one that is reminiscent of Wang Lung, the peasant character in *The Good Earth*.

Cognizant of the partnership between women and nature in producing life and providing sustenance, noted ecofeminist Vandana Shiva, affirms that 'women and nature are associated *not in passivity but in creativity and in the maintenance of life*' (47, emphasis in the original). This sense of identity and kinship with the earth, bonded by the life principle that pulsates in both, is at the root of the mother's relationship with nature and informs her sense of self.

A twin aspect of this relationship with nature is her equally strong and vibrant ties to the human community around her. Unlike O-lan who is essentially an isolated character and unlike Madame Wu who had sought to detach herself from others, the mother is depicted as an intensely social person. In her essay, 'Family Structure and Feminine Personality' (1974), woman writer Nancy Chodorow argues that the relational quotient is a fundamental factor in women's self-definition and development: 'feminine personality comes to define itself in relation and connection to other people' (44). This relationship and sense of connection, both with the human world and the non-human one, are at the heart of the mother's being and characterises her journey to selfhood.

According to Hong Jiang, the 'Chinese has one word, "*jia*", to express both home and family . . . [it refers] to both spatial belongs and emotional attachment' (1). In the mother, Buck delineates a character who constantly grows and evolves through the network of relationships and connections forged in the '*jia*', or the home space. She is at her most fulfilled and creative self within the context of her relationship with her family. 'Since the family occupies a central role in Chinese society, the "*jen-lun*" [defined as the basic relations within a family], between family members is particularly important' (Chang and Holt 253). Notwithstanding the betrayal of her husband, her deepest sense of contentment still flows from this most basic of relationships.

The familial bond not only shapes the character's daily sense of well-being but also provides healing and strength through the many crises in her journey. When abandoned by her husband, it is her children who quicken her back to life and living. In the aftermath of the agent's rejection and the abortion of the child, the mother's salvation and healing partially comes through her family, particularly her blind daughter, the 'small young hand feeling for her, called her back from some despair where she had lived these many months' (*Mother* 171–2).

Another important agency is the mother's relationship with other women. As emphasised in previous chapters, female bonding is perceived as a crucial element in women's growth toward self-awakening and self-discovery. This is a theme that constantly surfaces in Buck's work, springing from her own experience as a young wife in Nanjing, China. Through the early years of her first marriage, Buck found 'companionship, sisterhood and stimulation' in the community of 'missionary women' in Nanjing. Their 'presence seems to have spurted Pearl's literary productivity during the decade of the 20s – culminating in the birth of *The Good Earth*' (Thomson Jr 10).

In Chinese society, female bonding is regarded as a sacred tie. It is referred to as *Lao Tong*/friends for life (Murdoch), and *Lao Tang* or 'sworn sisters' (Chun). Thus, it is common to hear Chinese women refer to each other as 'sisters'. 'Sisterhood created a significant support network for women in rural region and give them strength' (Chun).

In *The Mother*, the character's support, too, comes from a network of women who constitute her immediate social circle. The relationship between women, depicted as one of reciprocity and interdependence, forms the backbone of their lives in the small, rural community where 'women helped each other when the need came' (*Mother* 33). The mother's friendship with the 'cousin's wife' is a key support in the mother's life and helps shape her journey to selfhood. At the hour of childbirth, the two women attend to each other and 'felt themselves the more deeply friends because of this hour common to them both and that must come again and yet again' (*Mother* 38). Again, it is the cousin's wife who stands with the mother through all the crises of her life. These shared experiences serve to bring a sense of solidarity and togetherness and make the trials life throws more endurable, giving the heart a brief respite from its loneliness.

The novel's ending affirms that the mother does arrive at a sense of internal freedom, ultimately. She does this by learning to come to terms with her own life, and with her own sexuality, and accept it for what it is. Eventually, therefore, it is in self-forgiveness and self-acceptance that the mother is released from the cycle of guilt and self-recrimination, one that also helps her to look forward to the future, symbolised by the birth of her grandson. Her closing words to the cousin's wife affirm this sense of release from bondage to the past: 'See cousin! I doubt I was so full of sin as once I thought I was, Cousin – you see my grandson' (*Mother* 302).

Chapter Five

I BELONG HERE

Kinfolk

> She lay in the darkness listening to the rain, breathing in a faint mustiness in the room, the smell of old wood and plastered walls and generations of her family . . . [t]he crude old room . . . the open-faced kind of country people, these were real and they were her own. She curled herself down into the huge bed. 'I like it here,' she murmured. 'I like it better than anywhere in the world'
> (*Kinfolk*, 188–89).

Kinfolk reiterates Buck's perennial preoccupation, which is, the interface between East and West, and its impact on the individual. Unlike the other novels discussed in this section which focus on the lives of Chinese characters lived out exclusively in China, *Kinfolk* is a study of a Chinese-American family's search for destiny and identity, played out against the dual backdrop of China and America. While the women protagonists function as the centre of consciousness in the preceding novels, in *Kinfolk*, the central consciousness shifts to the male figures, particularly, James Liang the eldest son of the family, and his father, the great Confucian scholar, Dr Liang.

The novel is conspicuously a satire on the attitudes of Chinese intellectuals living abroad who 'want the Chinese people represented [only] by the little handful of her intellectuals' (Buck, *The New York Times Book*

Review, 1933). Dr Liang clearly exemplifies this attitude in the novel: 'It was most unfortunate, he thought . . . that Chinese like himself were not the sole representatives of his country. It was a great pity that Chinatown had ever been allowed' (3). The chasm that polarises the intellectuals and the working-class people within the Chinese community is a theme that powerfully stands out in this novel. Affirming her awareness of this societal divide, Buck wrote in 1933: 'The cleavages between the common people and the intellectuals in China is portentous, a gulf that seems impassable' (*The New York Times Book Review*, 1933). Thus, it is within the framework of this social climate that the women protagonists' quest for identity and self-realisation is negotiated.

The novel's significance, however, lies in its exploration of a seminal post-colonial concern, which is, the quest for self and identity ubiquitous to the diasporic experience. This is a theme close to Buck's heart because she experienced first-hand the sense of dislocation and identity crisis that comes from living life on two different continents. In his biography on Buck, Peter Conn comments that Buck

> Was simultaneously an outsider and an insider in two different societies. Her divided situation rather resembled the 'two-ness' of American Blacks, as DuBois described it in *The Souls Of Black Folks* (1903) (24).

Karen Leong also reiterates this point when she remarks that Buck 'continually negotiated her in-between status as a foreigner and as someone who had been raised in China' (18).

The ever-present sense of divide and tension triggered by the simultaneous position of being both 'insider' and 'outsider', and the diverse ways by which the Liang family, individually, negotiate with the situation to arrive at a sense of self and identity, form the crux of the narrative.

The journey motif, largely metaphorical in the other novels discussed, is depicted here both in its metaphorical and literal sense. It is not unilateral, but a multilateral one: Even as it is a journey 'to', it is also a journey 'from', because the journey to the self also necessitates journeying out from somewhere/something that cramps one's growth and self-expression.

For the senior Liangs, particularly, Dr Liang, the journey to America entails leaving behind his homeland because he feels that a China wracked by war and revolution is no longer tenable for a sensitive scholar and philosopher like him. He comes to America, therefore, in search of a new destiny for himself and his family. However, the life in America, though marked by comfort and security, is also one of unease and tension, fraught with the perpetual consciousness of belonging neither here nor there. As Buck writes of herself in her personal memoir: 'In one world and not of it, and belonging to another world and yet not of it' (*My Several Worlds* 51). This discussion probes into a similar sense of diasporic angst felt by the three Liang women – Mary, Louise, and Mrs Liang – and the divergent paths traversed by them as they strive to engage with their 'in-between' status to forge identity and selfhood for themselves.

Mary Liang, the Liang's elder daughter, exhibits a marked inability and/or unwillingness to think of New York as home, even though she had practically no first-hand memories of China, the country of her birth. She tells her younger sister Louise, 'Do not forget – we are not American. Although we have never seen our own country, yet we are Chinese. We cannot behave like American girls' (*Kinfolk* 91). Her sense of self and identity emanates from, and is intertwined with a particular place – China – even though she has no personal memories of the place. Her deepest longing is always to go back 'home', to China, which is where she feels she truly belongs. 'Localism' or 'the desire to return home' as a means of reclaiming one's identity is an important theme in the exilic consciousness (Featherstone 47). The concept of 'Home' necessitates a broader exploration in this context. What is Home? Where is the idea of Home located? In his essay, 'Home(s) Abroad: Diasporic Identities in Third Spaces', Rath reconceptualises home as 'both a concrete location (a place or space in a geographic/cartographic sense) and an abstract space in the conceptual realm (an imaginary construct, at best)', circumscribed by culture, history, and community (85). For Mary, the idea of home/China encapsulates both concepts. China is both a specific, spatial entity that she eventually travels to in order to arrive at a fuller sense of self-knowledge and understanding. But it is also an imaginary construct, built on the memories and stories of her parents:

> Her heart was full of dreams about the country she had never
> seen, yet to which she belonged, where her own people lived. She
> could believe nothing but good about China, nothing but what
> was brave about her people. (17)

Dorinne Kondo, Japanese American critic, remarks on 'the necessity and inevitability of a desire for "home"' in an alienated environment, one that is often felt by people in diaspora. But she also talks of 'the accompanying danger of that desire', because oftentimes, 'it can elicit a nostalgia for a past golden age that never was' (97).

Mary's vision of China was shaped by the filtered and nostalgic account of her parents who, in an effort to kindle love and pride for one's roots in their children, recreate a romantic and unrealistic picture of China, a dream world that no longer exists, or perhaps, to use Kondo's words, 'never was'. This results in disillusionment and a sense of being cheated of the truth, when their four children finally made the trip to China and discover the glaring inconsistency between the ideal and the real, between what was portrayed and what is. Confronting poverty, oppression, ignorance, and injustice in pre-Communist China, Peter, the younger son, lashes out in rage: 'I shall never forgive Pa as long as I live – letting us believe that everything was wonderful, hiding it all under a Confucian mist' (269).

In more ways than one, perhaps, the characters' quest for the beloved homeland closely echoes the writer's own experience when she returned to the United States in 1934, 'in search of the America her mother had taught her to love, cherish and uphold'.

> The truth [however] is that Pearl never found the America she
> had come in search of. Like the sons and daughters of other
> missionaries before and after her, she found that her idealized
> America did not exist, even though a vision of it might shimmer
> on the horizon. (David D. Buck 40)

For the women characters in *Kinfolk*, the metaphorical journey to the self is undertaken by means of a literal journey to China. Indeed, the journey to China is central to the novel and to the characters' self-knowledge and self-discovery. For Louise, the trip to China was forced upon her by her parents, in a bid to distance her from her American boyfriend. For Mary, on the other hand, it is a conscious choice, because she believes that reclaiming, and reconnecting with her roots, is a necessary prelude to a deeper knowledge and understanding of herself. Her constant refrain is, 'I'd like to go back to our ancestral village . . . I want to know what kind of people we really are. Behind Pa and Ma who are we?' (173). The trip to China marks a turning point in their lives and sets the stage for their gradual self-realisation and discovery.

As previously mentioned, the journey, in this particular context, is a multilateral one. It entails not only a journeying 'to' but also journeying 'from' a space or situation that is not conducive to one's sense of self. For Mary, America represents a space of repression, one that thwarts her self-expression and authenticity. She is constantly conscious of the strain to be politically correct and not to give offence to 'the people in whose land they were aliens' (13). The sense of not belonging that characterises her American experience precludes her from thinking of America as home. Contrary to the definition of home as 'a safe place, where there is no need to explain oneself to outsiders' (Kondo 97), Mary finds herself the eternal 'outsider', the 'other', always 'explaining' oneself and one's family to others. The following conversation with the elevator attendant, a white American, illustrates this point:

> 'Yes, thank you,' she said, 'my brother in China is quite well. Yes, he likes it there. Yes, someday doubtless we will all return to China. Yes, of course we do like it here – but it is not our country'. (100)

Thus, for Mary, the first step in her journey to self-realisation necessitates breaking away from the confines of a space that threatens to stifle her self-expression and stunts her personhood. The voyage to China is a pivotal step in that direction. However, there is a marked discrepancy between the China woven in their imagination and the China they encounter. How do the protagonists respond to the disillusionment/discovery/reality that is China?

After the first shock of realising that the China of her parents does not really exists, or is long gone, Mary, though disappointed, does not allow herself to be embittered or disillusioned, like her two younger siblings, Peter and Louise. She writes to her parents:

> Really, Pa and Ma, you should have told us what things here are like, instead of letting us think that our country is one beautiful cloud of Confucianism. But maybe you have been away so long that you have forgotten. (208)

Practical by nature, she accepts the reality, like she does everything else, in her stride. She is convinced that behind the shattered visage and facade of brokenness lies a glorious China, enshrined not so much in the physical or external, but in the spirit, and character, and resilience of its people. Like her elder brother James, she passionately believes that 'ours are the best people in the world', notwithstanding the apparent ignorance, dirt, and disease (294).

Realising this, Mary is determined to rediscover the true spirit of China in its people, sharing Buck's own belief that 'the common people are China's strength and glory' (*The New York Times Book Review*, 1933). She attempts to do this by reconnecting and renewing ties with her own people, her kinfolk, with whom she feels an instinctive sense of kinship and affinity. This takes her on a further voyage, deep into the heart of the Chinese countryside, to her own ancestral village, Anming, to put down roots there and to live and work with, and for, her own people. Once there, she 'join[s] in the life' of the kinfolk, working and sitting with them, answering their constant questions (199).

No longer blinded by illusion, she sets herself to the task of educating the villagers, helping them to reinvent themselves and their lives and to bridge the great gulf of differences existing between themselves and the outside world. In the process, Mary succeeds in reinventing her own life and forming a sense of self. Many writers have commented on the role of 'social relationships . . . for developing a sense of belonging to a place', leading subsequently to a sense of self-affirmation and identity (Gerson *et al.*, qtd. in Hauge 8). Mary roots herself further into her community by choosing to marry Liu Chen, a doctor, who is as committed to China as she is. In so doing, she experienced a deeper sense of rootedness and belonging that nurtures within her a feeling of self-fulfilment and completion.

The process of reaching out to her roots, cultural and ancestral, is not an easy one to negotiate. Mary faces stiff resistance and opposition, initially, from the very people that she is trying to align herself with. This may be explained as an inevitable offshoot of the differences that exists between her and her kinfolk. Indeed, the spatiotemporal and cultural gulf between them is so wide that it cannot but spawn conflict and misunderstandings: 'There was a world of difference between themselves and these kinfolk, centuries of difference, space and time crowded together into a single generation' (193). These Chinese relatives, steeped in centuries-old habits and mindset, are sceptical and even suspicious of her efforts to bring change into their lives. She, in turn, is baffled by and impatient with their complacent acceptance of the status quo. In America, Mary had identified herself as wholly Chinese. Ironically, however, in China, the American sensibility that has been imbibed through her years in America unconsciously surfaces in her. Though married to a Chinese, she refuses to be the typical Chinese wife; she openly rebels against Uncle Tao, the patriarch of the Liang household, when she feels that her plans and purposes are being thwarted. As her mother reflects, 'although she [Mary] lived in the ancestral village, she behaved like an American' (348).

This paradox is best understood in the context of the diasporic experience, defined by Mandaville as the peculiar interplay of 'here' and 'there', characterising the strange diasporic ubiquity (qtd. in Mohapatra 1). In his seminal work, *The Location of Culture*, Homi Bhabha talks of the 'in-between spaces', or the interface between two cultures, resulting in the creation of a new culture which is a hybrid of the two opposing cultures, one that initiates 'new signs of identity' (1–2). Writing almost half a century before Bhabha, Buck had already articulated this situation in *Kinfolk*, one that is born of her own experience. What is observed in Mary is the overlapping and amalgamating of her Chinese heritage and American upbringing, thereby, birthing a new multivalent sensibility. Thus, her in-between situation which had earlier engendered a sense of belonging neither 'here' nor 'there' is now transformed into a new, creative space, one that enriches her perspective and her sense of self. 'The dehyphenated identity, the Chinese-American, takes the place of neither/nor as well as of both/and at once' (Lee, 2004, 109).

For Mary, her brother James and her husband Liu Chen prove to be a source of continual support and encouragement as she embarks on her new journey. Her relationship with these – the gendered other – provides her with the much needed strength and partnership indispensible to self-development. But the attempt to root herself in her new life is also aided by the visit of her mother to China.

Mrs Liang, the matriarch of the Liang family, is a pivotal character in the novel. It is she who helps Mary realise that if she is to re-enter her culture and take her place among her community, she must learn to see things from their perspective thus: 'Now these ancestral people do not understand that a person can read and at the same time work. It is necessary that you continually show them it is possible' (339). To reconnect with the villagers, therefore, throughout her stay in the ancestral village, Mrs Liang made it a point to identify with the village people. She 'washed her own garments and helped in the kitchens and in all ways surprised the Liang women who expected her to act as a learned and idle woman' (339). Watching her mother thus, Mary also learns to do the same, thereby, narrowing the gap between herself and the village folk. Mrs Liang, thus, functions as a bridge between tradition (epitomised by Uncle Tao and the villagers) and modernity (represented by her children), constantly attempting to explain one to the other. Having lived life in the same village once, she can clearly identify with the villagers' fear and distrust of change. At the same time, however, her years in America have opened her mind to the inevitability of, and the need for social change and development. She therefore, takes upon herself the role of a mediator, mediating between the rural folk and her own children, between the past and the present. As Mary and James look at their mother, they realise that she functions as 'the bridge between these centuries' (365). It is only by learning to bridge this gap between centuries and generations, as shown by their mother, that they can truly hope to belong and discover themselves in the lives that they have chosen to live.

The intrasocietal polarity that exists in China is re-enacted even in the Chinese immigrant circle in America. In New York, the Chinese working-class immigrants are represented by Chinatown. This place, bustling with life and activity, is often avoided by the sophisticated Dr Liang and other Chinese of his ilk: 'He did not often come here because he found it depressing.' It serves as a jarring reminder of 'what he habitually tried to forget, that the common people of his country were not in the least like himself' (5). Her husband's disapproval notwithstanding, Mrs Liang is a regular visitor to Chinatown. She finds in its environs, and in her compatriots there, a solid sense of home and comfort, which greatly adds to her well-being and confidence. In crossing the boundaries between Chinatown and her posh, riverside home, she, inadvertently, succeeds in forging a link between the working-class and the Chinese intellectuals in America.

As the narrative progresses, she reveals a multilayered depth to her being. Her trip to China brings to the fore the many dimensions of her character. When in America, Mrs Liang, like Mary, had regarded it as the alien other, a place that must be endured rather than enjoyed. Her years there, however, have unconsciously left their imprint upon her sensibility. When she revisited China, therefore, although she takes her place in the household 'as though she had never been away', 'she did not sink back into old ways. She approves of Mary's little school and goes about the village urging mothers to send their children to learn', which is what people in America do, she explains (338–9).

It is ironical that for Mrs Liang, it takes an absence, albeit a temporary one, from America to enable her to look at it objectively and appreciate certain values that it stands for. Thus, the geographical gap brought about by her distance from America serves, in a sense, to narrow the psychological gap between the two countries which was existent in her mind. When she returns to New York, she is pleasantly surprised to discover that 'there was a strange feeling of home here, too' (359). This eventual ability to create a sense of home both in China and in America enables the character to come to terms with her own bicultural reality. In the process, she discovers a sense of belonging that may be termed universal.

It is interesting to note that the spatiotemporal distancing brought about by the China trip serves not only to transform the protagonist's own thinking and perceptions but also transforms the way other characters perceive her. When she was in New York, Dr Liang was often 'ashamed of her' and what he thought of as her 'stupidity' before genteel society (6, 12). Her absence from him, however, brings home her worth and comfort in his life. As he looks at his wife through the veil of this temporary separation, he recognises her for the 'living and strong' individual that she is, one on whom his happiness is anchored, a feeling shared by the children (357). This new affirmation from her family serves to add greatly to Mrs Liang's confidence, self-esteem, and self-worth. As Sartre states, 'The "Other" has not only revealed to me what I was; he has established me in a new type of being which can support new qualifications' (302–03).

Through her characters, Buck dramatises the different ways in which immigrants respond to living life 'on the cusp' (Bhabha, qtd. in Mitchell, 1995), struggling to carve out a life and an identity for themselves in the situation that they are placed. Psychologist J. W. Berry (1997) identifies four acculturation strategies adopted by people in diaspora: (i) *integration*, marked by a strong ethnic identity while also identifying and integrating with the host culture; (ii) *separation*, when the individual separates himself/herself from the host culture and clings to one's own ethnicity; (iii) *assimilation*, when individuals take on the new culture's beliefs, values, and norms, deeming it relatively unimportant to maintain one's original cultural identity; (iv) *marginalisation*, when there is little or no possibility of cultural maintenance, or of having relations with others, often, because of exclusion or discrimination (9).

The abovementioned strategies characterise the experiences of the Liang women in their search for selfhood and identity. While Mary rediscovers her sense of self through the eventual return to her roots, for Louise her sister, the journey to self-actualisation takes a different turn altogether. Unlike her sister Mary, who had studiously clung to her own culture as a mean of preserving her identity, Louise's way of establishing herself is through the process of assimilation. She seeks her identity not in her Chinese roots but in the American present which is where, she feels, she belongs. Thus, Louise goes all out to inculcate the values and standards of the country in which she is born and bred. Repeated references are made in the text to her conscious attempt to always speak in English rather than Chinese, even when she is speaking with another Chinese person, like Chen. All her relationships are with American men – with Philip Morgan previously, and later with

Alec Weatherston whom she eventually married. If America represents the cultural other for Mary, for Louise, China is the other, notwithstanding her Chinese origin: 'She was frightened at the thought of China. She loved America' (32). Forced by her parents to go to China, Louise's only yearning while there was to come back home to New York. The journey to China only serves to bring to the fore, her deep sense of alienation and disconnect from her roots. She tells her brother James, 'I don't like it here . . . I wish I hadn't been born a Chinese. I wish I could stop being a Chinese' (153).

If excessive love for the homeland marks out her elder sister Mary, Louise, like her creator Pearl Buck, is characterised by extreme attachment to the adopted country. Of Buck, Liu Haiping opines, 'Not even after returning to settle in the United States in the mid 1930s could she detach herself wholly from China, which remained in many senses her true home' (56).

For Louise, one of the ways of identifying with the adopted nation is through her consistent and conscious attempt to always speak in English, the mainstream language. The role of language as an identity marker has been explored by many social psychologists. According to sociologist Rusi Jaspal, its role is often a double-edged one. It can constitute 'a means of asserting one's identity' through identification with the speakers of that same language, but it can also be a means of underlining 'one's distinctiveness from others' who do not speak the same (17–20).

For Louise, the English language, thus, becomes a powerful symbol both of her identification with America and, simultaneously, her non-identification with China and anything Chinese. Second, just like her sister Mary, Louise's way of rooting herself deeper into the culture and community of her choice, American in her case, is through marriage and relationships: 'How she hated being Chinese herself! She must go back to America. If she married an American, she could be an American, almost' (227). Her marriage to Alec Weatherston, an American soldier, provides her with the means of returning to America which is where she discovers her sense of belonging and home. When back in America, she says to herself, 'This is really my home, I belong here. I am really American' (284).

It is interesting to note that for the Liang women, identity and selfhood are strongly linked to place(s): Mary's journey culminates in China which is where she ultimately discovers her identity and sense of self; for Louise, the journey takes her to China, and then back to America; For Mrs Liang, however, the journey is one that encompasses both countries. She sees herself as a bridge going 'back and forth between the kinfolk' who have made their lives on both sides of the world, 'for she belonged to all of them' (363).

Through this novel, therefore, Buck explores the alternative modes by which the characters define their identities and realise selfhood. For each of these women, the journey to selfhood is one that is traversed differently and along diverse planes. The destination, however, is the same, which is, the discovery and realisation of self and personal fulfilment, even though this entails different meanings for each character. This reaffirms that the self is not a unitary or monolithic entity, but fluid, dynamic, and constantly evolving.

EPILOGUE

In rereading Pearl S. Buck, what may be said is that through her fiction, Buck succeeds, to a large extent, in correcting Western stereotypes of the Chinese people, particularly the Chinese woman. The subsequent reception and appraisal of her work by American readers and critics bear ample evidence to this. E. H. A. Carson, for example, notes that '[t]he central character in *The Mother* with little change might be typical of a sharecropper family in the southern states as of a peasant family in Central China' (56). Admittedly, her work is also motivated by her particular attempt to give voice and visibility to the long-marginalised Chinese woman, yet it is always laced with this clear political agenda of bringing about a better understanding between East and West. In using her work as an agent of cultural mediation, Buck shows her awareness of her art as being not only a means of personal self-expression but also a way of reaching out to the larger issues of society. In this sense, therefore, she may be described as a socially and politically conscious artist, who strives to make a difference through her work. Like her women characters, the self that Buck aspires to is a self-in-community, negotiated through active participation in, and dialogue with, the greater world outside oneself.

What she constantly strives to bring into focus through her work is that Chinese women are not inherently weak or inferior in any way. Their perceived powerlessness is rather the consequence of the oppressiveness of the culture and times that they are located in, which, as shown, is largely inimical to women. What is observed about these women, however, is that, in their own ways, they do manage to forge a sense of self in spite of the limited enclosures that define their lives. From victims, therefore, these women become survivors.

Further, what is fascinating to observe in Buck's work is that the image of the Chinese woman is one that is constantly evolving. There is a marked change and progression in the way the women characters have been depicted from one novel to the next. In *East Wind: West Wind* (1930) and in *The Good Earth* (1931), one encounters women like Kweilan and O-lan whose sense of self-awareness and self-expression is still largely dormant to a certain level. They accept their oppressed contexts unquestioningly, regarding it as the natural lot of women, rather than as something to be contested. It is only when they are propelled into a space of conflict and crises in their lives that their sense of self begins to surface, thereby initiating them in the journey of growth and maturity. In *The Mother* (1934), Buck portrays a woman whose values about life and about womanhood are still shaped and informed by the standards of her time and society. Simultaneously, however, what is also noticed is her attempt to explore and embrace other aspects of her female self, such as her own sexuality, rather than constricting herself to society's given roles about women. In her, Buck creates a woman who, historically speaking, is beginning to be aware of her own needs and desires, while at the same time still largely thwarted by the powerful conditioning impact of society. In *Pavilion of Women* (1946), the protagonist is depicted as not only being aware of her rights and desires as a woman, but as actively pursuing ways and means of achieving the same. The women characters in *Kinfolk* (1949), particularly Mary and Louise Liang, reflect the changing reality in the Chinese social milieu. More opportunities for women's education, and the Chinese diaspora, serve to connect these women with a larger world, other than the one they have known. They are, therefore, more aware and assertive of their needs and rights as women, exhibiting a growing confidence in themselves and a boldness in reaching out for what they feel they deserved.

These characters' journey to selfhood is one that is negotiated through a process of self-introspection, as well as through a network of relationships: with the gendered other, the racial other, and other personalities that constitute the characters' world. As such, the self that is realised by Pearl Buck's women characters is a self-in-community. It is in this constant dialogue between 'the I and the Thou, the self and the other, the individual and the community' (Gupta 2) that her characters succeed in defining and discovering themselves.

SECTION TWO

BRIDGING DIVIDES; SPANNING TWO WORLDS

Storytelling in Amy Tan's Fiction

PROLOGUE

'May my story be beautiful and unwind like a long thread. . .'
she recites as she begins her story. A story that stays inexhaustible
within its own limits.

(Trinh. T. Minh-ha, *Woman, Native, Other:*
Writing Post-Coloniality and Feminism 4)

We can only retell and live by the stories we have read or heard.
We live our lives through texts. They may be read, or chanted,
or experienced electronically, or come to us, like the murmurings
of our mothers, telling us what conventions demand. Whatever
their form or medium, these stories have formed us all; they are
what we must use to make new fictions, new narratives.

(Carolyn G. Heilbrun, *Writing a Woman's Life* 37)

Like many immigrant Americans, Amy Tan's identity is a 'hyphenated
identity' (Muthyala 103): a Chinese-American. Being thus situated, she is
fully aware of the dilemma and angst faced by such, especially women, in
their quest for identity in a context that has been described by Bhabha as the
'in-between, third-space' situation (2). Women's needs, and the strategies
they adopt, to reassert and redefine themselves in such a situation form
the crux of Tan's work. Almost all her novels chronicle the experiences of
Chinese immigrant women and Chinese-American women, both in their
past and in the present, as they struggle to reclaim the self and carve a
niche for themselves in a bicultural space. Lindo Jong, one of the characters
in Tan's first novel, *The Joy Luck Club*, sums up their situation succinctly

when she remarks thus: 'I think about our two faces . . . Which one is American? Which one is Chinese? Which one is better? If you show one, you must always sacrifice the other' (266). For these women, the journey towards self-discovery is fraught with complexities and ambiguities. They are constantly confronted by multiple, disparate realities that tries them, generating tension and conflict: the necessity of confronting their Chinese past with its patriarchal and suppressive overtones; their encounter with the American present which represents an opposite culture, a different way of life, and the oftentimes contradictoriness of the American Dream; and of course, negotiating the complex ritual of relationship, with their own selves, as well as with their children, namely, their daughters.

This section explores how these women forge and recreate an identity of their own in such a multivalent space. Thus, the quest for self becomes 'an archetypal journey' for these women (Foster 73): a simultaneous journey in space, in time, and out of time, as they attempt to bridge divides between geography, culture, generations, and between the past and the present, in the process seeking to heal their internal rifts and fragile relationships with each other.

One of the means undertaken by the characters to bridge these multilayered chasm(s) to work towards realising an integrated self is through the mode of storytelling. As she mentions in her essay, 'The Opposite of Fate', Tan grew up listening to stories: the read-stories from her father (336), and more importantly, listening, often surreptitiously, to talk-stories, family lore, and secrets that her mother and aunts 'gossip[ed]' amongst themselves 'as they shelled the fava beans and pummelled the dumpling dough at the kitchen table' (36), stories about her Chinese past and heritage which Tan later weaves into her fiction and which characterises her art. Thus, *The Joy Luck Club*, the first of Tan's novels to be published, is a series of sixteen stories set in four parts, told in the voice of four Chinese immigrant women and their four American-born daughters whose lives are interconnected through the Joy Luck Club. Similarly, ensuing novels such as *The Kitchen God's Wife*, *The Hundred Secret Senses*, and *The Bonesetter's Daughter* encapsulate layers of stories within the central narrative.

Critic-writer Marie Booth Foster states that 'storytelling – relating memories – allows for review, analysis, and sometimes understanding of ancestry and thus themselves' (74). For Tan, however, storytelling is not just a tool for self-knowledge and comprehension, but it also becomes a significant means of giving voice to countless women, like her own mother and grandmother, whose voices and stories have been suppressed and unheard through the centuries. 'For women living in male-dominated societies where they were silenced and excluded from public forms of involvement . . . storytelling provides a realm of voice and . . . a space for self-expression (H. Wong 4–5).

One of the dominant discourses in Tan's fiction is her employment of the 'Talk-stories' or the oral narratives. This is perfectly congruent with the Chinese and women-oriented context of her novels because it is directly connected with these women's sense of who they are, and the talk-story culture that they come from. According to Elizabeth Croll, in China, 'the art of storytelling [was] highly valued by women audiences, who loved to hear the simple stories, which were told in rhythmic and popular language' (qtd. in Ho 147).

At the same time, it also serves to validate and reinforce a mode of discourse and an art form that was, previously, largely undermined and negated by Western traditional discourses that privilege writing over other forms of expression. Traditionally, the oral narrative has been perceived as belonging to a 'savage, primitive, underdeveloped, backward, alienated' mentality (Lyotard 19). By foregrounding the oral in her work, Tan contests this assumption and shows that the oral discourse is as pivotal and legitimate as any other literary technique and expression. However, Tan refuses to be circumscribed solely within the realm of orality. In her fiction, she gives equal space to the significance of the written text as well as to the validity of the language of signs and gestures as powerful mediums by which these women share their stories. This is particularly brought out in *The Bonesetter's Daughter* and may be traced in the other three novels as well.

Another important aspect that is explored in her books is the relationship gap, or the divides, that characterises the protagonists' lives. Almost all scholars and critics have singled out the mother-daughter relationship and its inherent conflict as the most recurrent and conspicuous motif in Tan's work. While this is indeed the central strand informing all her narratives, other relationships – woman-woman, intercultural and intergenerational – also surface in her work, because the divide pertains to all these relationships.

With the sole exception of Ruth's story in *The Bonesetter's Daughter* which is a third-person narrative, the stories are told not in the voice of an omniscient author/third-person narrator but through the personal perspectives and individual voices of the multiple women characters. This serves to bring in an element of heteroglossia to Amy Tan's fiction and vastly enriched her work.

CHAPTER SIX

'FEATHERS FROM ACROSS THE SEAS'[1]

The Joy Luck Club

They go back to eating their soft boiled peanuts, saying stories among themselves. They are young girls again, dreaming of good times in the past and good times yet to come such good stories. The best. They are the lucky ones.

(Amy Tan's *The Joy Luck Club*, 41)

The Joy Luck Club, Tan's debut novel, revolves around eight women characters, namely, four Chinese mothers, local and *emigres*, and their four American-born daughters who are all given equal space to voice their own versions of truth and present their individual stories from their own perspectives. The narrative is thus structured around four interlinking parts, with the daughters' tales enclosed within the framing narratives of the mothers.

Tan's privileging of the female voice and silencing of the male voice has invited criticisms of feminist biasness in her work. While this may seem superficially true, as Gloria Shen asserts, it clearly signals Tan's

---

1   The title is based on the subtitle of the first part of Tan's novel *The Joy Luck Club*. The feathers referred to are the stories which the Joy Luck Club Chinese mothers brought back with them to their new land, America.

counter-attempt to correct the traditional gender imbalance in fiction which is often dismissive of women and their experience, 'to do away with "his story" and present "her life" from the perspectives of the individual women characters in the form of loosely connected monologues' (7).

These 'loosely connected monologues' of Tan's women characters are, as mentioned, rendered through means of the talk-story or oral narrative. The phrase 'talk-story' was originally a Hawaian pidgin expression which means 'to chat informally' or 'to shoot the breeze'. Linguistic scholar Karen Ann Watson describes it as 'a rambling personal experience mixed with folk materials' (54). In Chinese culture, the 'talk-story' or '*gong gu tsai*' is 'an ancient folk-art form' dating back to the 'storytellers of the Sung dynasty' and handed down – and embellished – by successive generations (Huntley 66). All these descriptions emphasise on the informal, personal, folk, and oral aspect of the talk-story. It is Chinese-American writer, Maxine Hong Kingston, however, who is credited with introducing the talk-story as a legitimate narrative strategy in her famous works, *The Woman Warrior* (1975) and *China Men* (1980). According to her, it is 'an oral tradition of history, mythology, genealogy, bedtime stories, and how-to stories that have been passed down through generations, an essential part of family and community life' (qtd. in Medoff 257).

Like Kingston, Amy Tan uses the talk-story culture extensively within her fiction. Unlike Kingston, however, for Tan, the talk-story is not employed as a structural framework, but is embedded within the body of the text through the narratives of the Chinese mothers. Thus, in contrast to Kingston where the novel itself is the talk-story, in Tan's work, the oral element is, as H. W. Wong asserts, 'more on a "textual" level rather than on a "structural" level' (201). It is not Tan the writer, *per se*, but her literary characters, who engage in talk-storytelling.

According to Tammy Conard, in *The Joy Luck Club*, the roots of the mothers' stories lie with the oral and aural tradition. That is, they were originally meant to be spoken and heard by an audience (28), the target audience being primarily the daughters and the reader-listener. Stephen Souris, on the other hand, argues that the novel 'seems to participate in the convention of having speakers speak into the void – or [only] to the reader as audience. No actual communication between mothers and daughters occurs' (26). Contrary to Souris' argument, however, what is seen in this novel is that the mothers' narratives are clearly addressed to a second-person listener(s) which encapsulates both the daughters, as well as the reader. In the chapter titled 'Magpies', for instance, An-Mei Hsu referring to the context of her daughter's failing marriage which results in regular visits to the psychiatrist, clearly addresses her daughter's situation – the 'you', being her daughter Rose:

> I know how it is to live your life like a dream. To listen and watch, to wake up and try to understand what has already happened. You do not need a psychiatrist to do this. A psychiatrist does not want you to wake up. He tells you to dream some more, to find the pond and pour more tears into it. And really, he is just another bird drinking from your misery. (240)

The 'bird' in question is the magpie and alludes to her own mother's story that An-Mei had, presumably, told Rose earlier, so that there is no need for her to qualify it in their present exchange. Again, in Lindo Jong's second narrative, the listener is clearly her daughter Waverley, as Lindo talks about the early days of her courtship by Waverley's father: '[W]e were shy at first, your father and I, neither of us able to speak to each other in our Chinese dialects . . . [b]ut I soon saw enough how much your father liked me' (263). These two examples clearly show that the mothers speak their stories not 'into the void', but to a specific listener – their daughters – thereby, opening up a channel of communication between them resulting in the potential bridging of the gap, or an attempt to do so. The ensuing discussion explores how the mothers' act of articulating their stories through the talk-story form is both deliberate, as well as necessitated by certain circumstances.

The mother-daughter relationship/rift is a dominant and recurrent theme in *The Joy Luck Club*, as in all of Tan's other novels. The rift is brought about by many factors – personal, cultural, and linguistic. When the Chinese immigrant women look at their American-born daughters, they are haunted by the fear that their daughters have virtually become strangers to them and to their own roots. The fable-like vignette in the opening section of *The Joy Luck Club* subtitled, 'Feathers from a Thousand Li Away' underlines this theme about an old woman who sails with her swan to America, full of dreams and hopes for herself and her life in the new country. 'In America,' she cooed to the swan, 'I will have a daughter just like me. But over there nobody will say her worth is measured by the loudness of her husband's belch. Over there nobody will look down on her, because I will make her speak only perfect American English. And over there she will always be too full to swallow any sorrow!' When she landed in America, however, the immigration officials pulled her swan away from her, leaving her with only one swan feather for a memory. In the subsequent struggle to adapt to the new country, she eventually 'forgot why she had come and what she had left behind'. Now that she is old, the mother laments that she has a daughter 'who grew up speaking only English and swallowing more Coca-Cola than sorrow'. Perceiving how distant the daughter has grown from her and her ancestry, the mother wants to give her the single, remaining swan feather and tell her, 'This feather may look worthless, but it comes from afar and carries with it all my good intentions.' The vignette ends with the mother waiting to tell her daughter this, 'in perfect American English' (17).

This vignette captures one of the major themes of the novel, which is, the theme of displacement, conflict, and alienation – personal, mother-daughter, cultural. The dynamics of the talk-story, because of its highly intimate and dialogic nature, is perfectly situated to address these gaps. In *The Joy Luck Club*, the mothers' stories are interspersed and fragmentary, told to the daughters in bits and pieces, over the years, or, as in Ying-Ying's case, the main story, concerning her past, is yet to be told to her daughter. Sometimes, the tales told are personal and about family history, while sometimes, they come as warning stories or 'didactic and cautionary pronouncements' (Huntley 66) and are employed by the mothers for a variety of reasons.

First, it is an attempt on the mothers' part to bridge the divide between themselves and their daughters. Both the mothers' as well as the daughters' narratives reveal the tension and distance existing between them. Jing-Mei Woo, one of the daughters, remarks, 'My mother and I never really understood one another. We translated each other's meanings and I seemed to hear less than what was said, while my mother heard more'(37). Later, when she is asked by the other mothers, the Joy Luck Club 'aunties', to tell about her dead mother Suyuan to her half-sisters in China, she realises, much to her own, and to their consternation, that she has never really known her mother. And as she looks at the dismay writ large on the faces of her mother's friends, it occurs to her that they, too, see in her their own

> Daughters who grow impatient when their mothers talk in Chinese, who think they are stupid when they explain things in fractured English. They see that joy and luck do not mean the same to their daughters, that to these closed American-born minds 'joy luck' is not a word, it does not exist. They see daughters who will bear grandchildren born without any connecting hope passed from generation to generation. (40–1)

This estrangement is a result of multiple factors. According to Wendy Ho, the mothers' 'unrealistic expectations of their daughters', and their fierce over-protectiveness and paranoia leading them to intrude and interfere in their lives make the daughters see them as 'demanding taskmasters' and to feel 'more misunderstood or devalued by their mothers than loved' (167). The daughters' narratives seem to lend support to this argument. Believing that in America, 'you could be anything you wanted to be', Suyuan tries to groom Jing-Mei into becoming a child-prodigy, a 'Chinese Shirley Temple', or one of the 'amazing children she had read in *Ripley's Believe it or Not*, or *Good Housekeeping, Reader's Digest*' (*Joy* 132–33); or a concert pianist. This leads to the daughter's frustration, resentment, the sense of being a failure, and eventually, outright rebellion, when she cannot match her mother's aspirations. In another mother-daughter conflict scenario in the novel, Waverley Jong narrates how as a child-genius in chess, she eventually gave up the sport out of resentment against her mother's belligerence and tendency to take credit for her daughter's accomplishment. She comes to regard her mother as an 'opponent' rather than the 'protective ally' that the former imagines herself to be (*Joy* 98–100). The simmering conflict between them spills over into Waverley's adult life where she constantly imagines that her mother's demanding and overly critical nature is responsible for wrecking her marriage to Marvin Chen and will probably wreck her current relationship with Rich Shields. It is only after a confrontation with Lindo that Waverley comes to realise that her perceptions of her mother were wrong all along. As the duo learn to talk to each other, sharing stories,

Waverley realises that the person she had thought of as her greatest opponent is in fact just 'an old woman, a wok for her armor, a knitting needle for her sword, getting a little crabby as she waited patiently for her daughter to invite her in' (183–84).

A study conducted among Asian families in America shows that high parental expectation and demand from children, leading to the child-parent conflict, is not peculiar to the Joy Luck Club mothers alone:

> The pressure to succeed academically among Asians is very strong. From early childhood, outstanding achievement is emphasized because it is a source of pride for the entire family. . . Parental expectations for achievement can be an additional stress factor in young Asian-Americans. (qtd. in Souris 33)

The experience of Suyuan and Jing-Mei, Lindo and Waverley, is representative of the reality of many Asian immigrants trying to etch out an identity and a chance of a better life by excelling, in their own right or through their children, in a predominantly alien culture. In this sense, Tan may be said to be a chronicler of the Asian-American experience as well, although this is a claim that she herself vigorously disavows.

For another daughter in the text, Lena St. Clair, the antagonism between her and her Chinese mother Ying-Ying is precipitated by a particular event that occurs when Lena was a young girl – the death of her baby brother at birth. In her narrative, 'The Voice from the Wall', she recounts:

> After the baby died, my mother fell apart, not all at once, but piece by piece, like plates falling off a shelf one by one. . . . Sometimes she would start to make dinner, but would stop halfway, . . .her knife poised in the air over half-chopped vegetables, silent, tears flowing. And sometimes we'd be eating and we would have to stop and put our forks down because she had dropped her face into her hands and was saying, *'Mei gwansyi'* – It doesn't matter. My father would just sit there, trying to figure out what it was that didn't matter this much. And I would leave the table, knowing it would happen again, always a next time. (112–13)

The sense of psychological imbalance that seems to characterise the mother and alienate the daughter serves to foster an atmosphere of tension and unease in the family. This eventually strains their relationship with each other. 'I had such fears inside,' Lena recalls, 'not in my head but in my stomach. I could no longer see what was so scary, but I could feel it' (113). The reader, however, privy to other/more information through the mothers' narratives, is made aware that the daughters' perspectives are incomplete, at times misinterpreted, and accounts for only part of the story. Ying-Ying's two narratives, 'The Moon Lady' and 'Waiting Between the Trees', give the reader an insight into why Ying-Ying seems perpetually displaced, lost, and isolated within herself. Unfortunately, however, the vital information(s) is not known to the daughter (yet) because of the gap/absence of communication between them. It is only when Ying-Ying decides to tell her part of the story, to 'tell Lena of my shame' (*Joy* 248), that there is hope of a possible reconciliation between them.

'The Moon Lady' is Ying-Ying's account of how she 'lost' herself, literally and metaphorically (*Joy* 83). It describes an episode in Ying-Ying's childhood. On a family outing in the river once, during the moon festival holiday, Ying-Ying accidentally falls into the water without any of her family knowing. About to drown, the child is rescued by fisher-folks. The attempt to locate her family in the passing boats, however, proves to be fruitless, filling her with terror, 'I had turned into a beggar girl, lost without my family' (79). On the dock, still searching for her family, she comes across the staging of the traditional Moon Lady myth which ends with the beautiful Moon Lady promising to grant the secret wish of any who petitions her. Desperate to be found, the young child rushes backstage to whisper her wish to the Moon Lady only to discover that the lady is actually a haggard-looking man. The sense of terror at being lost forever, coupled with a sense of disillusionment, and a childhood faith broken by the discovery of the Moon Lady's sham identity leave an indelible stamp in the young girl's consciousness. And though found later, she believes that her family never 'found the same girl' (82).

Her second narrative, 'Waiting Between the Trees', is a variation of the same theme and recounts yet another phase of her life in China, one that scars her personality for life – her marriage to a promiscuous man who consistently cheats on her and eventually, abandons her. Throughout the marriage, Ying-Ying's life had revolved entirely around her husband, so much so that:

> I became a stranger to myself. I was pretty for him. If I put slippers on my feet, it was to choose a pair that I knew would please him. I brushed my hair ninety-nine times a night to bring luck to our marital bed, in hopes of conceiving a son. (247)

These lines powerfully reiterate the negative social conditioning that occurs in women in a patriarchal culture. The eventual discovery of her husband's betrayal is like a deep gash. The abortion of the male child in her womb is her attempt to wound him as severely as he had wounded her, 'a passive aggressive negation of his proud family tree' (Snodgrass 148). In a lineage/clan-centred culture like China, the worst fate that can befall a man is to be deprived of a male heir. Ironically, therefore, the act of abortion acquires a certain potency and becomes a subversive form of power play, giving woman power and control over something that she alone is positioned to give or withhold. Though later retracting her view, third-wave feminist Rebecca Walker, the daughter of famous author Alice Walker, remarks in an article titled 'Rebecca's Story' that appeared in *Harper's Magazine* in 1992, that 'abortion can be a rebellious and empowering act. It is an act through which you can assert yourself'. To a certain extent, Ying-Ying's abortion may also be read as a symbolic and defiant gesture of asserting autonomy and agency over her life, and reappropriating the right to her own body, a right largely abrogated by patriarchy. The act is, in a negative sense, therefore, a deviant means of self-empowerment in a context of powerlessness and oppression. It is not, however, without its ambivalence. Ying-Ying's desperate attempt to assert power over her own body, unfortunately, entails losing part of the self in the process: 'I let myself become a wounded animal. . . I willingly gave up my *chi*, the spirit that caused me so much pain. . . I became an unseen spirit' (*Joy* 251).

Ignorance of these stories because of Ying-Ying's silence results in the daughter's ignorance and misunderstanding of her mother, thereby, widening the rift between them: 'When my daughter looks at me, she sees a small old lady. That is because she sees only with her outside eyes. She has no *chuming*, no inside knowing of things' (248). Now, however, Ying-Ying realises that Lena is also in danger of losing herself, married to a man who, 'in the name of feminism and right thinking', is taking her 'for every cent she's got' (see, qtd. in Foster 80). Love and concern for her daughter's well-being spurs Ying-Ying's decision to share her story, in the hope that Lena will learn some worthwhile lessons from her mother' mistakes and experience: 'All her life, I have watched her as though from another shore. And now I must tell her everything about my past. It is the only way to penetrate her skin and pull her to where she can be saved' (*Joy* 242).

A subtheme that emerges here is the daughters' need for rescue and redemption. Invariably, each of the daughters' narratives in the third section of *The Joy Luck Club* – 'American Translation' – reflect tales of dysfunctional lives and disoriented selves: Rose's narrative reveals her as an indecisive woman unable to think for herself, 'without wood', as her mother describes her (191); Lena is trapped in a bad marriage, unable to speak up for herself; Waverley lives her life in the constant fear of her relationships failing; while Jing-Mei suffers from a lack of confidence and self-esteem after a failed marriage and a career that never really seemed to take off. The desire to help their daughters come through and emerge stronger is one of the propelling factors that make these mothers share their stories which are often laced with a lot of pain. This theme is clearly underlined in the final vignette of the text – 'Queen Mother of the Western Skies' – which describes the woman talking to her baby granddaughter, comparing the child to Syi Wang Mu, Queen Mother of the Western Skies: 'Thank you, Little Queen. Then you must teach my daughter this same lesson. How to lose your innocence but not your hope. How to laugh forever' (213).

The process of opening up old wounds and revisiting the past through rememory and storytelling becomes an empowering experience for these mothers. It facilitates a kind of self-healing and enables them to help their daughters renegotiate the challenging terrain of their journey in the present, in order to chart out a more viable course for themselves in the future:

> I will gather together my past and look. I will see a thing that
> has already happened. The pain that cut my spirit loose. I will

hold that pain in my hand until it becomes hard and shiny, more clear. And then my fierceness can come back. . . I will use this sharp pain to penetrate my daughter's tough skin and cut her tiger spirit loose. She will fight me, because this is the nature of two tigers. But I will win and give her my spirit, because this is the way a mother loves her daughter. (*Joy* 252)

Apart from the intergenerational conflict and personality clash, the misunderstanding between mother and daughter is further accentuated by their cultural differences. At best, the mother-daughter relationship has always been a problematic one. In *Of Woman Born* (1976), Adrienne Rich talks of this relationship as being double-edged. She asserts that in every woman, there is always 'a girl-child' who still longs for a woman's tenderness and approval (184). Simultaneously, however, the female-child is also averse to the notion of 'becoming' like her mother, termed by Rich as 'matrophobia', and desires to become her own individual, free from the mother's bondage (194). This ambivalence is at the heart of every mother-daughter experience, resulting in 'the deepest mutuality and the most painful estrangement' (185).

In *The Joy Luck Club* mother-daughter dyad, 'the diaspora' has sharpened the problem further because of the 'total contrast in the experiences of mother and daughter' (Shear 199). The mothers came to America relatively late in life when their sensibilities are already informed and shaped by Chinese cultural norms and ideology so that they remain inherently Chinese in their thinking and behaving. The daughters, on the other hand, born and brought up in America, are thoroughly Western in values and mindset, '[o]nly her skin and her hair are Chinese. Inside – she is all American-made' (*Joy* 254). Moreover, these daughters have become this way because, in the beginning, their mothers have consciously moulded them to become thus. Excessive desire for their daughters to fit in and be assimilated into the adopted country so that they do not feel a stranger to it as they themselves feel largely accounts for the daughters' alienation from their own roots and culture later. As Lindo sadly admits:

It's my fault she is this way. I wanted my children to have the best combination: American circumstances and Chinese character. . . .

> I taught her how American circumstances work. . . .She learned
> these things, but I couldn't teach her about Chinese character.
> (254)

In successfully adapting to American circumstances, the 'Chinese character' is severely compromised in the process. As Lindo asks, 'how could I know these two things do not mix?' (254)

Scholars have pointed out that the conflict between Chinese mothers and their American daughters mirrors, at the micro-cosmic level, the deeper clash between cultures – the Chinese culture which is 'high context', and the American culture which is a 'low context' one. As Tan herself experienced it, the misunderstandings, most often than not, result from 'social contexts failing in translation' (*Fate* 281).

In his book, *Beyond Culture* (1976), American anthropologist Edward T. Hall describes a high-context culture as one where the individual has internalised meanings and information so that little is explicitly stated, in written or spoken messages. In conversation, the speaker assumes that the listener knows what is meant and can infer the speaker's meaning without it being explicitly spelled out. Simultaneously, a low-context culture is one in which information and meanings are explicitly stated in the communication. Explanations are expected when statements or situations are unclear. When Rose as a child asks her mother why she should be the one to look out for her younger siblings, on a day in the beach, the only answer she got was *'Yiding'*, which, in this context, roughly translates as 'because you must'. Within this single-word answer are implicitly underlined all the reasons as to why she should do so, namely, because they were her brothers; her sisters had once taken care of her; how else could she learn responsibility? How else could she appreciate what her parents had done (*Joy* 123)? It is instances such as these that lead Jing-Mei to assert: 'My mother and I never really understood one another. We translated each other's meanings and I seemed to hear less than what was said, while my mother heard more' (37).

Ignorance and misreading of cultural nuances, coupled with diametrically opposite worldviews, further play a role in generating misunderstanding between the characters. When Waverley declares, 'I'm my own person,' she is, in effect, telling her mother that she is a strong-willed individual, able to manage her life without being pushed around by others, which is, clearly, an American pride and virtue. Lindo, however, reads it as her daughter's repudiation of her relationship with her. Deeply wounded and hurt, she asks, 'How can she be her own person? When did I give her up?' (254). This reflects the deep cleavage between the family- and community-oriented Asian culture, represented by Lindo and the other mothers, and the highly individualistic American one assimilated by the daughters:

> American society has tended toward the ideal of the self-sufficient, self-reliant individual who is the master of his or her own fate and chooses his or her own destiny. High value is placed on the ability to stand on your own feet. . . In contrast, Asian philosophies tend toward an acknowledgement that individuals become what they are because of the efforts of many things and many people. They are the products of their relationship to nature and other people. (qtd. in Souris 32)

Whether such contrasting worldviews can ever 'mix' is a question that Tan leaves unanswered, because there is no ready or simplistic answer to the dilemma. What she succeeds in doing, however, through her characters, is to reaffirm with other diasporic writers, that the diasporic consciousness is never a singular entity. It is one that is marked by a sense of perpetual dualism, 'speaking in a double voice and living in a bicultural world characterize their dual cultural enmeshment' (V. Chen 3). It is only by learning to embrace both sides of the divide and accept it as part of their reality, rather than negating it, that the characters begin to discover a self that is complete and integrated. Thus, it is in accepting the Chinese part of herself, represented by her trip to China, and specifically, her reconnection with the long lost sisters of her mother's story, that Jing-Mei succeeds in discovering her identity. She remarks, '[a]nd now I also see what part of me is Chinese. It is so obvious. It is my family. It is in our blood' (*Joy* 288). For Waverley, too, the decision to go to China for her honeymoon is indicative of her growing desire to accept her Chinese origin, recognising it to be an integral part of her being, as integral as her American-ness. This eventual openness to explore and reconnect with their personal, familial, geographical, and cultural roots is prompted to a large extent by the stories that the mothers share, igniting an interest in the daughters to know more about their mothers and their culture. '[W]ithout the stories, the daughters would have no connection to their mothers and a culture from which they are at least partially separated' (Conard 26). Thus, in Tan's fiction, storytelling functions as a significant means of bridging divides, spatial, interpersonal, as well as intercultural.

Suyuan's story, told posthumously by her daughter, describes how stories become an integral means of combating the numbing despair and trauma of war, keeping them alive, metaphorically:

> At all hours of the night and day, I heard screaming sounds. I didn't know if it was a peasant slitting the throat of a runaway pig or an officer beating a half-dead peasant for lying in his way on the sidewalk. I didn't go to the window to find out. What use would it have been? And that's when I thought I needed something to do to help me move. (*Joy* 23)

The 'something' that Suyuan thought off became the start of the Joy Luck Club, a gathering of women, meeting once a week to play mah jong, 'to raise money and to raise our spirits' (23):

> And then we would talk into the night until the morning, saying stories about good times in the past and good times yet to come. . . . 'Oh, what good stories! Stories spilling out all over the place! We almost laughed to death. . . . We were all afraid. We all had our miseries. But to despair was to wish back for something already lost. (24)

In *The Postmodern Condition*, Lyotard talks of the relaying of traditional knowledge and values from one generation to the next, where 'the one-time listener becomes a speaker in his own turn' (21). As she looks back at the past, An-Mei realises that it is her mother's and grandmother's stories that have helped her face life's greatest tests and challenges. From these wisdom-stories, she learns about the uselessness of crying over one's fate, as well as the need to be strong and assert herself. 'Your tears do not wash away your sorrows,' her mother once told her, '[t]hey feed someone else's joy. And that is why you must learn to swallow your own tears' (*Joy* 217). This is the same truth that she tries to communicate to her daughter Rose, in the hope that the daughter will, in turn, pass it on to her children. Similarly, on the eve of her visit to China, Jing-Mei was exhorted by the Joy Luck Club aunts to continue her mother's tradition of storytelling to her family there:

> 'Tell them stories of your family here. How she became success,' offers Auntie Lin. . . . 'Tell them stories she told you, lessons she taught, what you know about her mind that has become your mind,' says Auntie Ying. 'You mother very smart lady.' I hear more choruses of 'Tell them, tell them' as each Auntie frantically tries to think what should be passed on. (40)

Thus, Tan envisions the ritual of storytelling as an invaluable and continuing legacy between generations.

Apart from their painful experience in China, their American experience also plays a role in undermining these women's self-esteem and exacerbating their sense of disconnect further. Like most immigrants, these women came to America in the hope of having a better life than the one they had had. The vignettes and narratives in the text repeatedly emphasise on the power and promise of the American Dream:

> My mother believed you could be anything you wanted to be in America. You could open a restaurant. You could work for the government and get good retirement. You could buy a house with almost no money down. You could become rich. You could become instantly famous. . . America was where all my mother's hopes lay. She had come here in 1949 after losing everything in China. (*Joy* 132)

For these immigrant women, however, the American reality turns out to be vastly different from the dream that had beckoned them there. They find themselves constantly marginalised in a society where the 'white-male-is-norm' culture/syndrome prevails (Minh-ha 6). Quoting Tan's essay, 'The Language of Discretion', Bella Adams notes that Chinese-American history, in particular, is marked by 'seemingly benign stereotypes' that tend to 'see

Chinese people from a limited and limiting perspective' (2005, 3). The sense of being the racial other in a predominantly Eurocentric society is constantly thrust upon them in the daily exchanges of life. Even the American-born daughters are not totally exempt from this. Rose's brief exchange with Mrs Jordan, her Caucasian mother-in-law, underlines this fact. Even while assuring Rose that 'she had nothing whatsoever against minorities', Mrs Jordan makes it clear that Rose's ethnic identity would stand in the way of her son's future career and advancement in life (*Joy* 118). Thus, as Japanese-American critic Dorinne Kondo claims, '[f]or mainland Asian Americans surely one of the most insistent features of our particular oppression is our ineradicable foreignness' (98).

The role of language in determining social acceptance/rejection, especially in the diasporic context, is an often-mooted point in Tan's writing, surfacing in almost all her work. The immigrant mothers' displacement in America is further problematised by their 'broken English' (*Joy* 34) and limited understanding of it. This has not only excluded and marginalised them from the dominant, mainstream discourse but also stifled their voices to a large extent. Ying-Ying's language is composed of 'a combination of English punctuated by hesitations and Chinese frustration': '*shwo buchulai*' – Words cannot come out', so that her husband 'would put words in her mouth' (106). The position of always having to express oneself, as well as understand things, through the mediation of another is a limiting factor putting these women at a disadvantage. This often leads to misrepresentations of self to others, as well as an incorrect grasp of situations, leading to distorted realities. Lena's narrative underscores this point:

> I often lied when I had to translate for her [her mother], the endless forms, instructions, notices from school, telephone calls. '*Shemma yisz?*' – What meaning? – she asked me when a man at a grocery store yelled at her for opening up jars to smell the insides. I was so embarrassed I told her that Chinese people were not allowed to shop there. (106–7)

The language factor has in fact marginalised and alienated these women even from their own daughters. These daughters have grown up speaking nothing but 'perfect American English' (*Joy* 17). Therefore, they grow 'impatient when their mothers talk in Chinese, . . . [and think that] they are stupid when they explain things in fractured English' (40). Tan recalls that when she was growing up, her mother's limited English also limited her perception of her:

It was the language that I grew up with, and it was also a language that

> I didn't want to listen to. Like many people, I thought that because
> the language was imperfect that the thoughts were imperfect –
> that the person was imperfect. (Ruiz, qtd. in Snodgrass 120)

The daughters' reductive estimate of their mothers because of their limited linguistic ability exposes the 'inappropriate evaluation of immigrant intelligence based on their spoken expertise with English' (Snodgrass 120). It also undermines their self-confidence and maternal worth. As H. W. Wong asserts, '[f]or the mothers, the daughters' persistent denial of the maternal experience and subjectivities is probably more disheartening than the denial and suppression from the patriarchal Chinese discourse and the mainstream American discourse' (218). It is only when they learn to acknowledge their mothers' stories that these daughters begin to appreciate the worth and uniqueness of their mother's tongue, recognising it to be 'their special language' (*Joy* 34), that defines who they are.

Storytelling, therefore, becomes a significant means for these women to reconfigure the events of their lives and thereby discover and reclaim their self-identity. At the same time, as H. W. Wong argues, it also succeeds in articulating female and immigrant subjectivities, experience, and voice (10). As they tell their personal stories, 'articulat[ing] their silenced lives, [and] their otherwise voiceless positions in this society' (V. Chen 6), these women achieve 'a political voice', because these stories also define the reality of 'many displaced Asian women' living in America (Conard 81).

Chinese myths and folklore define the quest for identity in Tan's women characters. In *The Joy Luck Club*, she interweaves Ying-Ying's personal narrative with an inversion of the popular Chinese myth of the Moon Lady which has dominant patriarchal and woman-as-villain overtones. Though there are regional variations, the broad outline of the myth is thus: Chang O, a mortal woman, steals a magic peach (purported to be the elixir of immortality) given by the Queen Mother of the Western Skies to Hou Yi, Master Archer of the Skies, who is Chang O's husband. When her husband discovers the theft, he banishes Chang O to the moon, a cold, barren place, where she is forced to live in perpetual exile. On the night of the Moon Festival she is believed to grant secret wishes. According to some scholars, her exile is the consequence of her own impulsive and thoughtless theft of something which she had not the wisdom to handle (Knapp, 194–95). In the myth, Chang O berates her own wantonness and selfish desires, forever lamenting the husband she has lost, and meekly accepting her fate 'to stay lost on the moon, forever seeking her own selfish wishes' (*Joy* 81). Henceforward, known only as the Moon Lady, Chang O is stripped of her name and identity, deprived of her husband's love and esteem, fallen low even in her own self-estimation, because of her misdemeanour. 'For woman is yin,' she cries sadly, 'the darkness within, where untempered passions lie. And man is yang, bright truth lighting our minds' (*Joy* 81).

In the context of the novel, the Moon Lady may be seen as an extended metaphor for Ying-Ying, whose experience is, in turn, broadly representative of the other women in the text. Like Chang O, these women, too, are 'lost' and rendered partially impotent by traumatic events of the past. The lost-ness and sense of displacement are further amplified by the marginalising impact of their American experience. In the United States, unable to fit her into any category, Ying-Ying was declared 'a Displaced Person, lost in a sea of immigration categories'. Her given name, Gu Ying-Ying, was replaced by Betty St. Clair. Instead of 1914, the year of the Tiger, her birth year was listed as 1916, the year of the Dragon. Thus, 'with the sweep of a pen', Ying-Ying lost both her identity as well as a birth date that determines who she is and what she is destined to be, in Chinese cosmology (*Joy* 104).

In Tan's novel, however, unlike the Moon Lady myth, Ying-Ying's journey maps out a different ending. She refuses to remain lost but becomes instead an active agent of reclamation, reclaiming herself, and reclaiming her broken relationship with her daughter through the act of communicating and articulating her story. Finding voice through storytelling becomes a self-liberating and self-empowering experience for Ying-Ying. But it also functions as a potential agency of empowering others, namely, her own daughter, who, like her mother, is also lost, and who needs to be helped through motherly wisdom and advice.

Ying-Ying's journey to selfhood, therefore, as with the other women protagonists in the novel, is constantly being negotiated between the tales of the past and the experience of the present. It is only by revisiting the past through storytelling that the characters succeed in reinventing their lives in the present and charting out a new future for themselves and the younger generation. Thus, by juxtaposing Ying-Ying's story and that of the Moon Lady and by having her character's story end differently from the traditional one, Tan readapts the myth to script a new story. She gives space for her women characters to articulate their version of truth, and in the process, they discover their own voices.

CHAPTER SEVEN

FROM SILENCE TO VOICE: RESCRIPTING A NEW MYTHOS

The Kitchen God's Wife

> I watch them . . . remembering together, dreaming together . . . the walk up the mountain, that time they were so young, when they believed their lives lay ahead of them and all good things were still possible. And the water is just as they imagined, heavy as gold, sweet as rare flower seeds. . . . I can taste it too. I can feel it. Only a little amount and it is enough to remember – all the things you thought you had forgotten but were never forgotten, all the hopes that can still be found.
>
> (*The Kitchen God's Wife*, 526)

> I could see this lady statue in her new house, the red temple altar with two candlesticks lighting up her face from both sides. She would live there, but no one would call her Mrs Kitchen God. Why would she want to be called that, now that she and her husband are divorced?
>
> (*The Kitchen God's Wife*, 531)

In *The Kitchen God's Wife*, which is her second novel, Tan explores the theme of silence and women's 'journey(s) to voice' and self-articulation (Foster 74) through storytelling. Finding voice is imperative to self-expression and self-definition, an assertion which is made by Marie Booth Foster in her essay, 'Voice, Mind, Self' (1996). As in *The Joy Luck Club*, Tan's first novel, *The Kitchen God's Wife* also centres on the mother-daughter relationship and its inherent ambiguity. Tan, however, narrows the canvas down to a single pair – Winnie, the immigrant mother who is also the fictional version of Daisy, Tan's own mother, and her American-born daughter Pearl. The relationship between the two is marked by a sense of distance and tension, if not outright conflict. Reflecting on their relationship, Pearl opines:

> I see my mother sitting one table away, and I feel as lonely as I imagine her to be. I think of the enormous distance that separates us and makes us unable to share the most important matters of our life. How did this happen? (*Kitchen* 33)

This 'enormous distance' that divides mother and daughter is an off-shoot of two major factors, their cultural differences and the cult of silence and secrecy that shrouds their lives. As in *The Joy Luck Club*, differing cultural markers and nuances do play a role in generating misunderstandings between the American-bred Pearl and her immigrant mother. For years, Winnie would complain to Pearl about being the only one who helped take care of her old friend Grand Auntie Du, while the old lady's niece, Helen, seems to do comparatively little. Pearl responds by saying that her mother should stop complaining to her and talk to Helen instead, thereby cutting right into the heart of the matter. But when she said that her mother looked at her 'with a blank face and absolute silence', Pearl remarks, 'after that she did stop complaining to me. In fact, she stopped talking to me for about two months. And when we did start talking again, there was no mention of Grand Auntie Du ever again' (6).

To Pearl's American mind, this was 'a perfectly reasonable way to get . . . [her] mother to realise what was making her miserable so she could finally take positive action' (6). What she does not realise, however, is that Winnie's 'complaint' is actually an unstated expression of pride, a circumlocutory way of talking about her loyalty and service to a friend. As Patricia Hamilton notes, the miscommunication is a result of the daughter's inability to understand 'the cultural referents behind the mother's words'

(126). It is only when she becomes more receptive to the Chinese way of thinking and conversing, a by-product of listening to her mother's story, that Pearl gradually begins to understand both her own mother's culture as well as her own mother.

But this enormous gulf between Winnie and Pearl is also the cumulative result of years of silence and secrets kept from each other. Foster describes Winnie and Pearl as 'keepers of secrets' (80), both hiding behind a veil of silence that threatens to dislodge their relationship and intensify their sense of inner isolation and disconnect. Pearl's silence involves a physical sickness, concealing from her mother the fact that she suffers from multiple sclerosis. Winnie's secret pertains to her life in China and to a past ridden with pain and personal tragedies. Cosseted by her mother as a child, the young Winnie's world fell apart when her mother suddenly disappeared, never to be seen or heard of again. Soon after, she was uprooted from her home and sent away to the countryside to live with relatives so that her father may be spared the reminder of the scandal and of his disgraced wife. The incident left Winnie, or Weiwei, as she was then called, with an inerasable pain and a yawning void in her life, one that she could never really come to terms with: 'Even to this day,' she tells her daughter when she finally talks about her loss, 'I still feel I am waiting for her to come back and tell me why it was this way' (*Kitchen* 102). But Winnie's most closely guarded secret concerns her first marriage to Wen Fu, a sadist and child-batterer who systematically abuses her and makes her life a living nightmare. The marriage leaves her physically and emotionally broken, with painful memories of three dead children, and a living issue – Pearl – who, however, is completely unaware of this fact.

The dynamics of silence/voice, a crucial element in feminist discourse, functions as an underlying subtext in this novel. This discussion probes into the many ramifications of silence, its connotation, and consequences, in the characters' lives and in their quest for meaning and selfhood. Primarily, silence, in this context, may be read, both as a result as well as a symptom of the lack of meaningful communication between mother and daughter, jeopardising their present relationship with each other. As Pearl remarks: 'Whenever my mother talks to me, she begins the conversation as if we were already in the middle of an argument' (3). Remarking on this, Foster asserts that the 'talks to' should be replaced with 'talks with', if a nurturing bond is to be built between Winnie and Pearl (81). While 'talking to' is often one-sided, privileging speaker over listener, 'talking with' is indicative of an equal exchange between both, one that seems painfully missing from the mother-daughter interaction here. The following instance in the text augments this point. Referring to her illness, Pearl says:

> I meant to tell her. There were several times when I planned to do exactly that. When I was first diagnosed, I said, 'Ma, you know that slight problem with my leg I told you about. Well, thank God, it turned out not to be cancer, but—' And right away, she told me about a customer of hers who had just died of cancer, how long he had suffered, how many wreaths the family had ordered. (26)

The above example is one of many, revealing the faulty communication line between the two, and the inability to really listen to one another. At the same time, it reinforces the argument that, without being 'listened to', articulation becomes a meaningless and futile effort, snuffing out the potential for interpersonal interaction and invalidating one's self-utterance, resulting in further silence: 'A voice is not a voice unless there is someone there to hear it' (Foster 75). And as Heather de Geest points out, prolonged 'preservation of silence leads to the loss of a voice and of a self for many individuals' (5). Pearl's inability to make herself heard, and Winnie's inability to hear, not only impairs the relationship between them but also negates the very essence of self-expression and self-legitimacy. Pearl must find a way to break the silence and be heard if she is to attain agency and recognition and meaningfully communicate with her mother. This is best achieved through storytelling because unlike in everyday, off-hand conversations, stories are generally told in an ambience where both speaker and listener(s) are prepared and attuned to listen and pay attention to one another. It is only when the two of them eventually engage in mutual talk-storytelling and listening, as they sit opposite each other in the intimacy of the kitchen table, that Pearl is finally able to disclose her secret to her mother; a telling that knits the two closer and forges a new bond between them.

But there are other factors responsible for the characters' long maintenance of silence and secrecy about their respective past and present situations. For Pearl, the wish to 'forget' and obliterate from constant consciousness a sickness that threatens to eat away the normalcy of life is one of the reasons for the non-disclosure:

> I did not want to be coddled by casseroles. . . . Kindness was a reminder that my life had changed, was always changing, that people thought I should just accept all this and become strong or brave, more enlightened, more peaceful. I wanted nothing to do with that. Instead, I wanted to live my life with the same focus as most people. . . . I wanted what had become impossible: I wanted to forget. (23)

Silence/refusal to talk about the stress-inducing reality becomes, in this context, a strategy for self-protection, blocking out all unwanted and anxiety-arousing thoughts and emotions. Described as 'motivated forgetting/ suppression' in psychological terminology, this strategy is widely recognised as one of the coping mechanisms in disease/stress-related situations. Aversion to talking about the disease partially accounts for Pearl's silence and subsequent distancing of herself from her mother, so that she rarely calls or visits though they live only a few miles apart because, 'Whenever I'm with my mother,' she says, 'I feel as though I have to spend the whole time avoiding land mines' (*Kitchen* 9). Like Pearl, Winnie too tries to deal with the pain of her past by refusing to talk about it, believing that somehow, 'not talking' makes the unpalatable truth less real. Therefore, just as Pearl tries to 'forget' her sickness by remaining silent about it, Winnie also attempts to 'forget' her painful past by obliterating it from her mind and her conversations. When Pearl asks her why she had never told her about her mother's disappearance before, Winnie answers, 'That's because I never wanted to believe it myself. So maybe that's why I did not tell you about her' (102). Similarly, silence regarding her marital history and Pearl's real parentage stems from the attempt to forget a chapter in her life that has deeply eroded her sense of self-esteem and self-worth. In this context, therefore, silence is employed as a self-protective mechanism, at the expense, however, of their relationship.

But Winnie's reasons for not divulging certain facts about her life to her own daughter go deeper than the mere wish to forget. In this novel, Tan explores the multilayered causes that are complicit in a person's silence. When the deeply disturbing story about her mother's first marriage is finally told to her, Pearl wonders why the truth was never disclosed to her before. Winnie's answer is, 'Because then you would know . . . how weak I was. You would think I was a bad mother' (510). Nanette Burton Mongelluzzo asserts that people consciously keep secrets about themselves due to shame, or perhaps guilt. We don't want others to know everything about us for fear of being judged, harmed, ridiculed, embarrassed, or even exiled in some fashion. Winnie's desire to be perceived as a good mother and a strong woman in her daughter's eyes leads her to hide a past which, she feels, reflects her vulnerability, little realising that the secret serves only to distance her from Pearl who often finds certain aspects of her mother's behaviour odd and inexplicably erratic. It is only after hearing her mother's tragic history through Winnie's storytelling that Pearl is able to empathise with her mother and understand her better. The knowledge that Winnie went through so much suffering and humiliation and yet comes out fighting makes Pearl see her with a new sense of respect, thereby validating her mother's experience and rekindling their connection and bond. As Helen, Winnie's friend says of the two, after their mutual disclosure to each other, 'Now you are closer, mother and daughter, I can already see this' (*Kitchen* 524).

At the same time, this atmosphere of closeness and shared confidences induced by Winnie's talk-story encourages Pearl to open up and talk about her own illness and fear. The act of voicing negative, pent-up emotions becomes a liberating experience and proves cathartic for Pearl. It enables her to come to terms with the disease and confront it in a more lucid manner, so that instead of denial, she now applies herself pro-actively to thinking how to deal with it. Moreover, the fact of being able to share the burden with her mother becomes a strengthening experience, binding the two closer and giving her a deep sense of comfort and assurance that she is not alone in this fight: 'She was tearing it away – my protective shell, my anger, my deepest fears, my despair. She was putting all this into her own heart, so that I could finally see what was left. Hope' (515).

Silence, in its negative aspect, can also be the result of terrible oppression and victimisation. According to Bella Adams, '[t]he brute fact of suffering' resists 'easy telling', thereby, pushing a person 'towards silence, not speech' (2005, 76). Winnie's ordeal with her first husband, Wen Fu, is so traumatic that she cannot even begin to articulate the experience either to herself or to her own daughter. It is only when Helen threatens to disclose the secret to Pearl that Winnie decides to tell her story, opening up thus an opportunity for Pearl to reveal hers. It is important to note here that the move to break silence is initiated not by Winnie but by Helen, Winnie's long-time friend who had witnessed her sufferings in China. Commenting on the role and importance of a network of strong female affiliations as fundamental in women's journey to self-discovery, Rita Felski notes that 'encounters with other women' almost always 'form(s) a part of the discovery process' (135). Thus, for Winnie as well as for Pearl, the journey to voice and, subsequently, rediscovery of themselves and of each other, is negotiated not in isolation, but through a network of female support and mediation.

Storytelling/revealing secrets becomes the means by which both women break their silence and embark on a journey towards voice and self-validation. What is noted here is that though Winnie's account is a private and personal history, in the telling, she also succeeds in evoking the history of an entire generation, particularly, 'the many privations and humiliations borne by the unseen and unheard victims', especially 'those who were female – in China's recent history' (Gillespie 34), marked both by war and patriarchy. Within the framework of her story, the untold narratives of other men and women, victims of war, and patriarchy are given space and hearing. In this sense, therefore, storytelling goes beyond the province of individual self-articulation by allowing the otherwise muted, collective voice of those who are caught in the same reality to be heard as well. This reiterates Minh-ha's argument that nothing is ever strictly private, because in many instances, 'the private is political' (37).

As in *The Joy Luck Club*, storytelling here occurs via the oral framework. In this novel, talk-story functions not only as a stylistic device but to effect certain ends. First, because it is a highly personal, reciprocal, and face-to-face encounter, talk-stories allow both speaker and audience to interact, explain, and corroborate issues at any given point in the narration, thereby, opening up space for meaningful dialogue and clarification. This is extremely important because Winnie's primary purpose in telling her story is to make her daughter understand not only what happened, but rather, 'why it happened, how it could not be any other way' (*Kitchen* 100). The talk-story is aptly conducive for this purpose. Second, talk-story is ideal in Winnie's situation because it allows her to speak out her pain and anger, providing an outlet for all the negative emotions and hurts of the past. H. W. Wong argues that in this novel, talk-story is more than just breaking silence. It is, in fact, a 'talking-cure', having 'a therapeutic effect' which is brought on by 'talking' about things . . . intentionally or unintentionally' forgotten (226). As Winnie tells her story, she is, in a sense, effecting her own emotional healing and bringing closure to the past, a past which, however, must be retraversed if she is to experience a sense of release and self-liberation. It is a testimony to Winnie's courage and strength, therefore, that she can ultimately revisit history by articulating her story to her daughter, even though doing so entails pain.

Rememory, a term coined by Toni Morrison to define the process of reliving past realities through memory, is one of the dominant motifs in Tan's work and is crucial to the characters' rehabilitation and rediscovery of self. It is a dynamic activity because it entails the unlocking of memories, long-buried or forgotten. 'These images brought back serve to heal the suffering brought on through past experiences' ('Rememory'). For Tan's women characters, rememory occurs through the process of storytelling, the unburdening of secrets, which, in many instances, unfolds a narrative of pain and loss. As they articulate the past through review and remembrance, it enables them to come to terms with what had happened and thereby find closure and healing. Tan writes in *The Opposite of Fate*: 'I wrote of pain that reaches from the past, how it can grab you, how it can also heal itself like a broken bone.' For that healing to happen, however, one has 'to dig them out, break them into pieces, then put them back together' (96–97).

As these characters introspect on the past, they become aware of their own courage and inner resources. This serves to instil in them a new sense of power, confidence, and hope for the future. What were once stories of oppression and hopelessness are now transformed, through the telling, into narratives of hope and personal empowerment. In the process, they rediscover and reclaim their lost/displaced selves. Storytelling, therefore, becomes a locus where past events converge with the present moment and opens up the potential for scripting new stories of hope and possibilities in the future. As Pearl reflects, after hearing Winnie's story, it is in the stories of the past, 'all the things you thought you had forgotten but were never forgotten', that wisdom for the present, and 'hopes' for the future, 'can still be found' (*Kitchen* 526). Storytelling, in this sense, functions as a bridge connecting the characters' past with the present and the future.

Another important dimension in this novel that cannot be overlooked is Tan's employment, or rather, manipulation of the traditional Chinese myth of the Kitchen God to create a new mythos, one that better defines the experience and reality of her women characters. The Kitchen God is a popular deity in Chinese culture, and his altar adorns almost each and every Chinese kitchen. In *The Kitchen God's Wife*, the altar of the Kitchen God was given as a gift to Pearl by Auntie Du before the old lady's death.

According to tradition, the Kitchen God was an ordinary mortal named Zhang whose fortune increased greatly through the industry and hard work of his wife Guo. Not satisfied with her, however, Zhang brought home a pretty woman who, together with him, mistreated Guo and eventually chased her out, leaving them to revel in the riches that Guo had made. After a few years of luxurious living, Zhang's fortune disappeared, his concubine left him, and he became a homeless wanderer begging from door to door. On one such occasion, his hunger was so great that he fainted. On recovering, he discovered himself in a warm and clean kitchen. Wanting to thank the mistress of the house for taking him in, Zhang was mortified to realise that it was none other than his first wife Guo. In shame and confusion, and in an attempt to hide from her, he accidentally jumped into the fireplace and was reduced to ashes in spite of Guo's attempt to save him. In heaven, the Jade Emperor who heard his story rewards Zhang's penitence by making him the Kitchen God to watch over the behaviour of people. Once a year, before the New Year, he was allowed to go to heaven and present his report on the doings of the mortals below, who, based on his report, are then rewarded, or punished, accordingly. In Chinese belief, the Kitchen God is thus one who determines people's fortunes throughout the year and must be placated with gifts and bribes. Ironically, however, his wife is denied a place in the Chinese pantheon of deities, even though she is 'the good one not him' (*Kitchen* 62).

The gender bias and androcentric slant of the myth is clearly obvious and is used by Tan to critique and highlight the suppression of women's voices and their dispossession in a male-dominated society. But Tan does not stop here. Rather, she exploits the myth of the Kitchen God to formulate a 'counter-myth' (Godard 170) – the Kitchen God's wife – to give voice to the untold, unheard stories of women like Winnie and Guo, whose version of truth had not been allowed fair hearing.

Parallels may be drawn between Winnie and the Kitchen God's wife. Like Guo, Winnie's story is one of abuse and oppression. Victimised by her husband, Winnie was further vilified by a society that punishes her with a jail sentence for daring to leave her husband and escape an abusive marriage. Wen Fu, on the other hand, went scot-free, portrayed in the tabloid as a war hero, the victim in the drama, deserted by a wife who is 'crazy for American sex' (*Kitchen* 478). Remarking on the similarities of her situation with that of the Kitchen God's wife, Winnie states:

> And when Jesus suffered, everyone worshipped him. Nobody worshipped me for living with Wen Fu. I was like that wife of Kitchen God. Nobody worshipped her either. He got all the excuses. He got all the credit. She was forgotten. (322)

This statement draws attention to a disturbing truth that surfaces in the narrative, namely, the complicity of society in the oppression and victimisation of women. Judith Caesar notes:

> Weili's victimization couldn't have taken place if Chinese society had not condoned it to such an extent that even her best friends didn't want to blemish their reputations by helping her escape – at least until the very end of the novel. (38)

Moreover, as Tan implies, this is an inevitable outcome of the values and ideologies of the society which are, in turn, shaped and patterned by its prevailing myths and lore. In her study on women and myth, Barbara Godard notes that 'the myths which have been dominant over the last few centuries are androcentric and have been overwhelming instruments in suppressing women' (171). It is imperative, therefore, to rescript new mythologies to replace the existing ones, a challenge and responsibility that Tan seriously and successfully undertakes in this novel, and in the corpus of her writing. In this regard, she shows herself conversant with the arguments of other feminist writers and critics such as Estelle Lauter who calls for a 'mythological change' (vii), to reframe the female experience, one that is 'untainted by patriarchy' (8).

In this text, Tan's rejection of the existing Chinese myth in favour of a new one is represented by Winnie's action of rejecting the Kitchen God in favour of his wife, because in her estimation, '(h)is wife was the good one, not him' (*Kitchen* 62). As Winnie gives Auntie Du's altar to Pearl, she consciously replaces the statue of the Kitchen God with the figure of a female goddess, that has no name and that has lain forgotten in the back quarters of a shop. She gives her a new name – 'Lady Sorrowfree, happiness winning over bitterness, no regrets in this world' (532).

It is important to observe that though Winnie's past history strongly parallels the myth of the Kitchen God's wife, there are marked departures in their stories. Unlike Guo, the silenced wife, who cannot speak up for herself because the patriarchal narrative assigns no space for her to do so, Winnie succeeds in reasserting herself and redeeming her voice through storytelling. As she articulates her story, she is not only reclaiming a personal self and voice, but also the lost history of Guo and others like her. It is interesting to note that unlike the Kitchen God who sits and judges and must be regularly appeased, the new icon, Lady Sorrowfree, is presented as a benevolent, understanding, and approachable figure, one who speaks and empower others to speak:

> But her smile is genuine, wise and innocent at the same time. And her hand, see how she just raised it? That means she is about to speak, or maybe she is telling you to speak. She is ready to listen. She understands English. You should tell her everything. (531)

In *The Kitchen God's Wife*, as in all of Tan's other novels, storytelling functions as a crucial media for creating bonds between characters and bridging the multilayered divides that their situations present. Both Winnie and Pearl are characters trapped in their self-imposed silence, a silence brought about by multiple factors, and one that thwarts their individual self-definition and distance them from each other. It is only as they break silence and discover voice through storytelling/disclosing personal truths to each other that they are individually liberated from the prison of fear, pain, and isolation that characterised their lives. In the process, they draw closer to one another. As the past is rescrutinised through the telling, it brings healing for both women. But it also unlocks, for the younger generation, a sense of history, culture, and ancestry, one that was in danger of being lost or forgotten in the buried annals of the past. Thus, Winnie's journey to selfhood, as that of Pearl's, is an odyssey travelled from silence to voice.

CHAPTER EIGHT

MY SISTER! THE TELLER OF STORIES
A Hundred Secret Senses

Through years of dream-life, I've tasted cold ash falling on a steamy night. I've seen a thousand spears flashing like flames on the crest of a hill. I've touched the tiny grains of a stone wall while waiting to be killed. I've smelled my own musky fear as the rope tightens around my neck. I've felt the heaviness of flying through weightless air. I've heard the sucking creak of my voice just before life snaps to an end.

(*The Hundred Secret Senses*, 31)

In *The Hundred Secret Senses*, Tan continues to develop her recurrent theme, which is, the exploration of the woman-to-woman relationship, and to show how this relationship is at the heart of female self/identity formation. Unlike her other novels, however, Tan moves the spotlight away from the mother-daughter dyad to focus on yet another element of the female relational model, which is, sisterhood. This text deals with the uneasy and problematic relationship between a Chinese immigrant woman, Kwan Li, and her American half-sister Olivia, who is twelve years her junior. The child of a Chinese immigrant man and his first wife, Kwan's existence came as a surprise to her father's American family who were oblivious of his earlier life and family back in China. Wracked by guilt at abandoning his first family, just before his death, Kwan's father expresses the wish that she be brought to America so that she can be reunited with her other three siblings born from his Caucasian wife. Thus, at the age of 18, Kwan finds herself unexpectedly transplanted in a new country, with a new life and a new family.

Interestingly, the theme of sibling reunion is one that keeps surfacing in most of Tan's work, albeit, under the overarching frame of the mother-daughter narrative. In *The Joy Luck Club*, June Woo's discovery of her Chinese identity is inextricably linked to her reunion with her long lost twin sisters from her mother's earlier marriage in China. In *The Kitchen God's Wife*, Pearl's eventual sense of wholeness and completeness stems, in part, from acknowledging and accepting as part of herself the long-dead siblings of her mother's story. This is suggested by the fact that the identity of the new icon of hope and healing, chosen by Winnie and Pearl for themselves, embodies the names of the three dead siblings: Sorrowfree, which is the name of the first child; Happiness Winning over Bitterness, from the name of the second daughter; and No Regrets in this World, the name of the third child (*Kitchen* 532). The significance of sibling relationship, particularly between sisters, as a facilitating agency to a better understanding of one's self and one's identity is a point that finds its genesis in Tan's own history. In 1987, Tan travelled to China and visited her three half-sisters from her mother's first marriage, for the first time. The reunion 'created an instant family bond that changed her outlook. As the warring sides of her ethnicity made peace, she felt complete for the first time' (Snodgrass 15). This theme, only partially developed in her previous novels, finds full expression in *The Hundred Secret Senses*.

However, in the attempt to position all of Tan's work within the matrilineal tradition, most Tan scholars, such as Tammy Conard and Lisa Dunick, among others, tend to under-emphasise the sisterhood theme in the novel. The Kwan-Olivia relationship is, therefore, also placed within the mother-daughter paradigm. This line of reasoning argues that Kwan functions more as a surrogate mother rather than as sister to Olivia, an argument based on Olivia's own account of the relationship. Recalling her childhood, she says:

When my teacher called Mom to say I was running a fever, it was Kwan who showed up at the nurse's office to take me home. When I fell while roller-skating, Kwan bandaged my elbows. She braided my hair. . . . She tried to teach me to sing Chinese nursery songs. She soothed me when I lost a tooth. She ran the washcloth over my neck while I took my bath. (*Hundred* 12)

Rather than being grateful to Kwan, however, Olivia realises with mixed feelings that most of the time, she resents her for taking her 'mother's place' (12).

However, to read the novel solely as a matrilineal narrative is to unfairly limit the scope and intent of Tan's work. While matrilineal overtones do surface in the text, the relationship in this novel is best understood through the lens of sisterhood and its built-in constraints and ties. Situating the text thus is highly pertinent: first, it reveals Tan's awareness of evolving trends and development within feminist studies, particularly, second-wave feminism, which shows a marked shift from matriliny to sisterhood:

With its possibilities of mutuality, the paradigm of sisterhood has the advantage of freeing women from the biological function of giving birth, but still offers a specifically feminine relational model. (Yu 143)

Second, it widens the parameters of Tan's fictional world and shows her openness to explore the complex and multinuanced world of female relationships without allowing herself to be frozen or typecast into a single mould.

Su-lin Yu, whose study of Tan's *The Hundred Secret Senses* reads it as a sisterhood text, notes that the movement from matriliny to sisterhood is very much a part of the evolving feminist discourse. According to her, the construction of 'sisterhood' as an independent discourse stems from 'the feminist desire to separate from the maternal discourse' (143). Furthermore, this relationship is seen as offering wider scope and possibilities for the development of a sense of self in women because it is a relationship 'between female equals' (Downing 20). The sense of equivalence that defines this relationship allows more space and freedom for individual 'differences' between women to be 'constructed, displayed and negotiated' (Yu 146), without the undue constraints that marks other, and more, hierarchical relationships. In his essay 'On Narcissism' (1914), Freud contends that in the mother-daughter dynamic, for instance, there is lesser scope for the daughter's individuation and sense of self to emerge because of the child's over-identification with her mother, at least in the early stages. Differences are suppressed, therefore, rather than negotiated. This, according to Adrienne Rich, is because in every woman, there is always a 'girl-child' who longs for a mother's 'nurture, tenderness, and approval' (184–5). In the process, however, she risks submerging her own individuality and personality.

While Freud's assertions are debatable and have been contested by writers such as Nancy Chodorow, who argues that the relationship which a woman shares with her mother continues to exert a profound influence upon her all through her adult life and shapes her 'creation and experience of self' (1978, xii), what clearly emerges here is that motherhood is not and cannot be the sole model to define female experience and development. Sibling relationship, particularly the sister or sororal bond, is as crucial to female self-development as the maternal one. In the sibling dynamic, differences are recognised and negotiated rather than resisted, thereby allowing room for each other's individuality and identity to form and emerge. What may be seen in Tan's work, therefore, is that both the maternal and the sororal bond play an indispensible role in defining a woman's journey to selfhood and identity.

In this, her third novel, Tan depicts the relationship, or rather, the difficult journey towards bonding and closeness that defines her two female protagonists, Olivia and Kwan, and shows how this is crucial to the women's realisation and discovery of themselves. To begin with, the relationship between the two is fraught with tension and is a one-sided affair. It is characterised by fierce love and devotion on Kwan's side, while Olivia's feelings for Kwan verges between toleration, irritation, and even resentment. In Olivia's perspective, her antipathy towards Kwan begins in childhood and is attributed to both generic as well as specific factors. Like in most sibling-rivalry situations, Olivia feels threatened by the arrival of a new sister into the familial scene. Already starved of maternal attention, the young Olivia sees Kwan as a competitor for her mother's 'divided attention' and 'meagre souvenirs' of love (*Hundred* 8). The situation is rendered even more complex, however, by Kwan's apparent strangeness and peculiarity. In fact, Olivia, who is the central narrative voice in the novel, begins by highlighting this particular aspect about her half-sister:

> My sister Kwan believes she has yin eyes. She sees those who have died and now dwell in the world of Yin, ghosts who leave the mists just to visit her kitchen on Balboa Street in San Francisco. (3)

Further on, the reader is told that Kwan not only converses with ghosts and seeks their advice on a regular basis, but she also believes in past lives and existence. One of the most impelling evidence of Kwan's eccentricity, according to Olivia, is her apparent belief in the truth of the tales that she tells Olivia. These tales, which are episodic and interspersed throughout the narrative, concerns Kwan's past life in China as well as in her other previous existences. Of all the stories, the most recurring, however, concerns her previous life in mid-nineteenth century China during the time of the Taiping Rebellion. In the story, Kwan is a one-eyed Hakka girl named Nunumu, serving as a maid in an English mission compound in Changmian, China. She forms a close friendship with Nelly Banner, an American woman who gave herself to the wrong man and eventually lost her true love, the half-breed Yiban Johnson. The account ends with the death of the two women at the hands of Manchu soldiers. In Kwan's belief, Olivia is the reincarnation of Miss Banner to whom she has pledged love and loyalty. Her excessive devotion to Olivia in their present lifetime is, for her, a fulfilment of her promise made in the past. Kwan's stories, therefore, provide a linkage between the remote past and the immediate present.

As the narrative progresses, however, the reader is made aware that the tension between the sisters goes beyond the personal issue of Kwan's so-called oddity. The text, in fact, sets up a tension between hugely differing worldviews: Western empiricism and rationalism, as opposed to Eastern mysticism with its thrust on intuition, subjective knowledge, and extraempirical experience. Roland Walter contends that in the Western worldview, truth is always equated with verifiable facts and data; and imagination, with falsehood (4). Confronted with Kwan's fantastical tales, Olivia declares, 'I'm not Chinese like Kwan. To me, yin isn't yang, and yang isn't yin. I can't accept two contradictory stories as the whole truth' (*Hundred* 277). Kwan's stories of and belief in the paranormal is clearly at odds with Olivia's empirically trained Western mind and contributes, in part, to their incompatibility and conflict. In the American set-up, therefore, Kwan's unusual gift is viewed as a psychological aberration, one that merits a mental asylum. When the 7-year-old Olivia mentions to her family that Kwan sees ghosts, Kwan was immediately packed off to a mental hospital where she was diagnosed as catatonic and given electroshock treatment in an attempt to cure her of her 'Chinese ghosts' (17). This episode is extremely revealing, as well as symbolic, because it also exposes the power-play at work between cultures, and contradictory worldviews and mindsets. As Ken-Fang Lee observes, 'the dominant discourse' will always try to silence or 'suppress different values or ways of thinking' that does not fit in with its own, 'in order to consolidate its supreme authority' (118). In Tan's novel, however, the minority voice, represented by Kwan and her stories, comes to the fore in this power struggle, as characterised by Kwan's resilience and unquenchable spirit: 'They do this to me, hah, still I don't change. See? I stay strong' (*Hundred* 18).

It is interesting to note that, at this point in the narrative, Kwan's storytelling seems to widen the rift between the sisters instead of bridging it. What are for Kwan accounts of a past that she perceives as true are for Olivia mere figments of her sister's delusional imagination. The different ways they react to these stories highlight their cultural differences and pulls Olivia further away from Kwan. Recalling her childhood, Olivia remarks, '(e)very night, she'd tell me these stories. And I would lie there silently, helplessly, wishing she'd shut up' (32). Critic Ruth Pavey made the same point when she asserts that for Olivia, 'Kwan's stories have always represented a strain', because they threaten to pull her away from the sane, safe, world of 'her own reality', back to her father's culture with its element of the unfamiliar and unknown (38). Thus, Olivia resists Kwan's stories and, by extension, Kwan herself, because at this point in her life, she is not yet ready/willing to open herself to other possibilities and realities other than her own. According to Ben Xu, in storytelling, timing is extremely crucial if the stories are to have any significance and meaning. Reflecting on the Joy Luck Club daughters, who, like Olivia, refuse to accept their mothers' stories initially, Xu notes that it is only 'after their own sufferings in life' that the daughters become more receptive to 'the humble wisdom' and truth of their mothers' stories (15). It is only later, as she matures, and after a series of events that unfold during her visit to China, that Olivia, too, comes to accept and acknowledge Kwan's stories. In so doing, she comes closer to a better understanding of herself and recovers her relationship with her sister. This is symbolised by her eventual adoption of Kwan's matronym, Li, as the identity she chooses both for herself and her daughter Samantha, born nine months after the China trip.

But there are other deeper issues behind Olivia's initial discounting of Kwan and her stories. At the beginning of the narrative, Olivia states:

> But just to set the genetic record straight, Kwan and I share a father, *only that*. She was born in China. My brothers, Kevin and Tommy, and I were born in San Francisco after my father, Jack Yee, immigrated here and married our mother, Louise Kenfield. (emphasis added, *Hundred* 3)

Olivia's obvious desire to distance herself from Kwan clearly points to her own aversion and resistance to the idea of China, and simultaneously, her own Chinese heritage and ancestry. In repudiating her relationship with Kwan, the American-born Olivia is, in a sense, rejecting the Chinese part of her being. This leads to a deep sense of divide and fragmented identity. At one point, in a bid to recover her identity, Olivia briefly toys with the idea of reverting back to her father's name. The Chinese-ness of the patronym, however, repels her: 'Olivia Yee. I say the name aloud several times. It sounds alien, as though I'd become totally Chinese, just like Kwan. That bothers me a little' (174). For Olivia, China, represented by Kwan, stands for something totally 'alien' and incomprehensible, the 'threatening Other from the East' (Yu 149) that must be resisted at all costs if she is to maintain her place in the dominant culture. According to Wendy Ho, the mainstream/ Eurocentric stereotypes of Asians, which tend towards the negative and derogatory, have seriously impaired the way younger generations of Asian-American read their immigrant parents and their own ethnic communities (165). In this text, for instance, Olivia's two brothers, and even Olivia initially, preferred to take the Italian-American name of their stepfather, Laguni (even though it is just a given name for foundlings), rather than their own Chinese name of Yee, because of the stigma attached to being Chinese, or the 'dumb Chink' (*Hundred* 12).

In this novel, as in all her other novels, Tan, like other Asian-American writers, critiques the denigrating impact of Western stereotypes upon the immigrant consciousness, particularly that of the Chinese woman. In her famous work, *Between Worlds* (1990), Amy Ling notes that the Western perception of the Chinese woman is limited to two common stereotypes: she is either the 'shy Lotus Blossom' or the aggressive 'Dragon Lady' (12). This limiting stereotype, in part, accounts for Olivia's condescending and blinkered perception of Kwan. Before Kwan's arrival, both Olivia and the family had envisioned Kwan as 'a Chinese Cinderella', a 'starving waif', 'shy' and 'skinny as a beanpole', in need of rescue by her American family (*Hundred* 7, 10). The chubby and effervescent girl that greeted them at the airport, however, completely debunks the stereotype, adding to their discomfiture and quashing their imagined role of Western saviour to third-world beneficiary. It is only later, in adulthood, as she learns to relate to her sister, that Olivia realises that, in fact, Kwan is just 'like anyone else, standing in line, shopping for bargains, counting success in small change' (21). The creation of a character like Kwan may be seen as Tan's way of contesting and breaking the myth of the Asian woman stereotype. Thus, Olivia's initial resistance to, and depreciation of, her Chinese heritage may be attributed to her having imbibed and internalised Western mindsets and negative stereotyping of the East. This is a conspicuous feature that defines almost all of Tan's Amerasian protagonists, particularly, the American-assimilated daughters in her novels.

Apart from the factors already discussed, this discussion traces the link between Olivia's inability/unwillingness to identify herself with her Chinese roots, to the fact that her Chinese lineage comes through the father, rather than the mother. The significant role that a mother figure plays in the awakening and formation of women's cultural consciousness has long been recognised by many female Asian-descent writers. In her essay, '*Daughter-Text/Mother-Text*' (1993), Marina Heung asserts that the mother is a 'potent symbol of ethnic identity' (20). On the same note, Shirley Lim also concurs that the mother is a 'figure not only of maternality but also of racial consciousness' (293). Based on these assumptions, it may be argued that in this context, Olivia's lack of cultural pride and identity (in particular, Chinese) stems from her mother's lack of it. Unlike the other mothers in Tan's work, Olivia's mother is non-Chinese and has no real connection with the culture, except for her brief marriage to a Chinese man. Describing herself as 'American mixed grill, a bit of everything' (*Hundred* 3), Louise Kenfield is a self-professed multiculturalist with no specific ties to any one culture. This multicultural facade, as displayed by her succession of multiracial husbands and love affairs, however, masks a deep sense of rootlessness and cultural insecurity. With no clear sense of roots, or of belonging anywhere, Louise is clearly, an inadequate model for her daughter. Therefore, Olivia's estrangement from her familial and racial heritage is one that leads to a severe crisis of identity.

It is interesting to note that, initially, Olivia blames her identity crisis on Kwan, the eternal scapegoat, rather than on herself, or her own mother. She remarks: 'Being forced to grow up with Kwan was probably one of the reasons I never knew who I was or wanted to become' (174). It is only later, as she re-evaluates herself and the events of her life, after Kwan's disappearance, that Olivia realises the falsity of her presumptions. She discovers that, all along, it is Kwan, who, through stories, seeks to open her mind to new experiences and to a more comprehensive understanding of the vastness and mystery of human reality. Whether Kwan's stories of reincarnation are true or just a projection of the human desire for immortality is not the focus here but, rather, the construction of meaning(s) behind the stories. As she retrospects on the stories, Olivia remarks, 'I think Kwan intended to show me the world is not a place but the vastness of the soul' (399), teaching her important life-lessons that 'life repeats itself, that our hopes endure, that we get another chance. . . What's so terrible about that?' (361). As Christine Downing notes, Kwan is the unconscious guide in Olivia's journey to self, psyche, and towards an increased consciousness of roots and ethnic identity (qtd. in Yu 147). Thus, what Olivia lacks in her own mother is made up for, to a certain extent, by the presence of Kwan, the sister/mother figure in her life. It is Kwan, who, through stories, challenges her assumptions of truth and reality and enlarges her perceptions about life and self, while also seeking to regenerate in Olivia, an appreciation for, and knowledge of, the Chinese heritage.

An important element of Chinese culture that Kwan imparts to Olivia through storytelling is language, particularly, the Chinese Mandarin dialect. Interestingly, while in their day-to-day transaction, Kwan would communicate with Olivia in Pidgin English, Mandarin is the language she reverts to, to articulate her secret tales and personal lore. Though not perfect in the language, Olivia recalls that in her childhood, 'Kwan would jabber away in Chinese', whenever she told her stories:

> That's how I became the only one in our family who learned Chinese. Kwan infected me with it. I absorbed her language through my pores while I was sleeping. She pushed her Chinese secrets into my brain and changed how I thought about the world. Soon I was even having nightmares in Chinese. (*Hundred* 13)

The role of language as an important cultural marker that facilitates the production of cultural identity has been acknowledged by many social psychologists and writers. Joshua Fishman asserts that language, though not the sole component, is nevertheless a strong 'symbol of ethnic identity' (144), facilitating 'identity formation, maintenance and transformation' (Berquist 64). Kwan tells Olivia that speaking in '[m]andarin lets me think like a Chinese person' (359). The relatedness of language and identity is clearly alluded to in this statement. Therefore, by using a Chinese dialect to tell her stories, Kwan is not only maintaining her own ethnic identity and ethos but also succeeds in imparting something of that culture to Olivia. At the same time, this shared language, described by Olivia as 'our secret language of Chinese' (*Hundred* 13) becomes a mean of bonding for the sisters, albeit, reluctantly, on Olivia's part.

As in most of Tan's novels, Kwan's stories are told through the talk-story mode. This is extremely important because it reflects the Chinese heritage and tradition that Kwan comes from. At the same time, it is deeply reflective of the diasporic tendency to cling to one's own cultural expressions and identity in the midst of cultural dislocation. As Vijay Agnew asserts in his book, *Diaspora, Memory, and Identity* (2005), diasporic individuals, severed from their roots, are often attached to various 'symbols of their ethnicity' (14), because these represent the familiar and comfortable in an otherwise new and alien milieu. Like the other immigrants in Tan's fiction, Kwan's experience in the new country is one of ambivalence. The relative comfort of life in America is simultaneously off-set by a sense of alienation and displacement. But Kwan's otherness is more pronounced than that of Tan's other immigrant characters because she is perceived as such, both by mainstream society as well as by her family. Olivia remarks, 'In so many ways, Kwan never fit into our family', before adding that time did nothing 'to Americanise' her either (*Hundred* 22). Kwan's talk-stories, which may be read as a potent 'symbol' of her ethnicity and told in her own language, provide her with a sense of comfort, because it invokes memories of '*laojia*' or 'home' (Laurence Ma 32), and, therefore, serve to mitigate an otherwise, intolerable situation. At the same time, these tales of the past, laced with personal and cultural memory, reinforce her cultural identity in the present context of displacement that she finds herself in. As bell hooks notes, 'memories of the traditional' are important, 'for they "illuminate and transform the present"' (1991, 147). Thus, storytelling becomes a strategy of helping Kwan negotiate with the contradictions and paradoxes of the American present.

In these narratives, Kwan's personal past(s), whether as Nunumu in a previous existence, or of her childhood in Changmian in the present one, is enmeshed with the historical past of China, particularly, the Taiping Rebellion during the mid-nineteenth century which was quelled by the Ching Manchus, the last ruling dynasty of imperial China. As she shares these stories with Olivia, Kwan is, in a sense, retrieving not only her own past but also the historical past of her country and ancestral homeland. Retrieval of the past, both personal and national, through storytelling, is a dominant theme in Tan's work. Her first two novels both trace eventful periods in China's history, such as the Japanese occupation during the 1930s and the 1940s, the Rape of Nanking in 1937, and the internal civil wars, which form the backdrop of her characters' early lives in China. The role of stories as an act of cultural and historical transmission is also explored by Bella Adams in her essay 'Representing History in Amy Tan's The Kitchen God's Wife' (2003). Through the telling, Kwan reintroduces Olivia to her own culture and tradition and reconnects her with the history of a country that she has not learnt to claim as her own. Thus, storytelling, in Tan's fiction, addresses the gap in knowledge between 'what was' and 'what is'.

As a result of these stories, Olivia comes to know more about Kwan and her life, marking the first step in their journey to bonding and closeness. At the same time, it brings her into touch with the history of the country from which she draws, at least, part, of her origin and being.

According to Sheng-mei Ma, however, it is not only China's historical past that is invoked in *The Hundred Secret Senses*, but 'the social history of the United States', as well, 'a history which constructs the American identity' (113). When Olivia and Simon renovated their newly purchased home in the Pacific Heights area of San Francisco, she unerringly identifies layers of paint she strips from the wall, with different periods of American social history:

> First to peel off was a yuppie skin of Chardonnay-colored latex . . . followed by flaky crusts of the preceding decades – eighties money green, seventies psychedelic orange, sixties hippie black, fifties baby pastels. (*Hundred* 132)

This recital of America's cultural history by Olivia is juxtaposed with Kwan's narrative of China's imperial past, a significant juxtaposition because it reflects the bicultural status of the protagonists. What Tan, along with other Chinese Americans, constantly affirms through her fiction is that the bicultural, biracial situation of immigrant communities is a reality that must be negotiated and accepted, rather than denied or resisted, if one is to realise an integrated identity. In an interview reprinted in *Conversations with Maxine Hong Kingston* (1998), Kingston affirms this view:

> I don't want to become an American by wiping out all my Chineseness. Nor do I want to stay Chinese and never participate in the wonderful American world that's out there. So instead of destroying part of myself or denying . . . reality, . . . I now see that there can be an amalgam. (qtd. in Skenazy 156)

Olivia's fluency with American history depicts the exclusive identification of herself with the American narrative, while her rejection of Kwan's Chinese 'yin-talk' (*Hundred* 129) represents her rejection of the Chinese part of herself. The amalgamated reality, therefore, is what Olivia must learn to embrace if she is to discover a self that is whole and complete.

Thus, although Olivia was introduced to Chinese cultural ambience quite early in life through Kwan and her stories, she remains largely aloof from it and, in fact, actively resistant to it throughout her early years. It is only during, and after, her trip to China that she comes to fully grasp the importance of embracing her bicultural reality to attain some resolution in her quest for identity. This may lead to the inference that Kwan's storytelling has not been effective, or at best, has only a minimal role to play in the eventual awakening of Olivia's cultural leanings and self-discovery. A reading of the text, however, shows that the self-realisation brought about by the China journey is but the culmination of an awakening process already seeded through Kwan's stories. As Olivia acknowledges to herself later, 'I've known since I was a child, really I have', although she admits to having 'buried' that knowledge about herself, 'in a safe place, just as she [Kwan] had done with her music box' (358).

The journey to China, undertaken by Kwan, Olivia, and the latter's estranged husband Simon, is a pivotal episode in the text. It is in China that Kwan's story reaches its climax and ends with her strange disappearance inside a labyrinthine maze in Changmian, her childhood home. 'The journey to China completes an emotional quest to find and understand a part of her ethnic heritage that Olivia has been undergoing since childhood' (Conard 69). Along with the American landscape that forms the backdrop of her characters' present lives, China as a physical and spatial entity features as a dominant motif in Tan's work. Almost all her novels depict the physical journey to China as crucial to the American-born characters' understanding and rediscovery of self. In *The Joy Luck Club*, Jing-Mei records that it is in China that she rediscovers her Chinese identity, which is an inseparable part of who she is:

> The minute our train leaves the Hong Kong border and enters Shenzhen, China, I feel different. I can feel the skin on my forehead tingling, my blood rushing through a new course, my bones aching with a familiar old pain. And I think, my mother was right. I am becoming Chinese. (267)

For Lindo and Waverley, the proposed trip to China is anticipated as a further means of healing the rift between mother and daughter and working out their differences with one another. Waverley states:

> Three week's worth of her complaining about dirty chopsticks and cold soup, three meals a day – well, it would be a disaster.
>
> Yet part of me also thinks the whole idea makes perfect sense . . . leaving our differences behind, stepping on the plane together, sitting side by side, lifting off, moving West to reach the East. (*Joy* 184)

Similarly, in *The Kitchen God's Wife*, though China functions as a site where Winnie's tragedies and bitter experiences were played out, it is also depicted as a source of potential healing and regeneration for both Winnie and Pearl. Towards the end of the novel, a trip to China is planned by Winnie, Helen, and Pearl in order to seek a cure for her disease, to revisit 'that magic spring' in Hangchow, where 'the water is just as they imagined, heavy as gold, sweet as rare flower seeds' (525–6). Holt-Jensen asserts that places are not just portions of geographical space, but 'territories of meaning' (224), processing meanings 'at different levels, spiritual, historical, and personal' (Mastoraki 16). In *The Hundred Secret Senses*, Tan depicts China as the ultimate point of resolution to Olivia's quest for self-knowledge and identity. On reaching Kwan's village, Olivia remarks:

> I gaze at the mountains and realize why Changmian seems so familiar. It's the setting for Kwan's stories, the ones that filter into my dreams. . . And being here, I feel as if the membrane separating the two halves of my life has finally been shed. (*Hundred* 230)

Thus, for Olivia, the process of self-exploration and awakening, begun through Kwan's stories, finds resolution in the actual visit to China. 'Before the knowing arrives, however, un-knowing, or the unlearning of rationality has to occur' (Sheng-Mei Ma 122). In China, confronted with overwhelming physical relics from the past (Miss Banner's journal and music box, and the buried duck's eggs), Olivia is compelled to acknowledge the veracity of Kwan's stories and rethinks her own previous assumptions about reality and self. She says, 'I now believe truth lies not in logic but in hope, both past and future. (*Hundred* 398). In acknowledging Kwan's legacies, Olivia is also, in a sense, accepting her own cultural heritage. As she inhales the air in Guilin, China, Olivia imagines herself 'filling my lungs with the very air that inspired *my ancestors*, whoever they might have been' (212, emphasis added). It is important to note this shift in Olivia's consciousness from the earlier denial and detachment of herself from her Chinese forebears, to the present acknowledgement of them, and of her own Chinese lineage.

What must be noted, however, is that the self that Olivia ultimately realises is one that incorporates not only her new-found Chinese affiliations, but one that also spans the American part of her being. After Kwan's disappearance and their futile efforts to trace her, Olivia and Simon decide to leave China and return 'home' (393). Home, for Olivia, is situated in the present context of America. Thus, though acknowledging China to be a part of her, the American reality is not discounted either. The identity that Olivia carves out for herself, therefore, is one that spans both worlds.

Chapter Nine

MY MOTHER IS IN MY BONES

The Bonesetter's Daughter

They write stories of things that are but should not have been. They write about what could have been, what still might be. They write of a past that can be changed. After all, Bao Bomu says, what is the past but what we choose to remember? . . . Ruth remembers this as she writes a story. It is for her grandmother, for herself, for the little girl who became her mother.

(*The Bonesetter's Daughter*, 403)

The significance of speaking out and giving voice to one's own life and stories through writing, as a means of self-affirmation and self-recovery, is highlighted by Tan in her fourth novel, *The Bonesetter's Daughter*. This novel spans the lives of three generations of women: Ruth, the second-generation Chinese-American daughter, her immigrant mother Luling, and Precious Auntie, her Chinese grandmother. As in her other novels, Tan depicts the mother-daughter relationship as the central focus of the text, a relationship, however, which has been undermined by several factors. Through Ruth's narrative, which is told in the third person and functions as the central narrative frame of the novel, the reader is made aware of the complex relationship that she shares with her mother. They are like 'two people caught in a sandstorm, blasted by pain and each blaming the other as the origin of the wind' (*Bonesetter* 158). From Ruth's point of view, 'her mother had always been, difficult, oppressive, and odd' (64), given to frequent bouts of depression, a morbid fascination with death, and the constant threat of suicide as a way of emotionally blackmailing her daughter. An incident in Ruth's adolescence illustrates this point. Entering Ruth's bedroom one day, Luling discovers her smoking. Highly incensed, she storms at her daughter, who answers back that as 'an American', she is entitled 'to privacy, to pursue [her] own happiness', not her mother's. The conflict escalates with Luling's usual threat of killing herself. Rebellious and angry, Ruth writes back in her diary, 'You talk about killing yourself, so why don't you ever do it? I wish you would. Just do it, do it, do it!' knowing full well that her mother will read it. The next day, she is horrified to find that her mother had fallen from the upstairs window and suffered broken bones and a concussion. Whether by accident or intentionally, Ruth had no means of knowing because, like many other things in their lives, the incident is never discussed, building up layers of silence between mother and daughter (158–62). Incidents like these, as well as the avoidance of meaningful talks between the two, has largely strained their relationship in the past and still makes it difficult for Ruth to relate easily with her mother in the present.

As in Tan's other novels, the conflict between the Americanised daughter Ruth and her Chinese-immigrant mother may also be traced to their culturally dissimilar mindsets and expectations. For instance, for Ruth, her mother's frequent entries into her room 'without knocking' is considered an act of parental high-handedness and a breach of privacy, which, as 'an American' she feels entitled to (158). For Luling, however, it is simply a means of knowing what her daughter is up to, to ensure her safety and prevent her from getting into any potential trouble or danger. Furthermore, brought up in the filial-conscious climate of prerevolutionary China, Luling expects the same standard of obedience and submission from her own daughter. Thus, as Amy Ling points out, 'the source of familial combat' in most Chinese-American homes 'is the possessiveness of Chinese mothers' as against the 'American-style liberation and autonomy' of their children (qtd. in Snodgrass 116).

It is interesting to note that in the absence of direct, personal talks between them, Ruth resorts to diary writing in order to communicate her frustrations to her mother. Similarly, in her childhood, 'sand-writing', communicating via the medium of a tea tray filled with sand, serves as Ruth's means of communication with Luling, when she temporarily lost her voice in an accident, after disobeying her mother. And though Ruth realises, soon after the initial shock, that nothing is wrong with her voice, she chooses to remain literally voiceless for quite some time afterward and continues to sand-write to her mother. For Ruth, sand-writing offers a better option of communicating with Luling because it is relatively free of the long arguments and heated confrontations that usually accompany their normal interactions with each other. At the same time, it provides an escape route, allowing Ruth to skirt the real issues and conflict between her and her mother, by burying it under the superficial and monosyllabic small talks afforded by the limited space of the sand tray. This clearly reflects the relationship between them which is characterised by the absence of any real talk and meaningful discussions. As Ruth reflects in her adulthood, 'in all the years gone by, she and her mother had never talked about what had happened' (*Bonesetter* 166). The talk-story/face-to-face dialogue, which features as an important element in Tan's other novels, is clearly missing here. Even when communication occurs, it is not direct or immediate but is mediated through the pages of a diary or a tray of sand. Incidentally, Luling's storytelling to her daughter is also told via a written manuscript rather than verbally.

In *The Bonesetter's Daughter*, Tan explores the centrality of the written discourse as an important means of communication between mother(s) and daughter(s). This clearly marks a departure from the oral talk-story mode employed by the characters in her previous novels. According to Lisa Dunick, Tan's employment of the written text in this novel endows her women characters with 'the agency to write themselves, an agency that critics have not yet recognised in the over-emphasis on talk-story' (10). In this regard, this text may be described as a literal *L'ecriture feminine*, to use Helene Cixous' term. In *The Laugh of the Medusa* (1976), Cixous asserts: 'Woman must write herself: must write about women and bring women to writing. . . Woman must put herself into the text – as into the world and into history – by her own movement' (875).

The written discourse is employed by all three of the women characters in this novel. This is Tan's way of emphasising the literacy and literary ability not only of the American-educated Ruth but also of her Chinese mother and grandmother. Liu Xin or Precious Auntie, Ruth's maternal grandmother, is depicted as a skilled calligrapher and poet, well-versed in the literary techniques and traditions of the day such as the 'eight-legged poems' (*Bonesetter* 187). Born in imperial China to a family of traditional bonesetters, she learns not only the art of folk-healing from her father but also how to read and write, an unusual accomplishment for a village girl at that time: 'she could write the names of every flower, seed, and bush, as well as say their medicinal uses' (205). It is ironic that in the prime of life, the fiercely independent Liu Xin is rendered voiceless and mute, figuratively and literally, through a series of misfortunes and tragedies. Betrothed to Liu Hu Sen, the youngest son of a family of a renowned inkstick maker, Liu Xin is rendered orphaned and husbandless on her wedding day when both Hu Sen and her father were killed by Chang, a man whose marriage proposal she had earlier rejected. Distraught by grief, she swallows burning resin in a bid to end her life but is discovered by Hu Sen's family, who manages to save her and the child she had already conceived. The suicide attempt permanently disfigures the lower part of her face and neck and robs her of her voice. And though the Liu clan allows her to remain in the household out of fear of being avenged by their son's ghost, her position is that of a servant. But the greatest pain in Liu Xin's life is having to give up her claims to her child Luling, who grows up thinking her to be only her nursemaid, Precious Auntie, and not her mother. In her accounts, Luling recalls that 'the bigger I grew, the more she shrank in importance. The smarter I thought I had become, the more I was able to reason that Precious Auntie was only a servant, a woman who held no great position in our household, a person no one liked' (205).

What is remarkable about Liu Xin is that though she is rendered voiceless, physically and metaphorically, she manages to transcend her voiceless position through the act of writing herself. In her context, the written text is employed for three distinct purposes: first, the calligraphy that she employs becomes a profound means of expressing her creative, artistic self. When 'writing characters', she tells Luling, 'a person must think about her intentions, how her *ch'i* flowed from her body into her arm, through the brush, and into the stroke. Every stroke had meaning, and since every word had many strokes, it also had many meanings' (269); second, the autobiography that she writes for her daughter Luling is a means of archiving her family history and relaying significant ancestral traditions to the next generation; third, through her written life story, Liu Xin attempts to reclaim and recover her status and maternal identity as Luling's mother, an identity denied to her in her lifetime. 'Your mother, your mother, I am your mother' (243), she writes on the last few pages of her manuscript to Luling, a disclosure, however, that her daughter fails to read. It is only after Liu Xin's final suicide and death that Luling reads the fateful words and embraces the truth of Precious Auntie's real identity. Liu Xin, thus, does manage to reclaim selfhood and identity through the act of writing herself into existence, although posthumously.

The tradition of woman writing herself is depicted in this text as a living tradition that passes on from mother to daughter and, eventually, to granddaughter. Like Precious Auntie, Luling, too, writes out her story, rather than tell it verbally to her daughter Ruth. Unlike Liu Xin, however, for whom 'story-writing' is necessitated by her physical muteness, for Luling, it is a deliberate and conscious choice. This choice is motivated by several factors: Luling sees the craft of writing as the continuation of a family tradition. Like her mother, she too takes up the art of calligraphy and poem-painting as a means of artistic self-expression. She tells Ruth, '[e]ach character is a thought, a feeling, meanings, history, all mixed into one' (*Bonesetter* 59). Through this particular act of self-articulation, Luling achieves a certain measure of calmness and healing in her otherwise volatile life. It serves to mend her sense of disquietude and internal incoherence. As Ruth says, she 'was different when she was writing and painting. She was calm, organised, and decisive' (58). It is also by virtue of these accomplishments that she eventually managed to get a visa to America, 'a land without curses or ghosts', going there as a 'Famous Visiting Artist' (338). Thus, in a sense, writing redeems Luling, both psychologically and materially. At the same time, '[b]y replicating her own mother's autobiographical writing, she displays reverence' not only for 'the importance and power of literacy' (Dunick 14) but also for a family tradition started by the mother that she had disavowed. It, therefore, assumes ancestral significance for her and her family. But Luling is also prompted by other more pragmatic reasons. Realising that her memory is failing, she takes to writing her autobiography as a means of preserving her life history and the history of her forebears, particularly, Precious Auntie. Thus, she begins her memoir with the statement, 'These are the things I must not forget' (*Bonesetter* 173). According to Nigerian scholar-writer, Emevwo Biakolo, one of the primary virtues of writing is 'permanence', the ability to 'preserve the word from vanishing' (qtd. in Akoma 10). Writing, therefore, becomes not just an act of performance but an active agency of counteracting the erasure and gaps that the human memory is invariably subject to.

It is important to remember that Ruth's access to the family genealogy and history would not have been possible without Luling's written narrative. In this context, the talk-story would not have sufficed or been possible because by the time Ruth is ready and willing to listen to her mother's story, Luling is already suffering the onset of dementia. The indelible nature of writing, therefore, preserves memory in a way that the oral narrative cannot. As Teacher Pan reminds Luling when he gave her his *duan* inkstone, 'once you put the ink to paper, it becomes unforgiving' (*Bonesetter* 295) and cannot be easily erased. In this novel, the physicality of 'ink' is used as a pervasive motif. Both Precious Auntie's and Luling's work involves the production of inkstick in the Liu family industry of inkstick making. Again, in the orphanage she was sent to, Luling works closely with inkstick and inkstone to teach the other children calligraphy and painting. Ink, therefore, comes to symbolise the power and endurance of the written word. The written record is Luling's attempt to ensure that the family history endures and that it is never forgotten. At the same time, it becomes a valuable material legacy that can be passed on from one generation to the next, functioning as a bridge between generations.

For Ruth, the importance and power of the written word are something that she has come to recognise since she was a child. Given to avid diary writing, words are her solace and companionship in the absence of a listening other brought about by the problematic relationship with her mother. It is in and through her diary that she seeks to validate her own self and existence. For her, the diary is 'proof of her existence, that she mattered, and more important, that someone somewhere would one day understand her, even if it was not in her lifetime' (156). Diary writing is often understood as an intimate and private activity allowing for the revelation and articulation of a very personal self. It represents 'the record of an "I" who constructs a view on him/herself in connection to the world at large' (Van Dijck). In Ruth's case, however, the diary is more than a channel of self-expression. It is, in fact, a representation of her inner need and desire to dialogue and communicate with her mother. As she writes, she is perfectly aware that she is addressing her words not only to herself but to her mother:

> Over sobs of righteous indignation, she began to write in her diary, knowing full well her mother would read the words: 'I hate her! She's the worst mother a person could have. She doesn't love me. She doesn't listen to me. She doesn't understand anything about me. All she does is pick on me, get mad, and make me feel worse.' (*Bonesetter* 159)

Thus, for Ruth, diary writing is a tentative attempt to reach out to her mother, to make her pay attention to her frustrations and feelings of being misunderstood, and to address the hurt between them. It is ironic, therefore, that Luling succeeds in reading only the bitter and accusatory part of Ruth's diary, prompting an immediate reaction from her in the attempt to injure herself. The misunderstanding between mother and daughter is never resolved through means of the diary because Luling fails to read what Ruth had written on the very last page: 'I'm sorry. Sometimes I just wish you would say you're sorry too' (166).

This incident draws attention to the fact that with all its advantages, the written discourse does have its limitations and problems because according to H. W. Wong, the reader(s) may select what he/she wants to hear/read by leaving out certain sections of the written text (258). Thus, the onus lies with the reader who decides what to elide and what to read. This may result in erasures and gaps within the story and the loss of certain truths that may distort and even destroy the meaning altogether. Incidentally, in Luling's case, Precious Auntie's suicide and death, leading to the former's lifelong sorrow, guilt, and an unhealthy obsession with death that disturbs her own relationship with her daughter, stem from Luling's negligence to read out the whole of her mother's written story: 'Out of spite, I did not read most of those pages' (*Bonesetter* 189). She, therefore, misses the most essential information, Precious Auntie's revelation of her identity as her mother that could have changed their lives.

Another drawback of the written narrative lies in the fact that it remains virtually a static text until the reader reads and engages with it. In *Literature as Exploration* (1938), Louise Rosenblatt, one of the earliest proponents of the reader-response theory, states that literature or any written text 'remains merely inkspots on paper until a reader transforms them into a set of meaningful symbols' (1995 ed, 24). Interestingly, Luling's memoir was written and given to Ruth some few years before she actually peruses it. The fact that it is written in Chinese and necessitates translation into English further adds to her disinterestedness and delay in reading. Though the text is in existence, it fails to have any impact on Ruth until she chooses to have it translated and reads it.

However, the potency of the written word is impressed most strongly upon Ruth through her temporary experience with sand-writing. When Ruth inscribes the word 'Doggie' on her sand tray to ask her mother if she can have a dog, Luling immediately imagines that Precious Auntie is trying to communicate with her from the other world. She comes to this strange conclusion because 'Doggie' happens to be Precious Auntie's nickname for her. At the same time, this reveals Luling's tragic preoccupation with her dead mother, a life constantly haunted by the ghosts of the past. Thereafter, Ruth had only to sand-write pretend-messages from Precious Auntie to get her mother to acquiesce to whatever she asks. She realises, with a thrill, that she 'had never experienced such power with words' (*Bonesetter* 85). Though most times Ruth uses the sand tray to get her way with trivial demands, there is one occasion when it literally saves her from a potentially harmful situation. Realising that she is in danger of being abused by a neighbour when they were still living in Berkeley, Ruth uses the aid of sand-writing to get her mother to move away from the neighbourhood.

Ironically, however, it is this conviction of the potential power of words that holds Ruth back from being a creative writer. She had often dreamed of being a writer in the style of Jane Austen, to write 'a book that had nothing to do with her own life . . . [to] revise her life and become someone else' (31). The thought of doing that, however, frightens her:

> In her imagination she could change everything, herself, her
> mother, her past. But the idea of revising her life also frightened
> her, as if by imagination alone she were condemning what she
> did not like about herself or others. Writing what you wished was
> the most dangerous form of wishful thinking. (31)

She opts to be a freelance ghostwriter for authors of self-help books instead, moulding the words of others without allowing them to affect her own life. Dunick remarks that the 'fear that revising her mother out of her fictional life may erase her from reality hinders Ruth from claiming any sense of agency she might find through original authorship' (13). It is only after reading her mother's autobiography that Ruth comes to realise the importance of inscribing one's self in paper.

The discovery of her mother's story, and simultaneously, her grandmother's story-within-the-story, marks a turning point in Ruth's journey. It gives her access to a past and to a rich familial history, particularly, the matrilineal one, which was previously a blank to her; the story enables Ruth to understand her mother more and perceive her differently, leading to their reconciliation. It also reinstates her grandmother to her rightful place in the family and in Ruth's own life. Before this, Ruth had always imagined Precious Auntie as 'the crazy ghost' (*Bonesetter* 58), the 'lady with bloody hair' (87), resenting 'her presence in their lives, [and blaming] her for her mother's quirkiness, her feelings of doom' (353). Now, however, she realises that these women, her mother and her grandmother, are the ones 'who shaped her life, who are in her bones' (402). More importantly, however, it releases Ruth from her fear and gives her the impetus to write her own self, her own family, her own story, into existence: 'Before, she never had a reason to write for herself, only for others. Now she has that reason' (401). The novel ends with Ruth continuing the family craft of writing as a means of affirming the past, a way of envisioning the future afresh, and more significantly, to give herself voice. As she begins to write, she visualises her mother and the spirit of her grandmother, inspiring and partnering with her in this joint venture of women writing themselves:

> They write about what happened, why it happened, how they
> can make other things happen. They write stories of things that

are but should not have been. They write about what could have been, what still might be. They write of a past that can be changed. . . . Ruth remembers this as she writes a story. It is for her grandmother, for herself, for the little girl who became her mother. (403)

Like all of Tan's novels, this text depicts the significance of storytelling as a means of self-articulation while, at the same time, serving to bridge the interpersonal, intercultural, and intergenerational fissures that divide her women characters. Though this text focuses largely on the medium of the written word as the vehicle by which her characters tell, and retell, their stories, it by no means discounts other modes of communication. In fact, in this novel, Tan explores the multiple ways that people connect to one another. Orality is as important as the written discourse in this novel. What is noted is that the reconciliation between mother and daughter, initiated by Ruth's reading of her mother's story, finds complete resolution when Luling verbally talks to Ruth, apologising for past hurts. Echoing Ruth's apologies in her diary years earlier, Luling tells her over the telephone, 'I hope you can forget just as I've forgotten. I hope you can forgive me, because if I hurt you, I'm sorry.' After they hang up, 'Ruth cried for an hour she was so happy. It was not too late for them to forgive each other and themselves' (402). This conversation, which is almost a word-by-word transcription of her own mother's talk with her six months before she died, is described by Tan as the 'most healing words' that her mother had ever bequeathed to her (*Fate* 220).

The orality that is depicted here, however, differs from the primary orality that features in Tan's other novels, where the characters have face-to-face encounters with one another as they engage in talk-story. This long-deferred conversation that, in a sense, sets the seal on their reconciliation is done through the medium of the telephone. Thus, the orality that is presented here is what Walter Ong describes as 'a secondary orality', the technologising of the word, which occurs through 'telephone, radio, television, and other electronic device[s]' (11). By interposing the cultural heritage of China symbolised by the oral/talk-story element into the American context with its highly technological culture, a bridge is created between the Chinese mythic past and the American present which constitutes the 'between-worlds' (Ling

20) reality of the characters. This is a distinctive feature in Tan's work and serves as a leitmotif in each and every one of her novels.

Another instance of bicultural welding in this novel is Tan's employment of autobiography as the express mode by which her Chinese women characters tell their story. In her assessment of Asian-American literature, Elaine Kim notes that the autobiography may be identified more as a Western genre, rather than an Asian one. In China, particularly, an autobiography is 'virtually unknown, since for a scholar to write a book about himself would have been deemed egotistical in the extreme' (Kim 24). Even when autobiographies are written, such as Chinese-American, Jade Snow Wong's *Fifth Chinese Daughter* (1950), 'the word "I" almost never appears, . . . Even written in English, an "I" book by a Chinese would seem outrageously immodest to anyone raised in the spirit of Chinese propriety' (Jade Wong vii). In *The Bonesetter's Daughter*, however, Tan deliberately introduces the medium of autobiography/self-writing, into a novel which is predominantly Chinese in both content and context. In doing this, she opens up a literary space for her Chinese women characters to articulate the hitherto, suppressed 'I'. At the same time, this is Tan's way of asserting and claiming ownership over both Western and Chinese literary traditions that constitute her rich bicultural heritage. This is a heritage that she constantly celebrates, and one that informs her art. In *Cultures in Between* (1993), Homi Bhabha notes that when transactions and collaborations between opposing cultures are negotiated, it gives rise to a new 'hybrid culture' (167). This hybrid culture is invariably richer for having imbibed the elements of both. In Tan's fiction, the synthesis between her Chinese and American heritage finds full expression, leading thereby to the creation of a new and richer literary space.

The language of signs and gestures as an equally valid tool of communication and storytelling is also highlighted by Tan in this novel. This finds expression particularly in the interaction between Precious Auntie and Luling. Recalling these interactions, Luling remarks:

> She had no voice, just gasps and wheezes, the snorts of a ragged
> wind. She told me things with grimaces and groans, dancing
> eyebrows and darting eyes. She wrote about the world on my

carry-around chalkboard. . . . Hand-talk, face-talk, and chalk-talk were the languages I grew up with, soundless and strong. (*Bonesetter* 2)

Apart from writing, Precious Auntie has no other means of communicating and sharing her stories with her daughter except through sign language which serves as an important means of bonding between the two. Luling recalls, '[n]o one else understood Precious Auntie's kind of talk', the language she employs to tell 'our secret stories' (3). While the autobiography is a formal record of her life and her family's history and genealogy, these gestural narratives, much like talk-stories, encapsulate information which are of a more informal and varied nature. These tales are packed with childhood memories, family anecdotes, cultural history, and fable-like observations about people, life, and living. Sara Ruddick asserts that 'children are shaped by . . . the stories they are first told . . . storytelling at its best enables children to adapt, edit, and invent life stories they can live with' (qtd. in Ho 127). From this repertoire of gestural stories, which are sometimes tragic, sometimes humorous, and often laced with maternal wisdom, Luling learns to construct a personal reality that she tries to convey to her daughter Ruth, despite the barriers between them, to instil 'all kinds of wisdom in Ruth's mind' and warn her away 'from danger, disease, and death' (*Bonesetter* 76). Thus, Tan envisages storytelling as a continuing, living, female tradition, as '[e]very woman partakes in the chain of guardianship and of transmission. Every griotte who dies is a whole library that burns down' (Minh-ha 130).

EPILOGUE

What emerges from this discussion of Tan's work is that storytelling is a strategic means of female self-discovery and self-affirmation. The women are, in one way or the other, hemmed in by various limitations that hinder their journey to selfhood. This is because of their location as women in a highly patriarchal context, a position which is rendered even more complex by their diasporic experience. However, 'despite attempts by Chinese patriarchy and the intersectionality of race, class, and gender to silence them', these women 'did manage to leave behind a written and oral record of their lives, thoughts, and feelings' (Judy Yung 1999, 3), through the stories that they tell/write.

Storytelling also serves another function in Tan's novels. It enables the transmission and perpetuation of values, culture, and history, which, as she constantly depicts, are crucial to self-knowledge and to an understanding of one's place and identity in the universe. As Nancy Chodorow asserts, the creation and experience of self is constituted by 'the inextricable interconnectedness . . . of psyche, society, and culture' (1978, x). Indeed, the depiction of culture(s) and history(ies), particularly, relating to China and America, is an integral part of Tan's fiction because it informs the characters' lived experience and reality. The self that is represented in these novels, therefore, is not a self in isolation but a self that is a part and parcel of the human tapestry, where race, culture, and history intersect.

The diverse modes employed by these women to tell their stories reveal their creativity and versatility. They are not restricted to any, one, singular way of telling their stories, but express themselves through a variety of mediums such as the talk-story, the written text, and nonverbal sign language. At the same time, this attests to Tan's own creativity and versatility as a writer. Though the oral discourse features as a major literary technique in her work, she does not limit herself to it but engages with other stylistic and literary traditions as well. This has greatly broadened the scope and parameters of her work and enriched her art. Though often compared to Kingston in her ability to validate the talk-story as a recognisable art form, Tan has been able to create 'a literary tradition apart from Kingston'. Not dependent on orality alone, her characters 'are able to move between speech and writing' (Dunick 17).

Through her writing, Tan succeeds in giving a literary voice to the Chinese-American experience and paves the way for Amerasian writers like Gish Jen, Fae Myenne Ng, and others. As Chinese-American author Belle Yang puts it, 'Amy Tan kicked the door wide open for many of us; she made Chinese-Americans believe they had important stories to tell' (qtd. in Ganahl 40). However, while the strong strand of biculturalism does indeed pervade her work, to label Tan merely as a writer of the Asian-American experience would be to grossly limit her art. The mother-daughter relations that she writes about is a theme that resonates universally and 'creates universality in her fiction' (Assunta Ng, qtd. in Snodgrass 118). As Tan herself affirms, 'the heart' of her fiction 'involves emotions we all have' because it is 'about human nature' that happens to be depicted 'through Asian-Americans' (*Fate* 190-91). In the final assessment, therefore, Amy Tan may be described not only as a writer of the Chinese-American reality but also as a storyteller whose work is ultimately a chronicle of the human experience itself, its 'love and hope, pain, and loss':

> I write stories because I have questions about life, not answers. I believe life is mysterious and not dissectable. I think human nature is best described in even a long-winded story and not in a psychoanalytical diagnosis. I write because often I can't express myself any other way, and I think I'll implode if I can't find the words . . . *about love and hope, pain and loss.* (emphases added, Amy Tan, *Fate* 322)

TWO PERSPECTIVES! TWO VOICES!

PEARL S. BUCK AND AMY TAN: A SUMMING UP

> Each storyteller puts his or her personal stamp on the story, and
> each telling is different.
> (Debra Shostak, 'Maxine Hong Kingston's Fake Books' 54)

In reassessing Pearl Buck and Amy Tan, one finds an interchangeability
of sensibilities inherent in the two writers. Though American by birth,
Buck's sensibilities are largely shaped by China: 'During her formative
years,' she 'knew China as reality and the United States [only] as reflected
in the memories and conversations of others' (Leong 13). Buck, therefore,
grew up on Chinese folktales and stories told to her by her Chinese *amah*
(governess) and experienced first-hand what it meant to live in China during
the late nineteenth and early twentieth century. All these impressions and
experiences gradually found their way into her art and characterise her
fiction, particularly her novels about China and the Chinese people. Of her
work, it has been said that she 'presents China from within, as the Chinese
see it' (Bentley 793).

Amy Tan, on the other hand, though of Chinese descent, was born
and brought up in America and is therefore largely informed by American
sensibilities and assumptions. What is said of the Amerasian daughters in
The Joy Luck Club, 'who grew up speaking English and swallowing more
Coca-Cola than sorrow' (17), may well be said of her. Her experience of
China is gleaned not from any first-hand encounter with it, but through
the lens of her mother's stories and memories. Her vision of China is, thus,

a filtered one. This, however, does not make her work any less authentic. She remains true in rendering China as remembered and created by the impressions of her mother. The dedication of her first novel, *The Joy Luck Club*, to her mother, tellingly reads: 'You asked me once what I would remember. This, and much more' (9).

Women are given a central space in the fiction of both writers. This reflects their awareness as well as their attempt as writers to construct a feminine narrative as a means of countering the peripheral position that women occupied in traditional literature. As Helene Cixous argues, woman has always been in a position of otherness and alterity in Western phallogocentric culture, functioning always '"within" the discourse of man' (887). And though often depicted, and even enshrined in literature as 'an ideal, a model of selflessness and purity of heart' like Goethe's 'eternal feminine' (Eichner 620), she is represented mainly through the male gaze, as the object, rather than the subject.

By foregrounding stories about women, therefore, both Pearl Buck and Amy Tan decentre the traditional power structure in which man is often always the centre. This is particularly observed in the work of Amy Tan who has been criticised for her marginal and/or negative portrayal of male characters. Rhoda Koenig, for instance, feels that Tan's over-emphasis on female subjectivities limits the development of her male characters to either 'tyrants or simpletons' (82). This view is echoed by Asian-American critic Frank Chin, who charged Tan with caricaturing Asian males through her depiction of either insipid or villainous male characters. In almost all her novels, the male presence is a perfunctory one at best. Even when men feature in a more pronounced manner in the narratives, such as the sadistic Wen Fu in *The Kitchen God's Wife*, or the exploitative Chang in *The Bonesetter's Daughter*, their roles are unequivocally negative. Thus, it is true that male characters have been either, greatly sidelined, or vilified, in Tan's novels. However, it is important to realise that this is so because Tan's primary design in writing her fiction is to recover the lost lives of women, particularly, the women in her own family who have long been silenced and overlooked. Through fiction, 'she tries to do away with "his story" and presents "her life" from the perspectives of the individual women characters' (G. Shen 7). As she says in one of her essays, 'Lost Lives of Women' (1991), '[t]hese are the women who never let me forget why stories need to be told' (90). As such, it is inevitable, therefore, that women would constitute the centre of her fictional world, though often at the expense of the male characters. According to Bella Adams, this 'critique of patriarchy in both China and America' situates Tan in an 'Asian American feminist tradition' (2005, 27) and makes her part of a larger discourse.

In Buck's fiction, specifically the novels discussed in section 1, women are again the pivot of the text. *East Wind: West Wind*, *Pavilion of Women*, and *The Mother* are all unambiguously woman-centred narratives. Admittedly, in *The Good Earth* and *Kinfolk*, male figures such as Wang Lung, Doctor Liang, and James Liang function as the controlling consciousness in the narratives to a large extent. This may be read as Buck's way of drawing attention to the patriarchal reality that informs the social and cultural setting of the stories. However, even in these novels, the women protagonists, particularly O-lan, Mrs Liang, and Mary Liang, are so individually and powerfully delineated that their presence dominates the text and their stories resonate even through the male-centred framework.

As noted, it is not merely women characters, but Chinese women, in particular, who are the focus of the two writers' work. For Buck, the choice to portray Chinese women as the subject of her work is a natural outcome of her own experiences in China. As she asserts, 'I can write only what I know, and I know nothing but China, having always lived there' (qtd. in Critical Excerpts, *The Good Earth* 372). To her, the Chinese woman represents a highly complex subject. On one hand, she is a much oppressed figure, crushed under the weight of centuries-old male domination and subjugation:

> As a girl growing up in a relentlessly patriarchal, Christian household, Pearl was especially attentive to the Chinese girls and women she met. She found that they, too, were trapped in a sexual caste system throughout their lives, a system even more punishing than the one she had seen at home. (Conn 26)

At the same time, she also observes 'how powerful Chinese women often were . . . among farmers and gentry alike, homes were typically ruled by the senior women in a kind of domestic matriarchy' (Conn 26). It is this sense of duality and paradox surrounding the Chinese woman that Buck tries to capture in her art, ranging from the indomitable Madame Wu and independent Mary Liang, to the highly oppressed O-lan and the exploited Mother.

For Tan, the portrayal of Chinese women as the subject matter of her art is spurred by a more personal motive than Buck. On one hand, it is an exploration of her own Chinese roots and personal identity 'to find my own voice and tell my own story' as she says in *The Opposite of Fate* (350). Simultaneously, however, it is also a means of giving voice to the unheard and unarticulated stories of Chinese, and Chinese immigrant women, particularly, her own mother and grandmother. As she remarks in an interview, her fiction is her way of telling these once-silenced women that 'we have a voice now, we can give voice to this' (Bertodano). All her four novels, discussed in section 2, are, therefore, fictional renderings of their lives and lived realities. It is through the lives and experiences of these women, particularly her female forebears, that Tan seeks to know and understand herself. Thus, Tan's stories may be said to be an articulation of both the personal 'I' as well as the collective 'we' (the women in her family and community). In this sense, her work may also be termed as a 'biomythography', a term coined by Audre Lorde in her book *Zami: A New Spelling of My Name* (1982), which is a reworking of her autobiography to encapsulate both the personal self and the collective experience. In moving beyond what Virginia Woolf terms as the aridity of the 'I' (104), to a focus on collective lives and identities, Tan invests her fiction with greater universality and significance.

The women characters portrayed by the two writers are extremely different. Most of Buck's characters are invariably drawn from the world of feudal China. As such, their outlook and values are reflective of the worldview and mindset of their particular time and society. Except for the characters in *Kinfolk*, almost all of these women lived largely insular lives, unexposed to other ideas and thinking, apart from that of their own culture. Even when Western ideas and culture are brought to bear upon their lives, through Christian missionary presence or Western education as in *East Wind: West Wind* and *Pavilion of Women*, they remain but a marginal presence operating from the fringes. Thus, the world that she portrays in her fiction is one that is predominantly traditional Chinese in its milieu and ethos. And it is within this context that her women seek to redefine themselves and their existence. Amy Tan's women characters, on the other hand, are placed in a dual cultural context. Both China and America form an equally integral part of their lived realities. Their journey to selfhood is, thus, traced out within this bicultural context. But although the characters are situated in different cultural context(s), in this sense, the common theme that links these women together is their shared background of patriarchy and marginalisation.

Because of their location in China and the particular time in which they are situated, Buck's characters are directly governed by the strictures and norms of Chinese patriarchal standards. Being so much a part of the system and under-exposed to values and mindsets other than the ones they have been taught, some of these women, like O-lan, and even Kweilan initially, display a total lack of self-awareness or desire to change the status quo. They seem to accept whatever lot society metes out to them even when that is extremely unjust and discriminatory to them as women. It is only when they are pushed into situations and corners that compel them to interrogate their lives and inner selves that their sense of self is awakened. This, however, does not mean that these women are deficient or lacking in any respect. If anything, the fault lies with the social system that has conditioned these women to think that they do not deserve more than what society allows and that their happiness, in fact, lies in complying with the very system that binds them. Kweilan's attitude demonstrates this when she recounts her childhood with her brother thus:

> It did not occur to me to mark the difference made between him and me. I did not at any time dream of being on an equality with my brother. It was not necessary. I had no such important part to fulfil in the family as he, the first son and the heir of my father. (*Wind* 127–28)

As socioanthropologists Rosaldo and Lamphere point out, 'in learning to be women in our own society, we have accepted, and even internalised, what is all too often a derogatory and constraining image of ourselves' (1). However, not all of these women are acquiescent and passive victims of their fate and circumstances. In fact, some of them, like Madame Wu, the indomitable heroine of *Pavilion of Women*, demonstrate a high degree of consciousness about their own aspirations and desires in life. The creation of a character like Madame Wu reveals Buck's awareness of the social changes that were taking place in China during the late 1920s to the early 1940s (in which the novel is set), when women were beginning to be conscious of their own aspirations and desires. Even the Mother, protagonist of the novel that bears her nomenclature, may be regarded as a woman who is acutely conscious of her needs and female desires. However, what must be noted here is that even though these women are beginning to articulate and express themselves in a somewhat more open manner, they are still largely governed and dictated by male-defined rules and social conventions. It is within the parameters of this still largely male world, therefore, that their freedom must be worked out.

Tan's female protagonists are relatively more assertive and more aware of their plight and rights as women. They grew up at a period in China's history when new ideologies were considerably becoming more of a presence in China. These were the New Culture Movement in 1919, the international political treaties, and the various wars such as the two World Wars, and the Sino-Japanese war that marked China during the earlier half of the twentieth century. Most of Tan's women are, therefore, more exposed to and forced to interact with new thoughts and ideas that challenge the very tenets of Confucian patriarchy. Moreover, many of these characters have greater access to modern education than most of their female counterparts in Buck's fiction. As such, they display a greater sense of self-assertiveness and boldness, attempting to fight the oppressive system and eventually breaking away from it altogether.

Tan's characters like Lindo Jong, Winnie Louie, and Luling Liu may well be said to exemplify this new breed of Chinese women, 'the Girls of New Destiny', as described in *The Bonesetter's Daughter* (263). An important means by which these women try to reinvent their lives and rewrite their destinies is by emigrating to America where they feel they can change their own lives and circumstances. As Lindo Jong remarks, 'In America, nobody says you have to keep the circumstances somebody else gives you' (*Joy* 254). However, even in America, these women are subject to a different kind of oppression, marginalised on the basis of race, rather than just of sex, one that threatens to undermine their selfhood.

Noticeable differences may be observed in the ways that the protagonists of the two writers negotiate their journey to the self. Trapped, with no other recourse, within an age and a culture that allow women no avenues for self-expression and assertion, except those sanctioned by society, Buck's women still manage to forge their own personal meanings and self-realisation even 'within' the limitations of the patriarchal space that defines their lived reality. They do this by working within the system and, sometimes, by using that very system to achieve their own personal goals and desires. Madame Wu, for instance, resorts to providing her husband with a concubine in order to free herself for the pursuit of her own freedom and independence. Similarly, both Kweilan and O-lan choose to carve out their own happiness and self-fulfilment within the boundaries of marriage and motherhood rather than fight against these institutions.

Tan's characters, on the other hand, with more access to opportunities, succeed in reframing their lives and achieving self-autonomy and agency by breaking 'away' from the confines of patriarchal China and emigrating to America. The new synergistic space that is generated by their dual cultural experience is not without its share of conflict. Nonetheless, it is in this newly created 'third space', to use Bhabha's term (211), that these women's individuality and self-definition are negotiated. Thus, the odyssey to the self is traversed differently and along different routes for the women characters of Buck and Tan. The destination which is arrived at, however, is the same, which is a rediscovery and redefinition of self.

For all the characters, the journey to the self is a multilateral one. Apart from *Kinfolk*, which also involves a geographical and spatial journey, the journey motif in Buck's novels is largely psychological and metaphorical. It is a journey that takes the characters inward, into the recesses of their beings, leading them to a re-examination of their inner lives and selves. This is highlighted in *Pavilion of Women* which dramatises Madame Wu's constant self-introspection to arrive at some level of self-knowledge and self-understanding. Even Kweilan and the Mother demonstrate this tendency to look into themselves as a way of making sense of their lives and experiences, especially when they are faced with crises. This inward journey is a necessary one, therefore, for it enables the characters to come closer to a better knowledge and understanding of themselves.

However, the theme that is consistently underlined in almost all of Buck's work is that the psychical journey is not, and cannot be, the only access to the self. The journey is also one that takes the characters into a world beyond themselves, a world in which they are constantly pitched into the presence of the other. This other encompasses the community of women that they relate to as well as the gendered and racial other. Like Sartre, Buck firmly believes that the self must relate to and 'be aware of other knowing consciousnesses' or 'others' in order to be a fully realised one (152). Thus, in *East Wind: West Wind*, Kweilan's self-development and growth is traced out in the context of her relationships with a network of women, with her husband who represents the gendered other as well as the racial other(s) signified by Mary, her American sister-in-law, and the anonymous confidante of her story. Similarly, Madame Wu's quest for self-understanding and self-actualisation is facilitated by her interactions with her father-in-law, and Andre, the Western priest. In *Kinfolk*, it is against the bicultural backdrop of China and America, two different worlds intermeshed with each other, that the women protagonists recover their identity and manage to forge a sense of self. Even for the socially isolated O-lan, the recognition that she is an indispensable part of the unending chain of human generations is what finally gives meaning and purpose to her life. Thus, the self that is realised by Buck's women is one that is not self-contained or isolated within oneself but one that is arrived at through a network of relationships with the other.

In Tan's fiction, the journey to the self is also explored through a nexus of relationships, both interpersonal and intercultural. However, the personal relationship that she portrays as central to her characters' growth and self-affirmation is the woman-to-woman alliance rather than the woman-man relationship. In her novels, the theme of female bonding is particularly reflected in the mother-daughter relationship as well as in the various sororal bonds, whether it is between siblings as in *The Hundred Secret Senses*, or women's friendship with each other. Writing at a time when 'the power of sisterhood', a key slogan in the postmodern, second-wave feminism of the 1970s and early 1980s, is emphasised upon by women writers, such as Luce

Irigaray, as crucial to 'women's self-salvation in a phallocentric world' (cited in He 2012, 204), *The Hundred Secret Senses* also reflects this particular mode of thought. However, her reaffirmation of female bonding, specifically the matrilineal one, may also be traced to her own familial heritage and the sense of personal strength and self-worth that she derives from the matriarchs of the family. It is no coincidence, therefore, that almost all her works are either written for, or dedicated to, her mother and grandmother. *The Bonesetter's Daughter* ends with a reiteration of the matrilineal ties as a significant source of inspiration, identity, and female creativity: 'Ruth remembers this as she writes a story. It is for her grandmother, for herself, for the little girl who became her mother' (403).

Cross-cultural relationships, particularly Sino-American, feature as a key element in the works of both Pearl Buck and Amy Tan. This reflects the bicultural reality that defines these two writers' lives. According to Peter Conn, one of Buck's biographers, almost uniquely among white American writers, Pearl Buck spent the first half of her life as a minority person, a white person in a nation of nonwhites. This experience, according to him, birthed in her a lifelong and untiring passion for interracial understanding (26). Her attempt to reconcile East and West is done both through sociopolitical means, as well as literarily.

On the political front, Buck and Richard Walsh, her publisher-editor who later became her husband, led a successful campaign to repeal the notorious Chinese Exclusion Acts, a series of laws dating back to 1882 that prohibited Chinese immigration into the United States. In 1941, the husband-and-wife duo established the East and West Association as a vehicle of educational exchange. Similarly, in 1949, she founded Welcome House, which is one of the first international, interracial adoption agencies in the United States (Conn xxvii-ix). Simultaneously, it is through her fiction that Buck tries to bridge the yawning gap between Eastern and Western cultures. Her debut novel *East Wind: West Wind*, as well as her subsequent novels, clearly underlines her vision of promoting a better relationship between the Eastern and the Western world. Her mission, as she often declares, is to present, through literature, the real China to Westerners. The relevance of Buck's work in this regard may perhaps be best appreciated when one considers the anti-Asian and anti-Chinese sentiments that prevailed in

America during the nineteenth and early twentieth century. An article that appeared in the *New York Times* on the 3 September 1865 is a revealing instance:

> We are utterly opposed to any extensive emigration of Chinamen or other Asiatics to any part of the United States. . . . With Oriental thoughts will necessarily come Oriental social habits . . . a population befouled with all the social vices.(qtd. in Rath 89–90)

What Buck succeeds in doing through her novels, therefore, is to enable Western readers to know China with 'sanity, compassion and understanding' (Gray 33). Interestingly, what is noticed in Buck is that although the intercultural theme is present in most of her work, either explicitly or implicitly, it is China that is always given the centre stage, while the West is eased to the margins. This may be traced to the tension in Buck's own life, between her intention to be true to both the cultures that constitute her reality and the personal pull that she felt towards China. However, her personal inclination, notwithstanding, this does not annul her firm belief that it is in reaching out to one another, personally and culturally, that the self is upheld and affirmed. The relationships between people, the equality of the races, and the necessity for human understanding are, according to her, 'principles in which I have been reared, in which I do believe and must believe fearlessly until I die' (Buck, *My Several Worlds* 376).

The cross-cultural presence is also a prominent feature in Amy Tan's fiction. Unlike in Buck's work, however, both China and America are given equal space in her novels. Even as China and its culture are powerfully evoked in the narratives, the American presence is also undeniably real. This is clearly a reflection of Tan's own bicultural heritage, one that constitutes her identity and informs her art. Like other second-generation Amerasians struggling to assimilate into the mainstream, Tan actively resisted the Chinese part of her identity during her growing-up years. As she matures, however, she learns to accept and appreciate her Chinese ancestry and legacy, recognising it to be an integral part of her being. This, however, does not lead her to repudiate the American part of herself. Rather, it results in an amalgam of both the Chinese and American aspects of her life, one that she vigorously celebrates and consistently depicts in her work. As she says in *The Opposite of Fate*, 'I am Chinese by racial heritage. I am Chinese-American by family and social upbringing. . . My characters may be largely Chinese-Americans, but I think Chinese-Americans are part of America' (310). Unlike Buck, therefore, who uses the intercultural motif as part of a greater agenda (a means of presenting a more realistic portrayal of China to the West), for Tan, it has a deeply personal note. It features in her novels, mainly, because it is very much a part of her own reality as well as that of her fictional world. It plays an active role in defining her own identity as well as that of her women characters.

It is interesting to note that unlike Tan who finally manages to forge a sense of self within the bicultural reality that defines her, Pearl Buck perpetually struggles with the sense of duality that characterises her life. Though she permanently moves back to the United States in the 1930s, the sense of alienation that she feels in her own home culture is always palpable. She writes, 'I have few friends of my own race, almost none intimate' (qtd. in Critical Excerpts, *The Good Earth* 372). In her autobiographical work, *My Several Worlds*, published in 1954, Buck confesses to the underlying sense of unease and of not belonging anywhere that is generated by her dual cultural experience. She describes herself as 'in one world and not of it, and belonging to another world and yet not of it' (51). Novels like *Kinfolk* which depict characters who are caught between two worlds reflect this same sense of diasporic angst faced by Buck in her own life. And though this angst is one that, perhaps, Buck never quite succeeds in resolving throughout her life, on the other hand, as Liu Haiping notes, it is one that serves to lend depth to her work. The dual perspective of being 'at once an insider and an outsider' brings with it 'the rare combination of emotional attachment and rational distance to her observations' (55) and enriches her writing.

If, for Buck's characters, the metaphorical journey involves delving deep into their inner world and reaching outward to the other, for Tan's women, self-reclamation and internal healing come through a revisiting of the past via the realm of storytelling and 'rememory'. The reliving and articulation of past memories are extremely crucial for Tan's Chinese immigrant women. They serve a dual purpose, which, first, is to heal and bring closure to their own traumatic memories. It becomes, therefore, a 'talking cure', as H.

W. Wong asserts in her thesis, a therapeutic effect brought upon through 'talking about things . . . intentionally or unintentionally' forgotten or buried (226). Second, this helps in bridging the rift between them and their American-assimilated daughters. As these daughters glimpse their mothers' pasts through the recounting of the stories, they learn to understand and appreciate their mothers better, a gesture that draws them closer. At the same time, the recollection of past horrors that they survived and the life-lessons learnt serve to inculcate within them a sense of strength and confidence that enables them to negotiate the present and face the future more confidently. Thus, for Amy Tan's heroines, the journey is also one that transcends the time-space dimension. It takes them from the present into the past, but it does not end there. In Tan's fiction, the past is never the destination. It is simply a route that must be retravelled in order to facilitate a better understanding of one's bearing in the present and help one to steer one's path in the future. Simultaneously, the lessons gleaned from the past are, in turn, passed on to the next generation in an attempt to help them navigate their own lives better.

Another important theme in the novels of both Pearl Buck and Amy Tan is the nature of the physical journey that their characters undertake. Of all Buck's novels analysed here, it is only in *Kinfolk* that the journey motif is depicted literally. In Amy Tan, the trans-pacific crossing and recrossings are a central part of her characters' experience in all the novels discussed. This literal odyssey is depicted as a cyclical one in both writers. The characters' journey from China to America is prompted by various reasons. For the Liang family in Buck's novel, the relocation is initiated by Dr Liang, the family patriarch, who sees in America the hope of a better life and better opportunities for himself and his family. Simultaneously, it is also a means of escape from the turmoil of civil in-fightings between imperialists, nationalists, and communists in China, thereby posing a threat for a scholar like him. For Tan's Chinese women, the relocation is both a result of their attempt to escape oppressed and subjugated lives in patriarchal China, as well as a means of reinventing and rewriting their own lives and destinies. As such, the journey itself becomes a strategy for asserting agency and control over their own lives and circumstances. The vignette in the first part of Tan's *The Joy Luck Club* underlines this motif. This recurs in all the novels. For the characters in Amy Tan and Buck's *Kinfolk*, therefore, the journey to America is both an 'escape from' an untenable or oppressive situation(s), as well as a means of 'reaching out' for something that they perceive as better for themselves and their families.

The promise/lure of the American Dream is an implicitly embedded subtheme both in *Kinfolk* as well as in Tan's novels. The Chinese immigrants envision America as the proverbial land of milk and honey, full of promise and equal opportunities: 'You could be anything you wanted to be in America . . . [t]here were so many ways for things to get better' (*Joy* 132). This, in part, accounts for their journey to the United States. In the new country, however, these characters find themselves in an ambivalent space. On one hand, they do manage to realise, in part, the promise of the American Dream. This is attested by the fact that almost all these women live lives of relative comfort and material success in America. Their offspring, particularly, are depicted as being extremely successful in their careers, exceeding their parents' dreams and expectations. At the same time, however, confronted with racial marginalisation, they soon come to realise, like other nonwhite Americans, that the dream is often sullied by the reality of their experience. The frustration of African-American poet Langston Hughes may well be said to echo the frustrations of these Chinese immigrants as well: '(There's never been equality for me / Nor freedom in this "Homeland of the free")' (Hughes 178). The sense of being outsiders, or unwanted, is constantly thrust upon their consciousness in all of their daily interactions. The fact that most of these Chinese immigrant women cannot speak 'perfect American English' (*Joy* 17) further adds to their being discriminated against. As Tan remarks in one of her essays, 'poor service, bad treatment, no respect – that's the penalty for not speaking English well in America' (*Fate* 165). Thus, it is within this space that the characters' quest for selfhood is negotiated and transacted.

However, it is not only the voyage from China to America, but more importantly, the return-to-the-motherland journey that is projected as one of the core events in Tan's novels, especially in *The Joy Luck Club* and *The Hundred Secret Senses*, and in Buck's *Kinfolk*. For the second-generation Chinese Americans, the trip to China is an extremely significant one, embodying both a search for roots as well as for personal and cultural identity. According to sociopsychologists, the desire to reconnect with one's roots, particularly, for adopted and diasporic individuals who have been distanced in time and space from the ancestral homestead, springs from the innate need for identity and belonging and allows for the construction of 'a more coherent sense of self' (Kohler *et al.* 2002, 95). Susanne Wessendorf documents two categories of immigrant rejourneyings to the country of origin. She uses the term 'roots migration' to refer to the second-generation immigrant's permanent relocation to his/her ancestral homeland. She also refers to 'roots tourism', a term used by Paul Basu to describe those immigrants who temporarily visit their parents' original homeland. For the roots migrant, the odyssey is motivated by the quest for belonging and homecoming, and for the roots tourist, the journey is largely seen as a pilgrimage, a 'journey of discovery', and a 'life-changing experience' (Basu 151).

To use Wessendorf's terminology, Mary and James Liang in Buck's *Kinfolk* are, in many senses, roots migrants. The two Liang children relocate to their ancestral village in China and realign themselves with their kinfolk as a means of putting down roots and experiencing a true sense of belonging, one which eludes them back in New York: 'Home for them was now becoming the brown walls of the village rising out of the brown plain' (*Kinfolk* 203). It is as they reconnect with their ancestral home and their kinfolk, committing themselves to live with, and work for, their own people with whom they have come to identify, that James and Mary experience a sense of wholeness and personal meaning in life. They had finally 'found . . . [their] roots, and it was time to begin living' (366).

In Amy Tan's novels, the journey to China is also undertaken, specifically by Jing-Mei Woo (*The Joy Luck Club*) and Olivia (*The Hundred Secret Senses*), the American-born protagonists. Even the other Amerasian daughters such as Waverley Jong and Pearl Brandt are also depicted as preparing to take a trip to China in search of reaffirmation and, in Pearl's case, healing. Tan's women, however, may be described as roots tourists or sojourners because their trip to the homeland is more of a visit rather than a permanent relocation. In her novels, one is led to understand that ultimately, the protagonists' journey leads them back 'home' to America. After the disappearance of Kwan, in Changmian, China, Olivia remarks,

'We decided to take the plane *home* [to America] on the scheduled day' (*Hundred* 393, emphasis added).

Even though the journey to China is an intensely meaningful one for Tan's characters, providing them with a deep sense of identity and completeness, the touristic impression is not altogether absent. This is particularly observed in *The Hundred Secret Senses* when Olivia photographs the almost ritualistic killing of a chicken for a feast welcoming her, the American guest. When she inquires about the procedure of the killing, the old woman who killed it replies that her prolonging of the chicken's death throes is merely for the benefit of Olivia's camera (295–96). According to Sheng-Mei Ma, Olivia acts more as 'an ethnographer documenting some primitive initiation rite' (122), rather than as a personal seeker of her own roots and origin. However, although Olivia's primary motive in going to China is to garner photographs for a book that she plans to co-author with her estranged husband, Simon, the fact remains that as a result of the visit, Olivia discovers a new-found sense of self-identity and appreciation of her own roots and heritage. As she acknowledges to herself, 'being here [in China], I feel as if the membranes separating the two halves of my life ha[ve] finally been shed' (*Hundred* 230). Thus, for the Chinese-American characters of Amy Tan, and Buck's *Kinfolk*, the journey to China is an immensely crucial one. It awakens in them a profound sense of belonging and reconnection with their roots and leads them to the experience of a more complete and integrated sense of self.

It is interesting to note the varying sense of 'home' that is envisioned by the characters of Buck and Tan. For Buck's characters in *Kinfolk*, specifically James and Mary, home is portrayed as an eventual return to one's ancestral roots in China. Significantly enough, even though Pearl Buck ultimately returns to America in her later years, she asserts through her characters that, for her, home is in China where her spiritual roots lie. As Liu Haiping remarks, 'not even after returning to settle in the United States' could Buck 'detach herself wholly from China, which remained in many senses her true home' (55). This deep sense of emotional rootedness in China is a theme which is re-echoed in Buck's later novel *Letter from Peking* (1957). Like Buck, Elizabeth Macleod, the American protagonist who lived with her family in Peking, China, is compelled to move back to the United States because of circumstances beyond her control. And though she eventually manages to carve out a new life for herself and her son in the country of her origin, her heart is always in China with her half-Chinese husband Gerald. Thus, for Buck, as for many of her characters (though there are a few exceptions as in the case of Louise Liang in *Kinfolk* for whom, like Tan's American-born daughters, home is America), China is where they truly experience a sense of home.

For the protagonists of Amy Tan, however, home is located in the American present. Not unlike her characters, though affirming the Chinese part of her consciousness, Tan looks to America as home. In *The Opposite of Fate*, describing a four-month book tour that took her to various parts of the world, Tan writes that at the end of the whirlwind tour, 'I returned *home* to San Francisco' (emphasis added, 367).

A central point of departure between the two writers concerns the literary techniques that they employ in their fiction. Except for her first novel *East Wind: West Wind* which is written in the first-person narrative, all of Buck's novels discussed in this study follow the Chinese practice of submerging the narrating 'I' and rendering the work in second- and third-person narration. As Jade Snow Wong remarks, 'In written Chinese, prose or poetry, the word "I" almost never appears' even though it is understood (vii). In this regard, therefore, Buck adheres wholly to Chinese literary tradition. Because the 'I' is never directly invoked, the story in her novels is, therefore, presented mainly through the voice of the omniscient author/ narrator. The author exists outside of the characters in the story, and yet, it is her perspective and description that shape, inform, and control the story.

This has opened Buck's work to charges of authorial intrusion, manipulation, and didacticism, which, as Paul A. Doyle points out, 'weakened the objectivity of her creation' and limits the artistic and literary scope of her work (150–51). According to critics like Doyle and Hilary Spurling, it is the perceived lack of growth and development 'in the artistic features of novel writing' that partly accounts for Pearl Buck's long exclusion from the literary canon of traditional American literature (Doyle 152–53). However, it is important to remember that for Buck, the guiding principle in her storytelling, particularly her novels about China, is the Chinese storytelling tradition in which she has been reared. As she repeatedly asserts, just like the Chinese storytellers of old, her concern in writing fiction is primarily 'to please and to amuse', rather than to create a work of art (qtd. in Doyle 155). In this regard, therefore, to measure Buck's work by the literary yardstick of traditional Western literature would be highly unjust. In her Nobel lecture, *The Chinese Novel*, delivered before the Swedish Academy at Stockholm, on December 12, 1938, Buck categorically states that her paramount objective as a novelist/storyteller is the entertainment of the common people: 'My ambition, therefore, has not been trained toward the beauty of letters or the grace of art' (55). According to her, 'a novelist must not think of pure literature as his goal. . . . He must be satisfied if the common people hear him gladly. At least, so I have been taught in China' (59). In this endeavour, therefore, Buck shows herself highly successful.

In Amy Tan's fiction, on the other hand, what is observed is the predominance of the narrating 'I' or the first-person narrator(s). The stories in her novels are told, almost exclusively, through the individual voices of her multiple women characters, rather than that of the omniscient writer/ creator. This has served to bring in an element of heteroglossia to her work. The impression that is created in her novels is that it is the protagonists who are the storytellers, rather than Tan the author. The story emerges through their voices. Thus, her fiction is characterised by the absence of the authorial voice. Instead of the unitary author/storyteller that one encounters in Buck's fiction, in Tan, one is faced with a multiplicity of character(s)/storyteller(s), who are themselves actors within the story, and whose voices compete with one another to present their own versions of truth. In its dismissal of the grand narrative and in privileging what Lyotard terms as the *petits recits* or individual, 'localized' narratives, Tan's work, therefore, may also be read as a postmodern text (Nouvet xvi).

A conspicuous feature of Tan's fiction which may also be seen in one of Buck's novels (*East Wind: West Wind*) is the employment of the Chinese talk-story or the oral, conversation mode. In all of these talk-stories, the female 'I' is given a privileged space and hearing. In *East Wind: West Wind*, Buck broke with Chinese literary tradition by inserting a narrating 'I' into the narrative, something which she studiously avoids in the other novels. As noted earlier, this may be seen as a conscious attempt on her part to allow for the articulation of a female subject like Kweilan, the Chinese woman, whose voice has been stifled behind the feudal enclosure of her world. Thus, though Buck tries to adhere to Chinese literary standards as much as is possible in the novels relating to China in the attempt to authenticate her work, she does not allow herself to be limited to its confines but transcends it whenever the need arises. In this regard, she reveals her skill and maturity as a storyteller, as she negotiates competently with different ways and means of telling her story, in order to achieve her purpose.

For Tan, the use of the talk-story serves a dual objective. First, it is highly appropriate to the Chinese context of her stories. Her Chinese women characters choose to articulate and express themselves through the talk-story because it is very much a part of these women's 'social world' and practices (Ho 140). Second, it is a means of reclaiming and recovering female self-expression and articulation as a way of countering the masculinist and nationalist imperatives of mainstream American culture. In this sense, therefore, the talk-story becomes not just a mere literary device any longer but a political strategy to assert a very feminist agenda. To paraphrase Trinh T. Minh-ha, the 'personal', thus, becomes 'political' (37). What is observed in the work of Amy Tan, therefore, is her successful welding of both Western literary practices such as the insertion of a narrating 'I', as well as Chinese literary traditions (talk-stories), to give form and substance to her work. This is a powerful reflection of her own Chinese-American identity which constantly finds expression in her art.

In Buck's work, one finds her largely guided and influenced by the Chinese literary culture which marks her childhood and formative years. There are, however, strains of multicultural literary traditions that are also evident in her work, such as 'the traditional Chinese novel, the King James Bible, classic American and English fiction of the last two centuries as well as the models in other literary genres' (Rabb 7). The influence of European Naturalism, particularly that of Emile Zola, has also been noticed in her work. Oscar Cargill notes that *The Good Earth*, for instance, is naturalistic in many ways such as in its accurate setting and detail, its stress on factors of environment and heredity, and especially, its focus on the common poor, and compares it to Zola's *La Terre* (1887), which incidentally translates as *The Earth* (148). These naturalistic themes may also be traced in *The Mother*. Thus, like Tan, Buck's work also reflects the literary confluences and intellectual legacies of multiple cultures. This serves to lend depth and dimension to their work.

It is not one single culture, therefore, but a plurality of cultures and text(s) that shape the lives and inform the intellectual experiences of these two writers. Ferdinand de Saussure argues that a text is the product of the meetings of many and various texts. Concurring with this view, Mikhail Bakhtin also stresses on a matrix of 'utterances' which are 'aware of and mutually reflect one another' (91), to refer to the ongoing dialogism between texts. This is clearly borne out in the writings of both Pearl Buck and Amy Tan whose works evidence the interplay of multiple texts, cultures, and discourses. The intertextual and intercultural dialogues demonstrated in the writings of these two authors enhance the scope and universality of their work and enrich its meaning.

Another important theme that links the fiction of these two writers is the strong feminist tones that are embedded in their work. Living and writing at a time when women's rights and gender equality must still be fought for, Buck shows herself a passionate advocate for, and supporter of, the rights and equality of women. Though active in vigorously campaigning for women's rights through the political platform, it is through her writings that she really succeeds in drawing attention to women's needs and aspirations, as well as to the various oppressions and subjugations that mark their lives. Her collection of essays, *Of Men and Women* (1941), has been hailed as a pioneering feminist statement and compared to the work of Virginia Woolf. It is interesting to note that Buck's portrayal of many of the key issues relating to women's lives anticipates in many ways the issues that are raised by feminists much later.

In *Pavilion of Women*, written in 1946, Buck underlines women's need and desire for a space of their own, apart from the solely domestic and familial one that society conventionally assigns to them. Thus, the protagonist, Madame Wu, is depicted as carving out a space for herself, both literally and metaphorically, by appropriating for herself the family library or the realm of knowledge, which was traditionally recognised as a man's domain. This same theme resonates in Betty Friedan's book, *The Feminine Mystique* (1963), written almost two decades after Buck's novel: 'We can no longer ignore that voice within women that says, "I want something more than my husband, and my children, and my home"' (32). In this sense, therefore, Buck reveals a sensibility and an awareness that is far ahead of her times.

The feminist perception of marriage as a patriarchal enclosure is again a subtheme that is implicitly embedded within Buck's novels: 'Radical feminists view marriage as a cruel trap for women, perpetuating patriarchy and keeping women subservient to men' (Lukas 75). In three of Buck's texts examined here (*Pavilion of Women, The Good Earth*, and *The Mother*), marriage is seen as either stunting to women's growth and potentiality or as an institution that enslaves and oppresses women further. Madame Wu, for instance, reflects on her marriage to Mr Wu, a man whose calibre is far beneath her, mentally and intellectually, as one that thwarts her self-growth and inner development:

> Her being she had subdued to duty for how many years, and for how many years had her soul waited, growing slowly, it is true through the performance of duty, but growing in bondage and waiting to be freed. (*Pavilion* 390)

She therefore, frees herself from the marriage by procuring a concubine for her husband. Though this act results in disruptions to the family order, it allows her the individual space to pursue her personal goals and desires which would not have been possible within the confines of her marriage. In *The Good Earth* and in *The Mother*, marriage is depicted as a patriarchal bind that ties women even more firmly to societally prescribed gender roles and female drudgery, exemplifying de Beauvoir's description of 'the wife-servant' (481). In his assessment of the character of O-lan (*The Good Earth*), James C. Thomson Jr notes that she is a woman 'betrayed . . . as much by her husband's weak character as by social attitudes' (25).

The same may be said for the female protagonist in *The Mother*, whose life was nearly wrecked by her marriage to a shallow and irresponsible man, who subsequently abandons his family without a qualm. In *East Wind: West Wind*, however, and to a certain extent in *Kinfolk*, Buck deviates from this theme by projecting marriage as a partnership of equals, one that facilitates the heroines' journey to self-realisation and discovery. It is pertinent to remember, however, that in these texts, both Kweilan and Mary Liang marry men who are their equals or who consider them to be equals. In this context, therefore, Buck departs from the rigid stance held by radical feminism. Thus, unlike radical feminists, it is not the institution of marriage *per se* that Buck critiques, but rather, marriage when it is used as a tool to subjugate women, or when it fails to provide the needed stimulation and partnership that is essential for a person's growth and self-actualisation.

This ambivalent view of marriage may also be noted in Tan's work. In her fiction, marriage is depicted both as a patriarchal instrument of oppression and as a means of salvation. More often than not, however, it is the former idea that gets reinforced more frequently through the stories of her women characters. Winnie's marriage to the tyrannical Wen Fu threatens her well-being, both physically and psychologically. Bella Adams suggests that in *The Kitchen God's Wife*, marriage is represented as 'a form of physical and psychological enslavement for women, whether mythical (the Kitchen God's wife), fictional (Winnie Louie), or indeed factual (Daisy Tan)' (2003, 27). In *The Joy Luck Club*, Lindo Jong and Ying Ying's narratives of their previous lives in China also reveal oppressive marriages that threaten to obliterate these women's sense of self altogether. The very embodiment of de Beauvoir's 'wife-servant' (481), Lindo actually begins to think of her first husband Tyan-yu 'as a god, someone whose opinions were worth much more than my own life' (56). Similarly, Ying Ying's story discloses a life that is lived exclusively for her husband's attention and pleasure, so that her selfhood is completely 'lost' in the bargain (247), a cycle that seems repeated in her daughter's life, years later. It is only when these women finally find the courage to break away from these self-destructive alliances that they begin to grow.

Simultaneously, however, like Buck, Tan also projects marriage as a potential means of salvation and growth, when it exists in an environment of mutuality and equality. Winnie's escape from a bad marriage in China would not have been possible without the support and encouragement of Jimmy Louie who became her second husband. More importantly, it is the sense of security and assurance of being loved that she experiences in her second marriage that helps her to regain a sense of worth and self-esteem. For Winnie's daughter, Pearl, her marriage to Phil Brandt is again depicted as a nurturing and supporting experience, especially as she struggles to cope with the disease of multiple sclerosis. It is in *The Bonesetter's Daughter*, however, in Luling and Pan Kai Jing's marriage, that Tan explicitly depicts marriage as self-enriching and as a complementary relationship, 'like two people performing a dance', rather than an unequal one (276). Kai Jing's affirmation of his wife, 'You are brave, you are strong' (302), uttered before his capture by the Japanese, continues to inspire her even after his death and moulds Luling's perception of herself as a strong and resilient individual.

The general impression that is created in Tan's novels, however, is that it is the women-to-women alliances rather than the marriage relationship that are the bedrock of her character's strength and sustainability. As Mary Snodgrass notes, in Tan, the husbands 'drift in and out of the story without making significant impact' so that the few positive instances of marriage fail to cancel out the numerous bad ones (112). According to her, even Jimmy Louie 'seems more like a comic-book rescuer than a mate and equal of Winnie' (113). In this sense, therefore, Tan's work may be said to veer more strongly towards the feminist view of marriage.

Female silence/voice, a dominant feminist theme, finds expression in the work of both writers. Interestingly, there is a division of thought on the issue of silence, even within the feminist ranks. According to bell hooks, 'silence is often seen as the sexist "right speech of womanhood" – the sign of woman's submission to patriarchal authority' (1989, 6). Patti Duncan, on the other hand, argues in her book, *Tell this Silence: Asian American Women Writers and the Politics of Speech* (2004), that 'silence is not merely a sign of absence of voice or power . . . [it can also] signify resistance' to hegemonic power (2). A study of the novels of Buck and Tan, however, reveals that in these two writers, at least in the texts examined here, silence is depicted as oppressive and self-destructive to the characters, imposed upon rather than resorted to as a means of resistance.

In Pearl Buck, the theme of women's silence, or rather, silencing, is explored in detail in *The Good Earth*, through the character of O-lan. O-lan's silence is a consequence of the interlocking of powerful and prevalent systems of oppression such as patriarchal ideology, her socioeconomic status, and her physical appearance that further ostracises her. What Goellnicht remarks of the male protagonist in Kingston's *China Men* (1980) may well be said of Buck's O-lan: 'This is not a positive silence but the silence of resignation that signals withdrawal and humiliation' (237). O-lan, therefore, seems locked in her silence to the end of the novel which ends with her death. And though her story and experiences are given voice, it is Buck, the creator/author, who articulates O-lan's story, rather than the character herself.

In Tan's fiction, images of silent and silenced women function as a subtheme in almost all her novels, particularly in *The Kitchen God's Wife* and in *The Bonesetter's Daughter*. 'Like the archetypal figure of O-lan, the Chinese servant-wife in . . . Pearl Buck's classic *The Good Earth* (1931), the powerful image of women devoid of opportunities to speak their minds found its way into Tan's fiction from the first' (Snodgrass 148). Again, it is a combination of issues, personal and social, that account for these women's silences. For Winnie, it is a sense of personal shame and fear of being perceived a failed woman in her daughter's eyes that makes her hide her story behind a veil of silence. For Guo, the mythical Kitchen God's Wife, and Precious Auntie, Luling's mother in *The Bonesetter's Daughter*, silence is forced upon them by the patriarchal context in which they lived. Even Kwan (*The Hundred Secret Senses*) represents the silenced figure, to some extent, silenced by mainstream American society which tries to stop her from articulating her Chinese 'ghost talk' (25), through electroshock therapy. However, unlike Buck's O-lan, Tan's women refuse to stay trapped within the abyss of silence. They eventually recover their own voices through the telling/writing of their own stories. Thus, in a sense, they become active agents of their own self-reclamation and self-articulation.

Thus, in analysing the novels of Pearl Buck and Amy Tan, one notices certain features that link the work of these two writers. Both these writers are clearly seen as attempting, through their fiction, to articulate the experiences and struggles of Chinese, and Chinese-American women, in their journey in quest of the self. As noted, women, particularly Chinese women, the 'doubly refracted "other"' (*Anthropology* 3), on account of their sex and race, have long been relegated to the peripheral spaces of traditional Western literature. By making Chinese women the subject of their work, therefore, both Buck and Tan attempt to correct the skewed gender and racial imbalance in literature and give voice to the realities and subjectivities of these women. As such, therefore, there are many key feminist concerns that are addressed in their work: the marginalisation and silencing of women's voices by patriarchal and other hegemonic power structures; women's needs and aspirations for personal space; and individual autonomy over their own lives and bodies.

What is noticed in the work of both these writers is that most of their female protagonists (with the exception of O-lan) are not simply projected as passive victims of the male-dominated context in which they are located, but rather, as active agents of their own self-recovery and personal fulfilment. Some of them achieve this by working within the bounds of the system that they find themselves in, as many of Buck's women did. Tan's characters, on the other hand, choose to break away from the system by relocating to a new country and carving out a new space for themselves, one which again calls for constant renegotiations and transactions. In spite of the different strategies that these characters employ, yet, in one way or the other, they do manage to attain a measure of selfhood and personal realisation, in the process.

Another significant strain that connects these two authors and impacts their work is their shared experience of biculturalism and its accompanying factors. This has opened up a space of conflict for both the writers personally, as well as for their bicultural protagonists, as they seek to accommodate themselves to, and come to terms with, this reality in their lives. Simultaneously, however, as their writings attest, this dual-cultural experience is one that greatly lends depth and richness to their fiction and enlarges the scope of their work. Thus, in examining the novels of Pearl Buck and Amy Tan, one finds a plethora of themes and motifs that serve as a bridge between their work in spite of the different time frames which span their writing careers.

Within these overarching common domains, however, certain differences and dissimilarities may be traced out. Though these protagonists' common goal is the realisation and actualisation of the self, yet, their odyssey towards selfhood also takes them via different routes and varying paths. For Buck's women, the journey takes them inward into self-introspection, but also outward into a relationship with the other: the gendered other; the racial other; and the community of women forming their social circle. For

Tan's heroines, on the other hand, the journey is one that is traversed by revisiting the past through storytelling. The nature of the physical journey to China that is undertaken in Tan's novels and in Buck's *Kinfolk* is again one that varies greatly. For Buck's characters, the voyage is portrayed as a homecoming, a permanent return to one's roots, while in Tan, it is depicted more as a pilgrimage, a temporary visit to explore one's ancestral connections so as to understand oneself better in the present context. Home, for Tan and her characters, therefore, is America, and continues to be America, while for Buck and her protagonists, the idea of home is traced back to China.

In analysing the novels of Pearl S. Buck and Amy Tan, one observes certain features that link the work of these two authors. The common themes found in both the writers' work reinforce the Saussurean/Bakhtinian argument referred to earlier, that all texts, in one way, or the other, 'mutually reflect one another' and attests to the intertextual dialogue that exists between them (Bakhtin 91). This serves to give a universal approach and relevance to their work. There are, however, points of differences that may also be traced in their works. Though both project China and America, and the Chinese woman as the main subject of their fiction, the approach taken by the two writers are different and unique to each writer. What may be said of Pearl Buck and Amy Tan, therefore, is that in these two novelists, one finds two very individual writers who, through the stories that they tell, attempt to inscribe their own personal vision of life and reality. Therein, lies their originality and distinctiveness and mark the two women writers as unique in their own rights.

BIBLIOGRAPHY

Primary Sources

Buck, Pearl S. *East Wind: West Wind*. Kingston: Moyer Bell, 1930. Print.
------. *The Good Earth*. New York: Washington Square Press, 1931. Print.
------. 'Chinese Women'. *Pacific Affairs* (October 1931): 905–9. Print.
------. *The Mother*. New York: John Day, 1934. Print.
------. *The Exile*. New York: John Day, 1936. Print.
------. *This Proud Heart*. New York: John Day, 1938
------. *The Chinese Novel*. New York: John Day, 1939. Print.
------. *Of Men and Women*. New York: John Day, 1941. Print.
------. *Pavilion of Women*. New York: John Day, 1946. Print.
------. *Peony*. New York: John Day, 1948. Print.
------. *Kinfolk*. New York: John Day, 1949. Print.
------. *My Several Worlds*. New York: John Day, 1954. Print.
------. *Letter From Peking*. New York: John Day, 1957. Print.
------. *China: Past and Present*. New York: John Day, 1972. Print.
Buck, Pearl. Interview by Mike Wallace. 2 August. 1958. Web. 20 September 2009.
        <http://www.hrc.utexas.edu/multimedia/video/2008/wallace/buck-pearl-t.html>
Tan, Amy. *The Joy Luck Club*. New York: Vintage, 1989. Print.
------. *The Kitchen God's Wife*. New York: Ivy, 1991. Print.
------. 'Lost Lives of Women: My Grandmother's Choice'. *Life* (April 1991): 90. Print.
------. *The Hundred Secret Senses*. New York: Ivy, 1995. Print.

------. *The Bonesetter's Daughter.* New York: Ballantine, 2001. Print.

------. *The Opposite of Fate: A Book of Musings.* New York: Putnam and Sons, 2003. Print.

------. *Saving Fish from Drowning.* London: Harper Perennial, 2005. Print.

Secondary Sources: Books

Adams, Bella. *Amy Tan.* Manchester: Manchester UP, 2005. Print.

Adorno, Theodor W. *Minima Moralia: Reflections from Damaged Life.* 1951. Trans. E.F.N. Jephcott. London: Verso, 1974. Print.

Agnew, Vijay. *Diaspora, Memory, and Identity: A Search for Home.* Toronto: U of Toronto P, 2005. Print.

Anzaldua, Gloria. 'Now let us shift . . . the path of conocimiento . . . inner work, public acts'. *This bridge we call home: radical visions for transformation.* eds. Gloria Anzaldua and Ana Louise Keating. New York: Routledge, 2002. 540–78. Print.

Ashcroft, Bill., Gareth Griffiths, and Helen Tiffin. eds. *The Post Colonial Studies Reader.* London, New York: Routledge. 1995. Print.

Bakhtin, M. M. *Speech Genres and other Late Essays.* Trans. Vern W. Mcgee. Austin: U of Texas P, 1986. Print.

Basu, Paul. 'Route Metaphors of Roots-Tourism in the Scottish Highland Diaspora'. *Reframing Pilgrimage: Cultures in Motion.* eds. S. Coleman and J. Eade. London: Routledge, 2007. 153–178. Print.

Battersby, Christine. *Phenomenal Woman: Feminist Metaphysics and the Patterns of Identity.* New York: Routledge, 1998. Print.

Berquist, Jon L. 'Constructions of Identity in Postcolonial Yehud'. *Judah and the Judeans: In the Persian Period.* eds. Oded Lipschits and Manfred Oeming. Ind: Eisenbrauns, 2006. 53–66. Print.

Bhabha, Homi. 'The Third Space'. *Identity, Community, Culture, Difference.* ed. J. Rutherford. London: Lawrence and Wishhart, 1990. 207–221. Print.

------. *The Location of Culture.* London: Routledge, 1994. Print.

Breakwell, G. *Coping with Threatened Identities.* London: Methuen, 1986. Print.

Buck, David D. 'Pearl S. Buck in Search of America'. Lipscomb., Webb., and Conn. 29–43. Print.

Chang, Jung. *Wild Swans: Three Daughters of China*. New York: Simon and Schuster, 1991. Print.

Chin, Frank. *The Year of the Dragon*. Seattle: U of Washington P, 1981. Print.

Chinn, Thomas H. ed. *A History of the Chinese in America: A Syllabus*. San Francisco: Chinese Historical Society of America, 1969. Print.

Chodorow, Nancy J. 'Family Structure and Feminine Personality'. 1974. Rosaldo and Lamphere. 43–66. Print.

------. *The Reproduction of Mothering: Psychoanalysis and the Sociology of Gender*. LA: U of California P, 1978. Print.

Collins, Patricia Hill. *Black Feminist Thought: Knowledge, Consciousness and the Politics of Empowerment*. New York: Routledge, 2000. Print.

'Combahee River Collective Statement'. *Home Girls: A Black Feminist Anthology*. ed. Barbara Smith. New York: Women of Color Press, 1983. 264–274. Print.

Conn, Peter. *Pearl S. Buck: A Cultural Biography*. New York: Cambridge UP, 1996. Print.

------. Introduction. *The Good Earth*. 1931 By Pearl S. Buck. New York: Washington Square Press, 1994. xi–xxx. Print.

Cutler, Constance A. *Review* of *The Good Earth* by Pearl S. Buck. *Master Plot*. ed. Frank N. Magill. New Jersey: Salem, 1976. 2319–2323. Print.

Daly, Mary. *Gyn/Ecology: The Metaethics of Radical Feminism*. London: The Women's Press, 1979. Print.

de Beauvoir, Simone. *Le Deuxieme Sexe/The Second Sex*. 1949. Trans. H.M. Parshley. London: Picador/Pan, 1988. Print.

de Certeau, Michel. *The Practice of Everyday Life*. Trans. Steven Rendall. Berkeley: U of California P, 1984. Print.

d'Entremont, John. 'Pearl S. Buck and American Women's History'. Lipscomb, Webb, and Conn. 45–53. Print.

Deaux, K. 'Personalizing Identity and Socializing Self'. *Social Psychology of Identity and the Self-Concept*. ed. G. Breakwell. London: Academic Press, 1992. 9–33. Print.

Downing, Christine. *Psyche's Sisters: Re-imagining the Meaning of Sisterhood*. New York: Continuum, 1990. Print.

Doyle, Paul A. *Pearl S. Buck*. Rev. ed. *Twayne's United States Authors Series, 85*. New York: Twayne, 1980. Print.

Duncan, Patti. *Tell this Silence: Asian American Writers and the Politics of Speech*. Iowa: U of Iowa P. 2004. Print.

Eichner, Hans. 'The Eternal Feminine: An Aspect of Goethe's Ethics'. Trans. Walter Arndt. *Norton Critical Edition*. eds. Walter Arndt and Cyrus Hamlin. New York: Norton, 1976. 615–624. Print.

Estyuroy, Annie O. *Daughters of Self-Creation: The Contemporary Chicana Novel*. Albuquerque: U of New Mexico P, 1996. Print.

Faulkner, Mara. *Protest and Possibility in the Writing of Tillie Olsen*. Charlottesville and London: UP of Virginia, 1993. Print.

Featherstone, Mike. 'Localism, Globalism, and Cultural Identity'. *Global/ Local: Cultural Productions and the Transnational Imaginary*. eds. Rob Wilson and Wimal Dissayanake. Durham: Duke UP, 1996. 46–77. Print.

Fetterley, Judith. *The Resisting Reader: Feminist Approaches to American Fiction*. Indiana: U of Indiana P, 1978. Print.

Fishman, Joshua A. *Handbook of Language and Ethnic Identity*. New York: Oxford UP, 1999. Print.

Foster, Marie Booth. 'Voice, Mind, Self: Mother-Daughter relationships in Amy Tan's The Joy Luck Club and The Kitchen God's Wife'. *Contemporary Literary Criticism: Tan, Amy*. ed. Jeffrey W. Hunter. MI: The Gale Group, 1999. 72–82. Print.

Freud, Sigmund. 'On Narcissism: An Introduction'. *The Standard Edition of the Complete Works of Sigmund Freud*. Trans. and ed. James Strachey. Vol. 14. London: Hogarth Press, 1914. Print.

Friedan, Betty. *The Feminine Mystique*. New York: N.W. Norton and Company, 1963. Print.

Gao, Xiongya. *Pearl S. Buck's Chinese Women Characters*. Pa: Susquehanna UP. 2000. Print.

Gerson, K., S. Stueve, and C. Fisher. 'Attachment to Place'. *Networks and Places: Social Relations in the Urban Setting*. ed. C. Fisher *et al.* New York: Free Press, 1977. 139–161. Print.

Gilbert, Sandra and Susan Gubar. *The Madwoman in the Attic*. Conn: Yale UP, 1979. Print.

Godard, Barbara. 'Feminism and/as Myth: Feminist Literary Theory between Frye and Barthes.' *Theory and Praxis: Curriculum, Culture and English Studies.* eds. Prafulla C. Kar *et al.* New Delhi: Pencraft, 2003. 165–194. Print.

Goellnicht, Donald C. 'Tang Ao in America: Male Subject Positions in *China Men*'. *Critical Essays on Maxine Hong Kingston.* ed. Laura E. Skandera-Trombley. New York: G. K. Hall and Co, 1998. 229–45. Print.

Gombrowicz, Witold. *Cosmos.* Trans. E. Mosbacker. London: Macgibbon and Kee, 1967. Print.

Gray, James. *On Second Thought.* Minn: U of Minnesota P, 1946. Print.

Greene, Ellin. *Storytelling: Art and Technique.* 3rd ed. Westport, CT: Greenwood, 1996. Print.

Gregory, Horace. *Dorothy Richardson: An Adventure in Self-Discovery.* New York: Holt, Rinehart and Winston, 1967. Print.

Grice, Helena. 'The Beginning is Hers: The Political and Literary Legacies of Maxine Hong Kingston and Amy Tan'. *China Fictions of English Language: Literary Essays in Diaspora, Memory, Story.* ed. A. Robert. Lee. Amsterdam and NY: Rodopi, 2008. 33–55. Print.

Gupta, Santosh. Mini Nanda. *Literary Constructs of the Self: Socio-Cultural Contexts.* Jaipur: Rawat Publications, 2010. Print.

Haiping, Liu. 'Pearl S. Buck's Reception in China Reconsidered'. Lipscomb, Webb and Conn 55–67. Print.

Hall, Edward T. *Beyond Culture.* New York: Anchor Press, 1976. Print.

Hall, Stuart. 'Spectacle of the Other'. *Representation: Cultural Representations and Signifying Practices.* ed. Stuart Hall. London: Sage, 1997. 223–291. Print.

Harris, Theodore F. *Pearl S. Buck: A Biography.* New York: John Day, 1969. Print.

Harte, Bret., and Mark Twain. *Ah Sin.* ed. Frederick Anderson. San Francisco: The Book Club of California, 1861. Print.

Hayford, Charles W. 'The Good Earth, Revolution, and the American Raj in China'. Lipscomb, Webb, and Conn. 19–27. Print.

Heilbrun, Carolyn G. *Writing a Woman's Life.* New York: W. W. Norton, 1998. Print.

Heung, Marina. 'Daughter Text/Mother Text: Matrilineage in Amy Tan's *The Joy Luck Club*'. *Amy Tan*. New Edition ed. Harold Bloom. New York: Infobase Publishing, 2009. 17–36. Print.

Ho, Wendy. *In Her Mother's House: The Politics of Asian American Mother-Daughter Writing*. Oxford: Altamira Press, 1999. Print.

Holt-Jensen, Arild. *Geography, History, and Concepts*. London: Sage, 1999. Print.

hooks, bell. *Talking Back: Thinking Feminist, Thinking Black*. Boston, MA: South End Press, 1989. Print.

------. *Yearning: Race, Gender, and Cultural Politics*. London: Turnaround, 1991. Print.

Hughes, Langston. *The Collected Poems of Langston Hughes*. New York: Vintage, 1995. Print.

Huntley, E. D. *Maxine Hong Kingston: A Critical Companion*. Westport, CT: Greenwood Press, 2001.Print.

Irigaray, Luce. *Speculum of the Other Woman*. Trans. Gillian C. Gill. Ithaca: Cornell U. P., 1985. Print.

Jackson, M. *At Home in the World*. Sydney: Harper Perennial, 1995. Print.

Juhasz, Suzanne. 'Maxine Hong Kingston: Narrative Technique and Female Identity'. *Contemporary American Women Writers: Narrative Strategies*. eds. Catherine Rainwater., and William J. Scheick. KY: UP of Kentucky, 1985. 173–189. Print.

Kar, Prafulla C., Kailash C. Baral and Sura P. Rath. eds. *Theory and Praxis: Curriculum, Culture, and English Studies*. Delhi: Pencraft, 2003. Print.

Kaufman, Gershen. *Shame: The Power of Caring*. Cambridge: Schenman Books Inc, 1980. Print.

Kearney, Richard. 'Emmanuel Levinas'. *Dialogues with Contemporary Continental Thinkers: The Phenomenological Heritage*. Manchester: Manchester UP, 1984. 47–70. Print.

Kim, Elaine H. *Asian American Literature: An Introduction to the Writings and their Social Context*. Philadelphia: Temple UP, 1982. Print.

Kingston, Maxine Hong. *The Woman Warrior: Memoirs of a Girlhood Among Ghosts*. 1975. New York: Random House; New York: Vintage, 1989. Print.

------. *China Men*. London: Picador, 1980. Print.

Kit Wah Man, Eva. 'Female Bodily aesthetics, Politics, and Feminine Ideals of Beauty in China'. *Beauty Matters*. Ind: Indiana UP, 2000. 169–96. Print.

Knapp, Bettina L. 'China's Fragmented Goddess Images'. *Women in Myth*. New York: SUNY Press, 1997. 169–200. Print.

Kondo, Dorinne. 'The Narrative Production of 'Home', Community, and Political Identity in Asian American Theatre'. *Displacement, Diaspora, and the Geographies of Identity*. eds. Lavie, Smadar., and Ted Swedenburg. Durham: Duke UP, 1996. 97–118. Print.

Kristeva, Julia. *About Chinese Women*. New York: Urizen, 1974. Print.

Lacan, Jacques. 'The Mirror Image as Formative of the "I" as Revealed in Psychoanalytic Experience'. *Ecritis: A Selection*. Trans. Alan Sheridan. London: Tavistock, 1977. Print.

Lakoff, G., and M. Johnsen. *More Than Cool Reason: A Field Guide to Poetic Metaphor*. Chicago: Chicago UP, 1989. Print.

Lauter, Estella. *Women as Mythmakers: Poetry and Visual Art by Twentieth Century Women*. Bloomington: Indiana UP, 1984. Print.

Leard, Abha Prakash. 'A New and Wondrous Phase': Feminist Salvation in Markandaya's *A Silence of Desire* and Desai's *Clear Light of Day*.' *Contemporary Indian Women Writers in English: A Feminist Perspective*. ed. Surya Nath Pandey. Delhi: Atlantic Publisher, 1999. 67–76. Print.

Lee, Gregory B. *Troubadours, Trumpeters, Trouble-Makers: Lyricism, Nationalism, and Hybridity in China and Its Others*. Durham: Duke UP, 1996. Print.

Leong, Karen J. *The China Mystique: Pearl S. Buck, Anna May Wong, Mayling Soong, and the Transformation of American Orientalism*. Berkeley and LA: U of California P, 2005. Print.

Li, David Leiwei, 'The Production of Chinese American Production: Displacing American Orientalist Discourse'. *Reading the Literatures of Asian America*. eds. Shirley Geok – Lin Lim and Amy Ling. Philadelphia: Temple UP, 1992. 319–331. Print.

Liao, Kang. *Pearl S. Buck: A Cultural Bridge across the Pacific*. Westport: Greenwood Press, 1997. Print.

Lin, Yutang. *My Country and My People*. New York: John Day, 1935. Print.

Ling, Amy. *Between Worlds: Women Writers of Chinese Ancestry*. New York: Pergamon Press, 1990. Print.

Lipscomb, Elizabeth J., Frances E. Webb., Peter Conn. eds. *The Several Worlds of Pearl S. Buck: Essays presented at a Centennial Symposium, Randolph-Macon Woman's College, March 26–28 1992*. Westport, CT: Greenwood Press, 1994. Print.

Lorde, Audre. *Zami: A New Spelling of My Name*. Trumansburg, New York: Crossing Press, 1982. Print.

Lukas, Carrie L. *The Politically Incorrect Guide to Women, Sex, and Feminism*. Washington, D. C.: Regnery, 2006. Print.

Lyotard, Jean-Francois. *The Postmodern Condition: A Report on Knowledge*. Manchester, Manchester UP, 1984. Print.

Ma, Laurence J.C., Carolyn Cartier. eds. *The Chinese Diaspora: Space, Place, Mobility and Identity*. Maryland: Rowman and Littlefield, 2003. Print.

Ma, Sheng-Mei. 'Chinese and Dogs in Amy Tan's *The Hundred Secret Senses*: Ethnicizing the Primitive *a la* New Age'. *The Deathly Embrace: Orientalism and Asian American Identity*. Minn: U of Minnesota P, 2000. 112–27. Print.

Maslow, Abraham H. *Toward a Psychology of Being*. New York: Von Nostrand, 1968. Print.

McCann, Carole., Kim, Seung-Kyung. eds. *Feminist Theory Reader: Local and Global Perspectives*. New York: Routledge, 2003. Print.

Medoff, Jeslyn. 'Maxine Hong Kingston'. *Modern American Women Writers*. eds. Elaine Showalter, Lea Baechler, and A. Walton Litz. New York: Scribner, 1991. 251–259. Print.

Minh-ha, Trinh T. *Woman, Native, Other: Writing Postcoloniality and Feminism*. Bloomington and Indianapolis: Indiana UP, 1989. Print.

Moi, Toril. *What is a Woman? And Other Essays*. Oxford: Oxford UP, 1999. Print.

Morrison, Toni. *Beloved*. New York: Plume, 1987. Print.

Muthyala, John S. 'The Politics of Borrowing Theories'. Kar, Baral and Rath 99–115. Print.

Nouvet, Claire, Zrinka Stuhaljak and Kent Still. eds. *Minima Memoria: In the Wake of Jean-Francois Lyotard.* Stanford, Calif: Stanford UP, 2007. Print.

Ong, Walter J. *Orality and Literacy: The Technologizing of the Word.* New York: Routledge, 1982. Print.

Palkar, Sarla. 'Breaking the Silence: That Long Silence'. *Indian Women Novelists.* Vol. 5. ed. R.K. Dhawan. New Delhi: Prestige, 1991. 163–169. Print.

Papke, Mary E. *Verging on the Abyss: The Social Fiction of Kate Chopin and Edith Wharton.* New York: Greenwood, 1990. Print.

Pitchford, Nicola. *Tactical Readings: Feminist Postmodernism in the Novels of Kathy Acker and Angela Carter.* London: Associated UP, 2002. Print.

Pratt, Annis, Barbara White, Andrea Lowenstein and Mary Wyer. eds. *Archetypal Patterns in Women's Fiction.* Bloomington: Indiana UP, 1981. Print.

Rath, Sura P. 'Home(s) Abroad: Diasporic Identities in Third Spaces'. Kar, Baral and Rath 82–98. Print.

Rich, Adrienne. *Of Woman Born: Motherhood as Experience and Institution.* New York: W.W. Norton and Company, 1976. Print.

Rosaldo, Michelle Zimbalist., Louise Lamphere. eds. *Women, Culture and Society.* Stanford, California: Stanford UP, 1974. Print.

Rosenblatt, Louise. *Literature as Exploration.* New York: Appleton-Century, 1938; New York: MLA, 1995. Print.

Ruland, Richard and Malcolm Bradbury. eds. *From Puritanism to Post-Modernism: A History of American Literature.* New York: Penguin, 1991. Print.

Sartre, Jean-Paul. *Being and Nothingness.* Trans. Hazel E. Barnes. New York: Washington Square, 1956. Print.

Saussure, Ferdinand de. *Course in General Linguistics.* New York: The Philosophical Library, 1959. Print.

Shen, Gloria. 'Born of a Stranger: Mother-Daughter Relationships and Storytelling in Amy Tan's *The Joy Luck Club*'. *Bloom's Modern Critical Interpretations: The Joy Luck Club* – New Ed. ed. Harold Bloom. New York: Infobase Publishing, 2009. 3–16. Print.

Shiva, Vandana. *Staying Alive: Women, Ecology, and Survival in India*. New Delhi: Zed Press, 1988. Print.

Shostak, Debra. 'Maxine Hong Kingston's Fake Books'. *Critical Essays on Maxine Hong Kingston*. ed. Laura E. Skandera-Trombley. New York: G.K. Hall and Co, 1998. 51–74. Print.

Sivaramkrishna, M. Introduction. *The Great Gatsby*. By F. Scott-Fitzgerald. Delhi: Oxford UP, 1981. xxvii. Print.

Skenazy, Paul. 'Kingston at the University'. *Conversations with Maxine Hong Kingston*. eds. Paul Skenazy and Tera Martin. Jackson: UP of Mississippi, 1998. 118–158. Print.

Snodgrass, Mary Ellen. *Amy Tan: A Literary Companion*. Jefferson, N.C.: McFarland, 2004. Print.

Soja, Edward. 'History: Geography: Modernity'. *The Cultural Studies Reader*. ed. Simon During. New York: Routledge, 1999. 113–125. Print.

Spurling, Hilary, *Burying the Bones: Pearl Buck in China*. London: Profile Book Ltd, 2010. Print.

Stirling, Nora. *Pearl Buck: A Woman in Conflict*. Piscataway, NJ: New Century, 1983. Print.

Thiong'O, Ngugi Wa. 'The Language of African Literature'. Ashcroft, Griffiths and Tiffin. 285–290. Print.

Thomson Jr. James C. 'Keynote Address: Pearl S. Buck and the American Quest for China'. Lipscomb, Webb, and Conn. 7–10. Print.

Van Doren, Carl. *The American Novel 1789–1939*. New York: Macmillan, 1940. Print.

Van Gulik, Robert Hans. *Sexual Life in Ancient China*. 1961. Trans. Louis Evrard. Paris: Gallimard, 1971. Print.

Warner, Marina. *Managing Monsters: Six Myths of Our Time*. London: Vintage, 1994. Print.

Wessendorf, Susanne. *Second-Generation Transnationalism and Roots Migration: Cross-Border Lives*. Farnham, Surrey: Ashgate, 2013. Print.

Wolf, Margery and Roxane Witke. eds. *Women in Chinese Society*. Stanford: Stanford UP, 1975. Print.

Wolf, Margery. *Revolution Postponed: Women in Contemporary China.* Stanford, Calif: Stanford UP, 1985. Print.

Woolf, Virginia. *A Room of One's Own.* San Diego: Harvest/HBJ Book, 1929. Print.

Wong, Jade Snow. *Fifth Chinese Daughter.* Washington: U of Washington P, 1950. Print.

Wong, Sau-Ling Cynthia. 'Sugar Sisterhood: Situating the Amy Tan Phenomenon'. (1995). *Contemporary Literary Criticism: Tan, Amy.* ed. Jeffrey W. Hunter. MI: The Gale Group, 1999. 52–68. Print.

Wright, Charlotte M. *Plain and Ugly Janes: The Rise of the Ugly Woman in Contemporary American Fiction.* Iowa City: U of Iowa P, 2000. Print.

Xie, Lihong. *The Evolving Self in the Novels of Gail Godwin.* Louisiana: Louisiana State UP, 1995. Print.

Yung, Judy. *Unbound Feet: A Social History of Chinese Women in San Francisco.* Berkeley, LA: U of California P, 1995. Print.

------. *Unbound Voices: A Documentary History of Chinese Women in San Francisco.* Berkeley, L.A: U of California P, 1999. Print.

Zola, Emile. *La Terre/The Earth.* 1887. Trans. Douglas Parmee. Middlesex: Penguin, 1980. Print.

Articles/Journals

Adams, Bella. 'Representing History in Amy Tan's *The Kitchen God's Wife*'. *MELUS* 28. 2. (2003): 9–30. Print.

Akoma, Chiji. 'The "Trick" of Narratives: History, Memory and Performance in Toni Morrison's *Paradise.*' *Oral Tradition* 15.1 (2000): 3–25. Print.

Anthropology and Education Quarterly 24. 1. (1993): 3–32. Print.

Ardanzazu, Usandizaga. 'The Female Bildungsroman at the Fin de Siecle: the "Utopian Imperative" in Anita Brookner's A Closed Eye and Fraud'. *Critique* 39.4. (1998): 325–340. Print.

Bentley, Phyllis. 'The Art of Pearl S. Buck'. *English Journal* 24. 10. (December 1935): 791–800. Print.

Berry, John W. 'Immigration, Acculturation, and Adaptation'. *Applied Psychology: An International Review* 46.1. (January 1997): 5–68. Print.

Bertodano, Helene de. 'A Life Stranger than Fiction'. *Daily Telegraph* (11 November 2003). n.p. Print.

Bhabha, Homi. 'Cultures in Between'. *Artforum* 32.1. (1993): 167–68, 211–12. Print.

------. 'Interview with Cultural Theorist Homi Bhabha' by J. W. T. Mitchell. *Artforum* 33. 7. (March 1995): 80–84. Print.

Boa, Kenneth. 'Forming an Authentic Self in an Inauthentic World'. *Engage.* (April–June 2012): 8–15. Print.

Broughton, Panthea Reid. 'Rejection of the Feminine in Carson McCullers' *The Ballad of the Sad Café*'. *Twentieth Century Literature* 20.1. (Jan 1974): 34–43. Print.

Caesar, Judith. 'Patriarchy, Imperialism, and Knowledge in *The Kitchen God's Wife*'. *North Dakota Quarterley* 62. 4. (Fall 1994–95): 164–74. Print.

Carson, E.H.A. 'Pearl Buck's Chinese'. *Canadian Bookman* (June 1939): 55–59. Print.

Chang, Hui-Ching., and G. Richard Holt. 'More than Relationships: Chinese Interaction and the Principle of *Kuan-Hsi*'. *Communication Quarterly* 39. 3. (Summer 1991): 251–271. Print.

Chen, Victoria. 'Chinese American Women, Language, and Moving Subjectivity'. *Women and Language* 18. 1. (1995): 3–7. Print.

'Chinese Life'. Review of *East Wind: West Wind* by Pearl S. Buck. *New York Times* (April 1930): 8. Print.

Cisneros, Sandra. 'Notes to a Young(er) Writer'. *The American Review* 15. (Spring 1987): 74–6. Print.

Cixous, Helene. 'The Laugh of the Medusa'. Trans. Keith Cohen and Paula Cohen. *Signs*: *Journal of Women in Culture and Society* 1. 4. (Summer 1976): 875–893. Print.

Conard, Tammy S. 'Creating an Asian-American Mythology: Storytelling in Amy Tan's Fiction'. MA Thesis. Texas Tech. University. 1998. Print.

Doan, Caoly. 'Image of the Chinese Family in Pearl S. Buck's Novels'. Diss. St. John's University. Brooklyn, New York: 1965. Print.

Dunick, Lisa M.S. 'The Silencing Effect of Canonicity: Authorship and the Written Word in Amy Tan's Novels'. *MELUS* 31. 2. (2006): 3–20. Print.

Felski, Rita. 'The Novel of Self-Discovery: A Necessary Fiction?'. *Southern Review* 19. (1986): 131–148. Print.

Ganahl, Jane. 'Amy Tan Gets Her Voice Back'. *Book* (January 2001): 40. Print.

Garnett, David. Review of *The Mother* by Pearl S. Buck. *The New Statesman and Nation* 7 (27 January 1934): 120. Print.

Gillespie, Elgy. 'Amy, Angst, and the Second Novel'. *San Francisco Review of Books* 16. 1. (Summer 1991): 33–4. Print.

Goldensohn, Lorrie. Review of *The Voyage In: Fictions of Female Development* by Marianne Hirsch. *Studies in the Novel* 16.3. (Fall 1984): 339–341. Print.

Hamilton, Patricia L. 'Fengshui, Astrology, and the Five Elements'. *MELUS* 24. 2. (1999): 125–145. Print.

Harte, Bret. 'The Heathen Chinee'. Overland Monthly and Out West Magazine 5.3. (September 1870): 287. Print.

Hauge, Ashild L. 'Identity and Place: A Critical Comparison of Three Identity Theories'. *Architectural Science Review* (1 March 2007): 1–15. Print.

He, Jing. 'Farewell to Gender: A Postmodern Feminist and Existentialist Interpretation of Chen Ran's "Gender-Transcendent Consciousness"'. *Virginia Review of Asian Studies* (2011): 87–99. Print.

------. 'Sisterhood across Cultures – With Reference to Chen Ran's and Amy Tan's Fiction'. *Intercultural Communication Studies* XXI. 2. (2012): 201–218. Print.

Howell, Nancy R. 'Ecofeminism: What One needs to Know'. *Zygon* 32.2. (1997): 231–241. Print.

Jiang, Hong. 'Female Bonds: A Reading of Two Stories by Chinese Women Writers'. *International Journal of the Humanities* 8.7. (Oct 2010): 1–10. Print.

Kelley, Mary. 'Reading Women/Women Reading: The Making of Learned Women in Antebellum America'. *Journal of American History* 83. (Sept 1996): 401–24 Print.

Koenig, Rhoda. 'Heirloom China'. *New York* 22. 12. (20 March 1989): 82–83. Print.

Kohler, Dayton. 'Carson McCullers: Variations on a Theme'. *College English* 13. 1. (October 1951): 1–8. Print.

Kohler, J. K., H. D. Grotevant and R. G. Mcroy. 'Adopted Adolescents' Preoccupation with Adoption: The Impact on Adoptive Family Relationships'. *Journal of Marriage and Family* 64. 1. (2002): 93–104. Print.

Lee, Ken-Fang. 'Cultural Translation and the Exorcist: A Reading of Kingston's and Tan's Ghost Stories'. *MELUS* 29. 2. (2004): 105–27. Print.

Li, Bo. 'The Chinese as portrayed in the Writings of Several Prominent American Authors'. MA Thesis. Stephen F. Austin State University, 1989. Print.

Lim, Shirley Goek-lin. 'Japanese American Women's Life Stories: Maternality in Monica Sone's *Nisei Daughter* and Joy Kogawa's *Obasan*'. *Feminist Studies* 16. 2. (Summer 1990): 289–312. Print.

Mastoraki, Polyxeni. 'The Perception and Formation of the Landscape through Time and Space: The Ancient Greek Heritage'. MA Thesis. U of East London, 2012. Print.

McGrory, Mary. Review of *Pavilion of Women* by Pearl S. Buck. *New York Times* (24 November 1946): 6. Print.

McHenry, Elizabeth Ann. 'Setting Terms of Inclusion: Storytelling as a Narrative Technique and Theme in the Fiction of Zora Neale Hurston, Eudora Welty, Leslie Marmon Silko and Maxine Hong Kingston'. Diss. Stanford University, 1993. Print.

Mohapatra, A. K. 'The Paradox of Return: Origins, Home, and Identity in M. G. Vassanji's *The Gunny Sack*'. *Postcolonial Text* 2. 4. (2006): 1–21. Print.

Murdoch, Wendi Deng. 'The Meaning of Lao Tong'. *The Huffington Post*. 30 October 2012. Print.

Naylor, Gloria. 'A Conversation: Gloria Naylor and Toni Morrison'. *Southern Review* 21. (1985): 567–93. Print.

Pavey, Ruth. A Review of *The Hundred Secret Senses*. *New Statesman and Society* 9. 390. (16 February 1996): 38. Print.

Rabb, Jane M. 'Who's Afraid of Pearl S. Buck?' *Randolph – Macon Woman's College Bulletin*. (Fall 1992): 6–7. Print.

Rao, Kiran. Interview by Haimanti Mukherjee. *Sunday Times of India*. 18 August 2013. Print.

Rich, Adrienne. 'When We Dead Awaken: Writing as Re-Vision'. *College English* 34. 1. (October 1972): 18-30. Print.

Rotman, Deborah. 'Seperate Spheres? Beyond the Dichotomies of Domesticity'. *Current Anthropology* 47. 4. (2006): 666–674. Print.

Rusi, Jaspal. 'Language and Social Identity: A Psychological Approach'. *Psych – Talk* (September 2009): 17–20. Print.

Ryff, Carol D., and Burton H. Singer. 'Know Thyself and Become what You Are: A Eudaimonic Approach to Psychological Well-Being'. *Journal of Happiness Studies* 9. (2008): 13–39. Print.

Schneider, Isidore. Review of *East Wind: West Wind*, by Pearl S. Buck. *New Republic* 63. (May 1930): 24. Print.

Shear, Walter. 'Generational Differences and the Diaspora in *The Joy Luck Club*'. *Critique* (Spring 1993): 193–99. Print.

Showalter, Elaine. 'Feminist Criticism in the Wilderness'. *Critical Inquiry* 8.2. (Winter 1981): 179–205. Print.

Turner, Joan. 'Turns of Phrase and Routes to Learning: the Journey Metaphor'. *Educational Culture: Intercultural Communication Studies* vii.2. (1997–98): 23–35. Print.

Walter, Roland. 'Pan-American (Re)Visions: Magical realism and Amerindian Cultures in Susan Power's *The Grass Dancer*, Gioconda Belli's *La Mujer Habitada*, Linda Hogan's *Power*, and Mario Vargas Llosa's *El Hablador*'. *American Studies International*, 37.3. (1999): 63–80. Print.

Wang, Veronica. 'Reality and Fantasy: The Chinese-American's Quest for Identity'. *MELUS* 12. (1985): 23–31. Print.

Watson, Karen Ann. 'Transferable Communicative Routines: Strategies and Group Identity in Two Speech Events'. *Language in Society* 4. 1. (April 1975): 53–7. Print.

White, Julianne. 'The Mother/Daughter Dilemma: The Failure of Motherhood in Wilkie Collins' *The Woman in White*'. *WILLA* 5. (Fall 1996): 32–35. Print.

Xu, Ben. 'Memory and the Ethnic Self: Reading Amy Tan's *The Joy Luck Club*'. 325 *MELDS* 19. 1. (1994): 3–18. Print

Internet Reference

Cargill, Oscar. 'Intellectual America: Ideas on the March'. *Contemporary Literary Criticism: Buck, Pearl Sydenstricker.* Vol 7. Ed. Phyllis Carmel Mendelson. Web. 7 May 2009.
<http://www.enotes.com/contemporary-literary-criticism>

'Changing Minds'. Web. 2 May 2013.
http://changingminds.org/explanations/behaviours/coping/suppression.htm

Chun, Alice. 'Women's Life in China'. Web. 30 October 2009.
<http://www.dimsum.co.uk>
de Geest, Heather. 'The Negative Persona of Silence'. Web. 29 April 2013. <http://wfae.proscenia.net/library/articles/de_geest_persona.pdf>

Dennis, Helen. *Toni Morrison Lecture.* Web. 2 August 2013.
<http://www2.warwick.ac.uk/fac/arts/english/about/people/permanentacademicstaffstaff3/dennisdrhelen/archivedmaterials/en3>
Lennon, Kathleen. 'Feminist Perspectives on the Body'. *The Stanford Encyclopedia of Philosophy* (Fall 2010): no. pag. Web. 24 November 2011.
http://plato.stanford.edu/archives/fall2010/entries/feminist-body/

Mandaville, Peter G. 'Territory and Translocality: Discrepant Idioms of Political Locality'. *Columbia International Affairs Online* (July 2000) Web. 21 October 2011. <http://www.cionet.org/htm>

Mongelluzzo, Nanette Burton. 'Secrets, Shame, and Guilt'. Web. 2 May 2013.
http://blogs.psychcentral.com/angst-anxiety/2012.02/secrets-shame-and-guilt/

Mount, Dana C. 'Enduring Nature: Everyday Environmentalisms in Postcolonial Literature'. *Open Access Dissertations and Theses*. 7179. Web. 26 June 2012.
http://digitalcommon.mcmaster.ca/opendissertation/7179

'Rememory in Toni Morrison's *Beloved*'. Web. 17 May 2013.
<http://www.123helpme.com/preview.asp?id=9680>

Ruiz, Sophia. 'Amy Tan'. Web. 12 May 2012.
<http://www.ireadpages.com/archive/marapr01/amytan/amytan.html>

Souris, Stephen. '"Only Two Kinds of Daughters": Inter-Monologue Dialogicity in *The Joy Luck Club*'. *MELUS* 19.2. (Summer 1994): 99–124. *Contemporary Literary Criticism: Tan, Amy*. ed. Jeffrey W. Hunter. 1999. 21-35. Web. 9 June 2009.
<http://www. enotes.com/contemporary-literary-criticism>

'Talk Story: Sharing Stories, Sharing Culture'. Web. 6 March 2013.
<www.talkstorytogether.org/sites/default/files/download/TalkStory ProgramManual.pdf>

Van Dijck, Jose. 'Composing the Self: Of Diaries and Lifelogs'. *The Fibre Culture Journal* 3. Web. 5 July 2012.
<http://three.fibreculturejournal.org/fcj-012-composing-the-self-of-diaries-and-lifelogs/>

Walker, Rebecca. 'Rebecca's Story'. *Harper's Magazine* (November 1992). Web. 8 April 2013. <http://www.fwhc.org/stories/rebecca.html>

Wong, Hiu Wing. 'Talk Stories' in the Fictions of Maxine Hong Kingston and Amy Tan. Diss. U of Warwick, 2006. Web. 6 March 2012.
<http//wrap.warwick.ac.uk/id/eprint/1183>.

Yu, Su-lin. 'Ethnic Sisterhood in Amy Tan's *The Hundred Secret Senses*'. Web. 27 May 2013. <http://www.ncku.edu.tw/-gender/pdf/t-8.pdf>

Printed in the United States
By Bookmasters